THE SUBJECT IS

Writing

FOURTH EDITION

THE SUBJECT IS

Writing

Essays by Teachers and Students

Edited by Wendy Bishop and James Strickland

BOYNTON/COOK   HEINEMANN
Portsmouth, NH

Boynton/Cook Publishers, Inc.
A subsidiary of Reed Elsevier Inc.
361 Hanover Street
Portsmouth, NH 03801-3912
www.boyntoncook.com

Offices and agents throughout the world

© 2006 by Boynton /Cook Publishers, Inc.

Library of Congress Cataloging-in-Publication Data
The subject is writing : essays by teachers and students / edited by Wendy Bishop and James Strickland. — 4th ed.
    p. cm.
    Includes bibliographical references.
    ISBN 0-86709-586-5 (alk. paper)
    1. English language—Rhetoric—Study and teaching.   2. Report writing—Study and teaching.   3. English language—Rhetoric.   4. Readers—Rhetoric.
I. Bishop, Wendy, 1953–2003.   II. Strickland, James.

    PE1404.S85 2006
    808'.042—dc22   2005031815

Editor: Lisa Luedeke
Production coordinator: Sonja S. Chapman
Cover design: Night & Day Design
Compositor: Reuben Kantor, QEP Design
Manufacturing: Louise Richardson

Printed in the United States of America on acid-free paper
10   09   08   07   06   VP   1   2   3   4   5

Dedication

For Patrick M. Hartwell (1937–2000), whom we both loved, and
Wendy S. Bishop (1953–2003), whom everyone loved and still misses.

Contents

Preface to the Fourth Edition

James Strickland

Wendy Bishop and I shared many things—an enthusiasm for writing, liberal politics, a wry sense of humor, a commitment to our professional community through organizations such as the Conference on College Composition and Communication (CCCC)—but most of all we shared writing teachers. We were both mentored at Indiana University of Pennsylvania by Patrick M. Hartwell, one of the most artful academic writers, who taught us the meaning of extensive research, careful accounting, and graceful style (often most brilliantly in parenthetical comments, pointing out, for example, that I probably need to substantiate the claims made just then). Pat knew rhetoric and composition research so well he would include APA-style references in even his casual conversations and classroom talk. He might be speaking about how the trouble with basic writers wasn't that they don't know the rules but more that they've learned the wrong rules too well; then he'd add "Rose, 1980" or some such reference. The only time he ever got confused about dates was with his own publications; he was a humble man.

Wendy and I also shared the same dissertation director, Donald McAndrew, whom another classmate, Brian Huot, once called the best stand-up classroom teacher, hands down. Don's style of teaching was so influential that I changed my plans to be a William Blake scholar and became a composition specialist instead, and Wendy made Don's classroom the focus of her dissertation and subsequent monograph, *Something Old, Something New* (1990). Don has a way of changing the energy in a classroom and transforming teachers and students, as can be felt when reading his chapter included in this volume and his work that he coauthored with longtime friend Tom Reigstad, *Tutoring Writing* (2001).

And we shared a commitment that *The Subject Is Writing* be a textbook speaking directly to students, written by writing teachers and even students themselves. I remember talking about it with Wendy during a break at a business meeting of the CCCC Executive Board. I remember her feeling that the book, instead of dispensing generic prescriptions and nineteenth-century modes of discourse, should offer honest advice and nurture a love of the craft of writing in our students. She asked me to write about ways the computer would change the composition classroom, and though the advancements in technology have rendered some of my observations and advice obsolete, it remains one of my favorite pieces. In the end, *The Subject Is Writing* would be an extension of Wendy in the classroom (channeling Hartwell and McAndrew and all the other luminous writing teachers we've learned so much from).

It is my hope that this fourth edition continues what Wendy was able to establish through the first three editions, and that were she able to open this new volume, she would smile that wonderful smile of hers once more.

—James Strickland, 2005

Works Cited

Bishop, Wendy (1990). *Something Old, Something New: College Writing Teachers and Classroom Change*. Carbondale, IL: Southern Illinois University Press.

McAndrew, Donald A., and Thomas J. Reigstad (2001), *Tutoring Writing: A Practical Guide for Conferences*. Portsmouth, NH: Boynton/Cook.

From the Preface to the Third Edition

Wendy Bishop

In journals, at conferences, and in department meetings, I often hear assertions that writing classes have no "content," especially when compared to literature classes or other classes in other disciplines where famous texts by famous authors are commonly under discussion. Those of us who write, who teach writing, and who love writing and reading a variety of texts know that the *contentless* claim is simply not true. Student texts are valuable texts.

Maxine Hairston (1986) believes, as I do, that "a writing course has its own content, and that is the students' and teachers' writing and the writing process itself" (188). I believe her statement fully because I know my second-best hours as a writer are spent talking to writers, researching writing, and responding to writing. My best hours as a writer, of course, are spent writing, since *talking about* will never substitute for *writing about*. It is clear that we learn to write better by attempting writing and thinking through writing.

I know that not everyone shares my enthusiasm for writing and talking about writing. Still, I feel that shared enthusiasm—that of committed writing teachers and freshly engaged writing students in this text—will offer you the encouragement to begin and continue your own journey as a writer. I'd like to think that you might learn, in our company and the company of your writing class, the lesson shared by poet Marvin Bell: "I always feel better when I write, when I go to my study out back under the wild cherry tree. It only takes a few minutes before I say, 'Why didn't I come out here sooner?' It feels wonderful" (Murray 1990, 190).

Of course that wonderful feeling isn't easy to achieve, but I believe it is worth pursuing. The writing teachers in this book are all trying to create a new kind of writing classroom, one that makes students ask, "Why didn't I come sooner?" At the same time, in their essays they examine the institutional constraints that still exist to slow the development of better writing instruction.

You may be in a writing class because you were told you needed to be there, and we still need to convince you to stay willingly. On the other hand, you may have already discovered that writing has a special place in your life because writing is for *you* as well as for those you write to. Toni Morrison claims:

Writing was the only work I did that was for myself and by myself. In the process, one exercises sovereignty in a special way. All sensibilities are engaged, sometimes simultaneously, sometimes sequentially. While I'm writing, all of my experience is vital and useful and possibly important. (Murray 1990, 8)

In the writing classes described in these essays and created by you and your peers and your teacher, writing is for you and for others, work you do alone and work you do together, work that engages you and that authorizes your view and your experiences, work that remains central to your sense of self—important *work*. . . . None of these authors offers you pat answers. None intends his or her view to be the only way to look at writing. But all are trying to share their commitment to writing.

The essays in this textbook were reviewed before publication in writing classrooms across the country. Students responded to the essay drafts and suggested revisions to authors, who then revised, trying to improve the essays in light of those suggestions. These are, then, not esoteric academic journal essays but, we hope, essays in the best sense, exploratory and earnest communications from writers to readers.

—Wendy Bishop, 2002

Works Cited

Hairston, Maxine (1986). "Using Nonfiction Literature in the Composition Classroom." In B. T. Peterson (Ed.), *Convergences: Transactions in Reading and Writing* (pp. 179–188). Urbana, IL: National Council of Teachers of English.

Murray, Donald M. (1990). *Shoptalk: Learning to Write with Writers*. Portsmouth, NH: Boynton/Cook Heinemann.

Acknowledgments

Clearly *The Subject Is Writing* represents a group effort in the best sense. I thank all the essayists—in each edition—who added to this collection by sharing their work. Peter Stillman and the late Bob Boynton supported the first edition through every draft and revision, and the third edition would not have existed without their initial enthusiasm and vision. Dan Melzer contributed a new essay to this edition and shared his teaching expertise by revising the instructor's manual. Finally, the fourth edition owes its energy to the interest and continuing support of Lisa Luedeke, who put her trust in me to carry out what Wendy Bishop had begun. Many thanks.

Thanks to the following teachers and their writing students, who helped with the manuscript drafts: Susan Barron; Anne Bower; Roger Casey; Devan Cook; Gay Lynn Crossley; Beth Daniell; Kevin Davis; Diana Dreyer; Kim Haimes-Korn; Rich Haswell; Ruth Johnson; Ann Kalinak; Carolyn Kremers; Pat MacEnulty; Michael McMahon; Ruth Mirtz; Dean Newman; Elsie Rogers; Mary Jane Ryals; Jim Strickland; Kathleen Strickland, Craig Stroupe; Gretchen Thies; Cindy Wheatley-Lovoy; Ron Wiginton; Thia Wolf; and Trisha Yarborough. Wendy also expressed her appreciation for more than a decade of first-year through senior writing students who discussed these essays with her and helped her see how to improve her work as writer, teacher, and editor. Wendy's children, Morgan and Tait, shared the journey, and she always said she'd been educated by watching them move from writing in elementary school to writing in high school and college as these editions progressed. Finally, importantly, Wendy would acknowledge her husband, Dean, who helped—in every way.

I would add my gratitude to the teachers and students at Slippery Rock University of Pennsylvania, who helped by reading and responding to these chapters. I'd also thank my wife, Kathleen, who has always been at my side, for better or worse, in sickness and in health. And thanks to my production team at Heinemann; they truly are family.

Part I

How Do Writers Find Their Subjects?

Write before you know what you have to say or how to say it. Ignorance is a great starting place. Write as fast as you can—and then increase the speed! Don't worry about penmanship or typing, punctuation or correctness, making sense or being silly. Velocity is as important in writing as in bicycle riding—speed gets you ahead of the censor and causes the accidents of meaning and language essential to good writing. . . . Later you can read what you have written and the draft, rough as it is, will often reveal what you have to say and how you can say it.

—Donald Murray, Pulitzer Prize–winning journalist

The most powerful thing about journal writing, for me, can be visualized as a sort of wheel, a snake with its tail in its mouth. At some point, the wheel is labeled "writing." Somewhere on the other side, it's labeled "thinking" or "learning." Writing, in other words, *leads* to thinking and learning. Thinking and learning lead, in turn, to more writing. And on and on, like a mantra. I think this concept works especially well with journal writing because it suggests the exploratory nature of journals and emphasizes their chief value: contemplation.

—Chris M. Anson, writing teacher

One use of the journal is to extend or explore your thinking in order to construct your own knowledge. Rather than simply restate or rehearse ideas shared in a course, you're using the journal to reformulate and reflect on ideas *in your own words*. In that way, you're assimilating these ideas into what you already know and believe. . . . You may also use your journal entries as prewriting to develop ideas for your papers. As you begin to define and clarify a possible paper topic, you could highlight or circle material and entitle that material in the margin according to its relevance to your overall topic.

—Richard Beach, writing teacher

I've been learning to write since before I can remember—since first holding a crayon in my hand—yet I've only scratched the surface of what there is to learn and to write about. Some of my best writing has grown out of my journals, has come instantly, like magic. I didn't know what I was going to write, it just came out. Other writing has taken months to research, or years to simmer and season in my memory and my heart, before I could bear to write it down. I write better than I did, say, a year ago, but I still don't write as well as I want to.

—Carolyn Kremers, writing teacher

What matters, when you first sit down to write, is that the who you are writing for is yourself and the why is to make that writing a process of discovery. It is the act of writing that makes the search for new meaning possible. You may decide to share this initial thinking with a fellow student or with your teacher, but hold on to the certainty that whether to share or not, at this predraft stage, is your decision.

—Pat D'Arcy, writing teacher

1

Writing as a Tool for Learning and Discovery

Thia Wolf

Thia Wolf is Associate Professor of Composition Studies at California State University, Chico, where she coordinates the English Composition Program. She teaches courses in writing and rhetoric to undergraduates and courses in composition theory to graduate students. The birth of her son in 1995 has inspired her to investigate learning development in children. She resides in Richardson Springs, a canyon just outside of Chico, with her family and three rambunctious dogs.

This essay examines ways of using writing to improve memory, foster insights, and accelerate learning. Few of us stop to consider that writing can be more than a functional activity (something we do when we need to apply for a job or prepare for a trip to the grocery store) and different from mandatory assignments. Writing is a uniquely human tool, a means to stimulate memory, construct new knowledge, and explore both ourselves and our environment. Even people who don't like to write essays, letters, or research papers may find that they enjoy using writing to increase their learning potential. I want to introduce you to writing activities that can support you in learning and in living. You'll probably get the most out of this essay if you have paper and pencil handy. Rather than reading straight through, plan to sit down with the essay more than once. On each occasion of your reading, try one or two of the activities suggested here. They are scattered throughout the text.

Let's begin by looking at some ways that writing stimulates and enhances memory. Although researchers still have a long way to go before understanding all about the ways our brains work, they have created useful hypotheses, or theories, about brain function. Obviously, our brains store information over the entire course of our lives; this stored information forms the basic building blocks of our memories.

We'll try a simple writing activity that demonstrates how memory becomes activated through language. Start with a word that seems neutral, even uninteresting, and print it in the middle of a sheet of paper. (In my example, below, I started with the word *bread.*) After you've printed this word, print other words or phrases that it reminds you of. (You'll see that I wrote names of breads, but pretty soon I found myself writing names and places where I'd eaten bread, people I know who like bread, childhood memories about bread, etc.) Keep track of the thoughts that go through your mind by noting as many words and phrases as you can around other words and phrases on the page that trigger a memory or association. You may be surprised at how many memories come back to you and how many associations you have for simple words such as *tree, lamp,* or *blanket.*

The map below (Figure 1–1) is a visual representation of the ways my brain became stimulated when I thought of the word *bread.* I began by categorizing breads: sourdough, French. And I suddenly remembered something I think of only rarely—the Helm's Bakery Truck that used to visit our neighborhood when I was a child. The Helm's truck was like an ice cream truck,

Figure 1–1

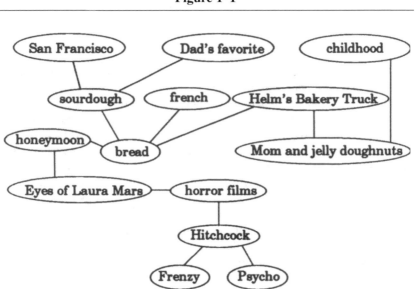

except that it was filled with shelves of breads, doughnuts, and other bakery goods. Although I didn't mention it in my map, remembering the Helm's truck brought back memories of some of the most delicious smells imaginable. When the Helm's man opened the large back doors to his truck and invited us up a step and into his bakery, my mother and I found ourselves enveloped in the thick, sweet smells of freshly baked treats.

Remembering what it felt like to enter the truck with my mother, I also remembered her favorite food: lemon jelly doughnuts. But my thinking didn't stop there. Coming back to my original word trigger, *bread,* I realized that sourdough bread reminds me both of my father, who loves it, and of San Francisco, a place renowned for its sourdough loaves. Thinking of San Francisco reminded me of my honeymoon and of a film my husband and I saw while we were there. That film, a horror film, made me think of other horror films I've known.

Create a map yourself and see what it shows you about how your memory works.

Activity

When I made my map and reviewed it, I realized how important the sense of smell is in my memory process: the smell of the Helm's Bakery Truck and the smell of the sourdough loaves on San Francisco's fisherman's wharf brought back the richest memories for me.

Writing researchers Linda Flower and John Hayes (1977) explain that we store memory in "rich bits," chemically encoded pieces of information that incorporate many experiences and associations. Flower and Hayes liken them to intuition and explain that without the intervention of language these bits never become useful to us. Although I have stored many complex bits of information about my family and my daily experience in my brain, I can only examine, enjoy, and use this information fully when I put it into words. Looking over my map I can also see that relationships occupy a central place in my memory process: Most of my memories center on my relationships with my family members. The words in my map serve as memory triggers, allowing me to relive significant moments in my life and to make new connections between my past experience and my present situation. If you examine your cognitive map, what memory triggers seem to matter most to you? Did you remember any details when you did your map that surprised or pleased you? What were they?

Most people who use writing as a way of remembering the past find that many small details they had entirely forgotten resurface during the writing activity. This is not to say that all of these memories are accurate. Experiments on the working of memory reveal that many factors—including stress, distorted self-assessment, and elapsed time—alter the way we remember past events. Also, the way others remember or represent the past can influence our memories of it (Loftus 1988).

To demonstrate how malleable memory really is, write a one-page description of something you remember from your childhood. Make sure that it's a memory that is fairly vivid for you and that someone in your family will probably also remember. After you've written your description down, talk to the family member who shared the experience with you. Ask for his or her description. What discrepancies did you find?

I've often found that my memory of a situation differs radically from others' memories. When I finished high school, I expected to be given my father's old Volkswagen Beetle; I clearly remembered that he had promised it to me when I was a freshman. My graduation day arrived at last, but my father had no memory of any such promise! He eventually traded the car in on a new car for himself. Because I know my father is an honest man, I know he really didn't remember having promised me the car. It's not impossible, in fact, that I made up the promise in my own mind and came to believe in it because I wanted it to be true.

The malleability of memory is one reason why some people like to keep daily journals: a written record of the highlights in one's life can help to keep memory more accurate. In business situations, many individuals like to create a "paper trail," a series of memos and notes that record each worker's responsibilities for a certain project. In these cases, writing becomes a way of preserving memory and creating a history of a business undertaking or a private life.

But writing has many more interesting uses than to preserve or explore memory. In and out of school settings, writing can help individuals synthesize new information with previously learned information and thus create new, complex structures of *understanding*. So let's move from the realm of memory and examine some writing activities that help us to think more clearly and create new ways of knowing what we need to know.

Activity

One writing activity my students and I both enjoy is the "teacher exercise," an activity passed on to me by a friend who took a workshop on creative diary keeping. The teacher exercise is an example of a dialogue activity, a way of externalizing some of the internal conversations that take place between different voices within yourself. To create a successful dialogue with one of your internal teaching voices, start by listing important teachers in your life. These may be people you have known and admired, people you've never met, characters in stories or film, places you've traveled, even objects. (For example, I learn a lot by watching the ways trees share ground and sky with one another; they're a cooperative group that live together peaceably unless dire necessity forces them to struggle for the same ground. From trees I've learned the importance of being as much as one can be wherever one stands.) I've included a partial list of my favorite teachers below:

My music teacher, Virginia Petersen

My dissertation director, Professor Don Daiker

My colleague, Elizabeth Renfro

My neighbor, Jean Graybeal

Trees

After you make a list that suits you, try writing a dialogue between yourself and one of your teachers about a problem you want to solve. Write as quickly as you can, allowing the dialogue to surprise you. Continue to write for several pages.

Written dialogue exercises like this one frequently allow writers to experience sudden insights about problems as diverse as family fights and difficult chemistry equations. Even if your internal teacher doesn't have an answer for your problem, he or she can often provide a strategy for approaching the problem so that you can think about it more calmly, analytically, and effectively.

Another useful dialogue exercise involves re-creating an argument you've had with someone, but approaching the argument from the other person's point of view. Include not only the spoken part of the argument, but also the thoughts of the person you argued against. How does that person respond internally to the things you did and said during the argument? When you consider the argument from his or her viewpoint, can you better understand why he or she responded to you in the way he or she did? Try this dialogue exercise here, including the other person's internal thoughts in parentheses.

Being able to understand your opponent's point of view has long been a recommended technique for learning how to persuade others to see your side of an argument. Psychologist Carl Rogers (1965) has claimed that only through validating the viewpoint of another can we hope to have our own viewpoints validated. Analyzing and validating an opponent's view before opposing it may lead to better negotiations for a third, socially constructed viewpoint between all of the parties involved. And you may surprise yourself by finding that, after studying someone else's view, you agree with his/her opinion more than you'd realized.

I recall a turbulent time in my household when I was still in my teens. During an argument with my mother, I claimed that she always put her own needs and interests ahead of my own. She countered by telling me that most of her activities (cooking, cleaning, driving, shopping) revolved around my needs, and that if I didn't understand this, I had better start trying some of her responsibilities on for size. If I had stopped to think about the world from her point of view, I would have seen that she contributed a generous share of her time and energy to keeping me happy. Because I didn't stop to think about her perspective, I made her angry, had some of my privileges revoked, and took on a new household responsibility, that of family cook. She and I didn't have a conversation about our misunderstandings: we had a fight. And fighting, although it produces a satisfactory amount of adrenaline and a momentary surge of self-righteous indignation, rarely transforms the problems it seeks to address.

Now that you've warmed up your imagination by creating the voices of a teacher and an opponent, consider some of the other ways that imagination can intersect with writing to help you create connections and new insights. Below, I've described a few activities that students of mine have found useful. Read them over, then try one.

Activity

Letter from the Future.   Write yourself a letter from an older version of yourself. What will you be like in twenty-five years? Where will you live? What will you do for a living? What will matter to you most? Write to yourself from this older perspective. What advice should your older self give your present self to make sure you arrive at the future you most want?

Intersection.   List five subjects you've studied in school. Choose the two that seem most different from each other and write a paragraph describing all of their similarities and connections, even if you really have to stretch to find these.

Drawing into Writing.   Draw three pictures of a recurring problem in your life, whether it's studying mathematics or making satisfying friendships. Date one of these pictures from an earlier time in your life, one from the present, and one from the future. Write a paragraph or two that explores the connections between these pictures. What patterns can you start to detect by exploring the ways these pictures relate to each other? What alternative behaviors or approaches might help you solve the problem you've explored?

These activities work equally well for advancing your understanding of your private life and of your scholastic endeavors. You can just as easily ask a future version of yourself about the many reasons why studying writing or mathematics now might help you later in life as you can ask that self about the benefits of vigorous exercise over the course of many years. One important feature of activities like these is that they give you a chance to become more involved in your learning process. Research on cognition, our internal thought processes, indicates that personal involvement in any learning activity increases the chances that learning will be sophisticated rather than superficial, and memorable rather than easily forgotten (Mandler 1984). With a little thought and creativity, you can see how activities such as these could help you in a variety of classes and situations. In a history course, you might write a journal entry from the point of view of a historical figure; in a chemistry course, you might write a conversation among the elements in an equation. You'll enjoy learning more and learn more effectively if you can construct approaches to learning that engage your attention and challenge your imagination.

One of the most powerful ways to challenge yourself through written language and to learn any lesson well is to develop a facility with metaphors and similes. Some researchers argue that metaphors—comparisons between like things—are the fundamental building blocks of all interpretive endeavors. This is because metaphors tap in to our most basic ways of knowing about the world—through our senses and our bodily motions. Everything we understand, every new piece of knowledge we add to what we already know, connects with some physical experience of our environment. This is the critical function of metaphor: to provide us with linguistic links between abstract or unexamined thoughts and our physical understanding of the world in which we live.

That last sentence may be hard to understand without a concrete example of the way metaphors and similes work. Let me provide you with an example from my own life. As a freshman in college, I enrolled in an astronomy course, a class I nearly failed. I have hated astronomy ever since but never stopped to think about why. By constructing a simile, I can begin to examine my reasons for responding so negatively to this academic subject. To construct the simile, I'll use the abstract, unexamined problem ("I hate studying astronomy") and a physical experience to which I can compare it. For my physical experience, I use the technique of association, jotting down the first example that comes to mind of something else I hate: eating a rotten bing cherry. So here's my simile: Studying astronomy is like *eating a rotten bing cherry.*

What sense can I make of this comparison? I'll start with the physical side of the equation. Bing cherries are my favorite food. I look forward to cherry season every year and have been known to consume a whole bag of cherries for lunch or dinner. So when I get a rotten cherry, I'm disappointed and disagreeably surprised. My mouth is all set for one kind of taste sensation, but the cherry feels mealy and tastes moldy on my tongue.

Having sorted through these reactions to the rotten cherry, I can start thinking about ways the eating experience reminds me of the astronomy class I took. I remember now that before I enrolled in the course, I expected to like it. I've always been a science fiction fan, and I assumed an astronomy class would focus mostly on facts about distant planets (with some speculation about extraterrestrial life-forms thrown in for good measure). In fact, the professor talked mostly about physics. He wanted us to learn a variety of mathematical calculations that would help us understand how scientists interpret the information they receive from telescopes. Because I expected one kind of experience in the course and got another (very much like expecting a good cherry but biting into a rotten one), I reacted to astronomy with distaste. Realizing this makes me wonder if I wouldn't be wise to give astronomy another try. After all, I may have caused my own problems in learning because of the expectations I carried with me into the class. Now that I'm older and a bit more open-minded, I might enjoy learning something about telescopes and the use of physics to understand the stars.

Writing theorist Peter Elbow (1981) suggests an interesting metaphor activity, which students in many of my writing classes tell me later is the single most useful discovery tool I taught them. This activity will help you make surprising, creative connections if you do the first half quickly and the second half thoughtfully. First, choose a problem (scholastic or personal) that you haven't yet solved. Quickly, without stopping to think about your response, write down its color, its shape, its size, its smell. Now take several minutes to explain, in writing, why you gave this problem each of these physical properties (for a whole series of metaphor activities, see Elbow 1981). Were you able to discover what some of your metaphors meant?

Often, using metaphors to redefine a problem can give you an entirely new perspective on your situation. Developing skill with metaphors will also enhance your use of descriptive and poetic language in your more formal writing tasks.

Finally, you can also employ writing in classes across the disciplines to help strengthen your learning process. Most students take notes during lectures, even though many classroom lectures only repeat material that can be found in the course textbook. If you notice that the professors in some of your classes go over reading material in their lectures, consider using writing in their classes to do something other than take notes. Here are some suggestions: periodically summarize the key points the lecturer has just covered; decide what puzzles you about what you've heard, and write down questions that you'd like to ask in class or during the teacher's office hours; listen for and jot down discrepancies between what the lecturer says and what you thought you knew about the subject (discrepancies should be cleared up in a conversation with the teacher or by rereading the course's text). All of these writing strategies allow you to interact with your learning, to question the material actively instead of sitting like a porous lump in the lecture hall waiting to be filled with someone else's knowledge. Students who take an assertive, interested approach to learning get more out of the courses they take and enjoy their educational experiences far more than students who learn material by rote for exams.

The writing strategies mentioned above can help you during your assigned reading. Keep blank paper handy to copy out intriguing or confusing portions of the text. Select some of these passages for brief writing: What questions do the passages raise or what new ideas do they give you? A particularly rewarding technique for examining your assigned reading is to make connections between unrelated courses. Ask yourself hard questions, such as How does this rule in physics connect with what I learned about the law of supply and demand in my economics course? or Did the conquest of the New World by the Spanish that I'm studying in my history course contain any of the ethical dilemmas I'm studying in my philosophy class? If you take a few minutes to note these questions and respond to them briefly in writing, you'll begin to see many opportunities for drawing on information from all of your classes in developing an educated worldview. You'll probably come up with some interesting paper topics this way, too.

Above all, remember that writing for learning need not be correct, sophisticated, or polished. Writing for learning should serve you as a tool for analyzing and synthesizing many kinds of information in your life. This is writing for *you*, not a teacher, employer, or classmate. Although you may choose to share some of this writing or to develop ideas from this writing into more formal prose, writing for learning should be stress-free, exploratory, and mind-opening. Use it to enjoy and enhance your mind's activity as you study, reflect, and live.

Works Cited

Elbow, Peter (1981). *Writing with Power*. New York: Oxford Press.

Flower, Linda, and John Hayes (1977). "Problem-Solving Strategies and the Writing Process." *College English, 39,* 456.

Loftus, Elisabeth (1988). *Mind and Body*. New York: Norton.

Mandler, G. (1984). *Mind and Body*. New York: Norton.

Rogers, Carl (1965). *Client-Centered Therapy*. Boston: Houghton Mifflin.

Sharing Ideas

- As you tried Thia Wolf's activities while you read, which proved most useful to you and why?

- In an essay later in this collection, Kate Ronald explains that "with computers and copier machines, we don't worry much anymore about memory." In Thia's essay, however, a writer's memories are very important, and writing is a way to "improve memory, foster insights, and accelerate learning." Are these essayists contradicting each other or are they discussing memory in different ways?

- Thia suggests that you can tap in to your memories through writing in general and through particular writing strategies like mapping, setting up dialogues with internal voices, and drawing. What, then, is the importance of memory to writers?

- You may have used memory maps before (the technique is sometimes called clustering) or you may freewrite or list to capture the vivid and important details of your past. Share your personal methods (listening to music, walking, etc.) for triggering memory.

- How have two different memories of the same event (yours and another family member's, for example) affected your life?

- Thia suggests that it can be very important for a writer to be able to understand the viewpoint(s) of others. Share a time in your life when that was true.

- Everyone knows that poets use similes and metaphors, and Thia claims they have a lot to offer to any writer. What do you think of her claim and her example (astronomy and rotten cherries)?

- Metaphors seem to come naturally to some people. Do you know anyone who regularly compares one thing to another? Write a sketch of that person, capturing his or her language, and the way he or she makes comparisons.

- If you don't normally make comparisons easily yourself, take a piece of your writing and try to consciously add some metaphors. What changes? How do you like the new version?

————————————

2

Composting with a Writer's Notebook

An Interactive Reading

Jim Mahoney

Jim Mahoney teaches composition at DeVry University and writing methods to future English teachers at The College of New Jersey, where he also supervises student teachers. A retired high school English teacher and department chairperson from Long Island, Jim lives in Yardley, Pennsylvania, and roots hard for his New York Mets and Jets but is even more passionate about his family and six grandchildren. He is an e-mail junkie who would love to hear from you at Campyhits@aol.com if you have any questions or comments regarding his chapter.

Did you know that most writers always keep a little book with them to write in? They carry this notebook because writers like to be able to write down ideas as they come to them. Some call it a day book; some call it a journal or a log; some use a lot of other names. I like to call it my writer's notebook—it's simple, direct and makes it hard to forget what the book is for. No matter what you call it, it helps writers learn to be prepared for those ideas and for opportunities to observe and then record small details of life that come at times when we least expect them.

In my classes I require students to keep a writer's notebook; your teacher might require it too. In any case, I recommend the practice if you want to participate in the life of being a writer.

Something else you should know is that all of this kind of writing should be done in a separate notebook, apart from anything else you do in this class or any other class. It's not a place for class notes or for rough drafts of your finished pieces. This is a place for thoughts and collections of ideas. I never collect the writer's notebook from my students and I never demand that anyone else read it or hear it be read from. (That doesn't mean, however, that you can't read something aloud from it to the class or show someone something you have written; that will always remain your choice.) I do require a page count, which I do with my students at my side, near the end of the semester, to give them credit for keeping their writer's notebook. I suggest that you to try to write at least twenty-five full pages. If there are pages that are partially filled out, I count them as half or quarter pages and add them up that way. Writing on the front and back of a page counts as two pages. You can use any kind of notebook you want—a marble notebook or a spiral, college ruled or wide lined, about seven to eight inches wide by ten or eleven inches long.

I also ask my students to write a reflection at the end of the semester on how they used their writer's notebook. This will be one of several reflections included in the portfolio that will serve as a final assessment of their work. You might not have much of a reaction to the writer's notebook at this time, but in the weeks ahead, you will come to develop some personal feelings for this book. Later in this chapter, I'll share some reflections of other students who have kept a writer's notebook. Now let's try some writing activities.

Quick Writes

This is an interactive reading, which means I'm going to ask you to stop reading and do some writing as we go. So, put today's date in the upper left-hand corner, out in the margin, and then write, "Quick Write #1." I'm going to give you a prompt and I'd like you to write for one minute—that's right, sixty seconds, that's all—moving your pen as fast as you can, not worrying if any of your words are correctly spelled, or even complete, or if you have complete sentences. I'd like you to pour out of your head as many words as possible in the next minute. I'll give you the prompt and you can change any single word of it or change everything about it. If you are halfway into writing about it and something else pops into your head, feel free to follow those thoughts and write rapidly about them. Oh yeah, get your watch out to time yourself, since I can't be there with you right now. Here's the first prompt; respond to it before reading further.

1. When I was in eighth grade, I . . .

This prompt always seems to work with students and teachers. There is just something about eighth grade when everything was changing and we were becoming aware of all sorts of new things. What I've noticed is that the average person will write about four or five lines in one minute. Go back and count your lines. Only four? Well, maybe you'll learn to write faster and even get up to five or six lines next time; most writers produce more words as they practice. It also depends on the size of your handwriting and the size of the paper you are using. And, by the way, college students aren't any faster or slower than younger or older people. Sometimes, though, they have trouble getting started because they begin to monitor their ideas, thinking that some ideas aren't fit or suitable for college writing. Forget about second-guessing—just write.

You might be interested in why I start with writing. Actually, if we could bring in contraptions to measure your brain activity, we'd discover more brain waves when you were writing than there are as you are reading this right now. Researchers working with Alzheimer's patients whose brains were faltering as they lost the capacity to remember learned that the brain does not necessarily deteriorate with aging and, in fact, can get stronger and larger. With activity and stimulation, it can actually grow new dendrites, getting stronger and fuller the more the brain works. Since writing is one of the best stimuli for brain activity, it's a good exercise to start with.

Now, skip a line, write "Quick Write #2," and write for one minute about this prompt:

2. I'll always remember that wonderful, glorious day.

Remember, if you want to change *wonderful, glorious* to *horrible* or *nightmarish*, feel free to do so. Write as if the pen were on fire, as if moving it fast were the only way to keep your hand from burning. Skip words if you like. See if this time you can write a line or two more than you did the last time.

Did you write any more than you did the last time? You probably did. And I guess you were wondering how this might help you become a better writer. If topics for each assignment are given by your teacher, it may not be so obvious how the writer's notebook might help. However, if you're not told what you have to write about and you have to come up with topics on your own, the writer's notebook can become a place to go to look for such topics, things from your past and things you've learned to notice about life going on around you. As a student, you may have been too busy to notice anything carefully. We'll spend some time slowing things down for you so that you'll have time to notice the world and you'll have some of those observations in there as well.

Ready for our third prompt? I generally do three at the start of each of my classes. My students always have their notebook open at the start of class, and some are even writing in it before class, coming up with their own things to write about. Skip a line, write "Quick Write #3," and write for one minute about this prompt:

**3. When I think about entering their house,
I remember that delicious smell of food.**

Remember, you are not trying to write anything perfect or polished. You are just gathering material to get as much as possible collected in this notebook in one minute. Your pen is on fire. Put it out by covering six or seven lines. Go!

Stop! I know; you just got started, were on a roll, and I stopped you. Sorry, but we've got lots more to do; you can always go back to a topic and continue it on another page of your writer's notebook. In that space you skipped after your quick write, just put a little note to remind you where you continued it. Number all your pages and simply write down the page number where it continues. Noted American writer Ernest Hemingway always stopped writing every day at about noon but made it a point to stop in the middle of a sentence, so he could easily pick up writing again in midthought. And the truth is that it's easy to pick up where you left off because it will still be hot.

Observing and Recording

Earlier, we used the writer's notebook to collect material from our past. I often refer to this notebook as a compost heap (trust me, it's a good thing), a place where we throw live and dead grass clippings, leaves, clippings from shrubs, even skins from fruits and vegetables, anything that will decompose to produce rich compost, what is referred to by gardeners as black gold because it is so organically powerful in helping other plants and vegetables grow. We'll use the stuff you throw into your writer's notebook to help grow rich, healthy pieces of writing.

Writers are good at noticing details. They see the little things because they train their eyes and ears to pick up on them. Did you ever notice how a very young child, perhaps one or two years old, finds the most interesting things on the ground? Perhaps it is because children are so close to it that they want to pick everything up, examine it carefully, and even taste it! They persist and find the smallest openings in things and burrow their little fingers in, inspecting all the angles. They are never too busy with other things. They notice everything, and even though they're only two or three years old, they are leading wide-awake lives. I am going to suggest you try an exercise in which you notice everything about the room you are in and about the people, sights, sounds, and smells around you. I even refer to this as spying. As you write about the things around you, stop and slyly notice someone in your view, how he or she holds a pen, how his head moves as he writes, what she does with her hands, feet, or other body parts. I'm not going to have you race through this as we did the quick writes. Here you are more laid-back, observing and writing, observing and writing. For the next two to three minutes, stop reading and observe and write. Go ahead; try spying.

Inner and Outer Observations

Most writers present to the reader views of what they have been observing. We'll refer to these as outer observations; that is to say, anyone who is looking at a particular thing, say a bumblebee climbing around in a flower, would agree to the details observed, the physical movements of the bee. However, while we observe, we also have things going on inside our head, things such as what the bumblebee reminds us of, other bees we've known in our lifetime, how beautiful the flower is, how lucky the flower is to so strongly attract the bee, or how this activity reminds us of another person, oddly enough. All of these thoughts and more are the inner observations. These inner thoughts may even focus on our own thoughts or causes of stress at that particular moment. Inner observations, then, can pay attention to feelings we have that may be quite contrary to the observed object.

Not too long ago, I was giving a session on using the writer's notebook at a teacher conference and we spent much of the session outside, recording and writing. This is what I wrote:

Hurrying Home

The cement slab I sit on, at first inviting, now forces me to shift and I pull my jacket tighter, or so I want to, but choose to keep on writing. The small brown leaves lie crumpling beneath my feet, having dropped, sadly, and all too soon for me, from the brilliant yellow-leafed tree.

Perched at picnic tables, sitting cross-legged on the ground, standing in the parking lot, fellow observers shiver and write while the whizzing trailer-trucks on the Thruway head happily, or maybe sadly, perhaps to someone's death, going to places I do not go.

But maybe the dead leaves I stand on will connect to their dead, or to new births, like that of my three-week-old granddaughter, MacKenzie, whom I hurry home to.

In the next two or three minutes, continue recording your observations, but when other thoughts jump up, demanding your attention, notice them or see how they connect to what you are observing. You will probably find yourself looking and writing, looking and writing, and then writing longer and looking less. Go ahead.

———— ◆ ————

How did you like it? You could even take a moment now to write about the experience you just went through as you wrote. Doing that kind of writing could be considered metacognitive thinking, thinking about your thinking. The writer's notebook will also be a place where you can do that kind of reflective writing about things.

Ranking, Rating, and Talking

Please look back over all that you have written since we began and rank the topics you wrote about in importance to you. Give the topic that is most important to you a 1 and continue ranking the other topics. Then put an asterisk (*) next to any topic that you think you might like to come back to at a future time and write more about, perhaps even develop into a finished piece.

If you were doing the writing or the quick writes and the observing as activities during the first day of my class, I'd ask you to get together in groups of three and talk about the kinds of things you wrote about. Introduce yourself first and make sure everyone gets an equal time to talk. You won't have to read anything you wrote, but you can if you want to. You could talk with each other about the things you rated highest and why or mention topics or activities that you didn't like and explain why. I usually allow ten minutes to do this, so I normally limit each student to no more than two minutes of talking at first. When each person in your group has had a turn, then you can go back to talk about other things you left out. If you're doing this alone in your room, try to find some others in your class who also read this article and did the writing as you did. You'll find it is so much better to talk with others about your thoughts and even your writing. It will be worth the effort to find a couple of friendly faces in your class to do this with.

Other Kinds of Quick Writes

My students have often found that they write best, at least at first, when I provide the prompts and allow time in class to do the writing. I worry that they'll grow to be dependent on their teacher to get started. Therefore, I'm going to show you a way to find your own prompts so that you can do this kind of fast writing on your own. It'll mean finding some poems that will get you going. For example, I'm looking at a poem by Mary Oliver called "The Journey." I might read this poem with you (or ask you to read it to yourself) and then select a line or phrase to use as your prompt, altering it just as you did when we started. Suppose you were attracted to the poem's opening words. You would copy that prompt into your notebook and write about that for the next minute or more. (In class, I always limit the quick writes to a minute because of the other things we have to do, but you can write longer when you're doing it outside of class.) Then you could look at other lines in the poem. You might select another line. Again, you could write for a minute or more. When we do this in class, I stop students after two minutes and urge them to find another prompt, and I repeat this again after another two minutes. You will find it hard to stop yourself when you are doing this alone, but just remind yourself that the writer's notebook is meant to get you started, and you can always return to any individual entry. By stopping you after two minutes, I am giving you more variations of topics to write about, thus increasing the different kinds of materials that you are placing in your own compost heap.

A Backward Glance:
Reflecting on the Writer's Notebook

I ask my students a couple of times during the semester to read through the entries in their writer's notebook and write a reflection on what they've observed. I hand out sheets of paper with some questions for them to think about as they are looking over their entries and then as they begin to reflect. You might use these questions or make up your own:

- What is your strongest (or most important) entry and what significance does it have for you as a person or as a writer?

- What is your weakest entry and why? What does it reveal to you?

- Where were you when you did most of your writing? Your best writing?

- Are you better off when a topic is given or put on the board, or do you write best when you are alone and with your own thoughts and observations?

- What kind of growth or change have you seen in your writer's notebook or in your attitude toward using it?

- How useful or tedious has the writer's notebook become?

- Did you write any entry because of something you read? Something you overheard?

- Has your writer's notebook helped you as a writer or helped in accomplishing anything for your English class or other classes?

Final Reflections

At the end of the semester, as my students revise some of their writing for their final portfolio, I ask them also to include a reflection on the writer's notebook. They return to some of those backward glances that they wrote during the semester and they think about the final entries. Below are some comments from students in a recent freshman composition class. Darianz, a foreign exchange student, wrote:

Upon Further Inspection

Glancing back at my writing in my writer's notebook, I find that it has helped me on more than one point. It is designed to stimulate a writer's mind and catalog ideas for future use. While writing in it, I have tried to avoid creating any pattern but when I read through all my notes at one time I found that there is a recurring theme: my fiancée. This brings me to the strongest and most important entry I wrote in the class, a first thought that would later become my first poem, entitled "Admiration with Love." Deciding to write about my lovely fiancée gave me an outlet for my emotions as a person and a familiar subject for me to write about as a writer. One of the first parts of the draft in question was, "The countless days they stayed apart, him working hard to get the visa." That was one of the driving sentences that got me on a straight path to creating a powerful poem.

Darianz went on later to explain when and how he wrote in his writer's notebook:

Regretfully, I did most of my writing during my bus ride to and from school, a ride that does not help when it comes to concentration and continuation. It is a bumpy, noisy, uncomfortable trip, interrupting me more often, making it hard to even finish a sentence. On the other hand, and not so surprising, my best writing was accomplished in the classroom where I had the opportunity to calmly write in a quiet environment. This is also the time that I wrote the fastest and the time it was easiest to get my thoughts down on paper, although most of the time, we were given the topic by the teacher. This made it easier for me to focus on the actual development of the topic and not spend all of my time figuring out what topic I should breech. A good example of a subject I wrote about in class are the lines, "The clearest memory I have of childhood is when me and my best friend were up on the top of this huge and very steep hill. We were just about to ride down it on our bikes and . . ." This part inspired my third finished piece, "Wheels."

Kirk wrote in his reflection:

Like every carpenter who has a belt of tools, in my book-bag I had valued instruments. Never in any other class did I have notebooks with such meaning and worth behind them. My Writer's Notebook and Literary Log were both unique in their influence to improve my writing.

Initially during the first day of class, I thought the Writer's Notebook was pointless and I would fill it with random drawings and non-sense babble. However, in my final pages, I realized these twenty-five pages in my notebook did not have a single sketch on them. Idea after idea was scribbled down in a single flow of thoughts about each topic. Writing as fast as I could without stopping to think about content was my goal. Further into the pages, you can actually notice where the paragraphs gradually get longer. The Writer's Notebook was a good place to jot down random thoughts I had, that I might possibly use in one of my finished pieces.

So that's it. If you're interested, accept my challenge and go out and get a notebook for yourself, a writer's notebook. Put the things you've written as you read along in the front and go from there, finding just ten minutes to write each day or every other day. In the end, you'll love the rich compost you've collected for growing new things. Let me know how it goes.

Sharing Ideas

- Have you tried keeping a journal or a writer's notebook before? If so, describe some of your experiences.

- Reflect on the quick writes that you tried while reading this chapter. Were they successful in generating material of interest in a short burst of writing time?

- What do you think of Jim Mahoney's idea that these writings should be accumulated as a kind of compost pile from which the ideas for rich writing topics emerge?

- What did you think of the idea of rapid writing? Were you frustrated at the idea of speed?

- How did you feel about being stopped after you'd just gotten started?

- Are you worried about writing things that are very personal and that someone might read without your permission? How do you feel about writing about your feelings or about your past?

3

Memories of Wandering Thoughts

Amanda McCorquodale

Amanda McCorquodale was a senior at Florida State University when she included this essay in her class writing portfolio.

"Hey, Amanda, do you need a ride?" The other kids didn't walk home from school.

"No thanks," I smiled and wiped away the sweat already forming on my forehead. "Actually I prefer to walk."

For most, walking is a last resort, something one does when they have exhausted all other options and just need to get somewhere. I, on the other hand, find excuses to go walking, a practice that started out quite innocently but has festered into a healthy compulsion. I walk because my peace of mind demands it. I walk because if I don't, I would go slowly insane. What is it about walking that feels so good?

My first walks arose out of necessity when I was a high school student and not yet old enough to drive. There was no one available to pick my brother and me up at dismissal, so we had to walk home instead. The mid-afternoon sun would beat down on us and my back would ache from the calculus and history textbooks that I brought home each night but did not read. It wasn't until my brother joined the football team and was unavailable to escort me home that I realized I relied on the walks home from Miami Country Day School for more than just transportation. But now, I was instructed not to walk home by myself, so on the way home, I had to invent daily stories about rides I got from friends.

23

I walked quickly off campus so that I was not seen by my brother as he ran around the field that sat on the edge of school. Once out of sight, I began my meandering pace, enjoying the first calm moment of the hectic day as I pulled my book bag around to the front to minimize the strain on my back. I was in no hurry to get home, piles of assignments tainted my after-school life. I took time to enjoy the walks home, I was being productive by getting myself from point A to point B, but I was able to relax in the fresh air and have some time to myself.

At first, I thought it was the therapeutic practice of exchanging my day's stories with my brother, using words to drop the day's hassles like bread crumbs on a path. Yet with the absence of my brother at my swaying side, I saw that solitude was very suitable for walks. Instead of listening to someone else's stress, I was given the full twenty minutes to untangle my own head. I arrived at the chain-link fence that lined my backyard; my T-shirt under my backpack felt damp against my warm skin. My lungs had expelled all the recycled air of the stale classrooms and replaced it with real air, the kind you inhale greedily as if it were a drug. I had reached home, refreshed and pleasantly exhausted.

——— ◆ ———

Walks allow you to creep up on a destination; the switch to the next phases of your day is gradual. This slow transition gives you space to wake up or wind down. And just as sleep is time for dreams that sort through all the day's stimulation, walking is a mini-dream sequence where your feet go on cruise control and your mind does a little spring cleaning.

What could be more natural than walking? Yet, the automobile threatens the sanctity of this natural activity. Thought to add convenience and save time, automobiles are seen as symbols of progress in American society. Although with cars, there is also traffic and parking. By the time you have reached your destination, almost all of your patience is worn away already. I should mention that I do own a car and am grateful for its convenience when grocery shopping or going to the laundromat. Sure, cars allow us the capacity of traveling far from home, but if you could work down the block and walk, why wouldn't you?

In my third year in college, I was the bookkeeper in a copy shop downtown. From early in the morning to late in the afternoon, I kept track of the shop's account activities, from minuscule five-cent copies to large payments on copying machines. My brain and eyes were pained with all the attention to detail, how was I going to get through a semester of this? One night while my roommate and her friends stayed up laughing, I lay in bed unable to sleep, realizing every minute I didn't fall asleep was going to make it that much harder to wake up the next morning. I felt as if I was in some whirlpool of bad days, everything compounding in a day of work that I dreaded doing. As I blinked away sleep, it occurred to me. What if I walked?

The next morning I laced up sneakers under my business casual clothes and walked up Park Avenue to work. I passed by the Tallahassee parks where, often, homeless men and women reclined asleep on the shaded benches. I watched students drive by, hurriedly shoving bagels into their mouths. Suited business men balanced cups of coffee in one hand while fishing their briefcase out of their backseats with the other. Downtown restaurants emitted smells of morning nutrients: fresh brewed java, eggs, sausage, and muffins which I watched the employees place in storefront windows. I wasn't alone, the world was waking up with me and we were in this thing called morning together.

By the time I arrived at work, not only my legs, but my mental faculties were stretched and awake. I didn't clutch endless cups of coffee, bribing my eyes to open. And when my boss greeted me at the door with "How are we three cents short from yesterday?" I was able to form complete sentences and explain how with a smile.

In the same respect, I was anxious to leave the office and begin the down-hill walk home, same terrain and sights but the shadows and scattered light were newly arranged. I exited the glass doors of the copy shop, the muscles in my back were knotted in elaborate patterns and my shoulders and wrists ached from hours of mindless data entry. I could still hear the grating voice of the caller who had called in with a complaint. I paced myself down the sidewalk, passed lanes of bumper to bumper five o'clock traffic. I tried not to look smug as my average walking speed gave me incredible forward progress when compared to their idling engines. I was *going home*. I soon left the gridlock of smoking exhaust pipes and squeaky brakes. I entered the chain of downtown parks and the caller's voice that had been echoing in my head turned into a distant murmur and finally, silence. I let my stride lengthen as the slope of the hill propelled my legs forward. This was almost too easy. I walked even further from the drone of car horns and general buzz of downtown closing time; I lingered in the moss-draped and oak-lined parks, a shaded purgatory between work and home. Soon I entered the student country, full of loud music and cigarettes, where I lived. I passed down College Avenue, the fraternity and sorority houses emitting the dinner smells of fried chicken and cornbread, before reaching the steep slope of my driveway that descended into my apartment complex. My neighbors, draped on beat-up couches outside their doors, had already started unwinding.

"Here comes Amanda," one remarked as I appeared at the driveway. "How was your day?" he asked as I approached.

I answered before I could realize that this was not the answer I had expected to give as I left the copy shop, not fifteen minutes earlier.

"Good" I smiled, "a nice day."

After four months of the trip up and back down the hill, I was connected to the unique sights and sounds of Tallahassee that I witnessed each morning and afternoon. That world seemed like a breathing organism and through my walks, I had intimate knowledge of its habits and schedules. I had my own version of

Tallahassee and my feet traced its seven hills, allowing me to unfold into its open spaces and onto its sidewalks.

———————— ◆ ————————

In Geoff Nicholson's novel, *Bleeding London*, Stuart, the protagonist, decides to walk down every single street in London. His calculations tell him this could be done in three years if he accomplished ten miles a day. Why all this walking? Well, as Nicholson states, "He [Stuart] did genuinely believe that if he walked long enough and far enough he might eventually work out why he was walking at all." Very simply, walking occupies your body while your thoughts are left to entertain you. It is much like the habit of social smoking, which permits a person to people watch, an activity that, by itself, would seem eerie and intrusive.

The following spring semester, my walking obsession helped me digest London as I studied abroad at the Florida State Study Center in London. Every morning for four months, I woke up unable to believe where I was. It seemed surreal, like I was watching a movie, like my life was happening to someone else. The only way I could fully comprehend that I was actually living in London was to touch my feet to the London pavement. *Pavement* is one of those words that distinguishes American English from British English and *pavement* just sounds more solid than *sidewalk*. To me, *pavement* meant reality and I needed its daily reassurance that my experience wasn't resting on clouds.

I left our flat on Great Russell Street each day, walking as far around our neighborhood of the West End as I could, exploring the bustling areas of Soho and Covent Garden. I passed by the pigeon-laced Trafalgar Square I had only seen in movies, walked past infamous galleries I had only read about, and saw illustrious museums that had only been alluded to in my textbooks. Sometimes I walked with a camera in hand, never really stopping long enough to use it. I would lose all sense of time and finally, realizing how far I had wandered into truly foreign territory, had to head back. Yet, getting lost is quite a nice treat when walking.

One Sunday morning, I went exploring in the business district, the square mile of London that is referred to as the City. I was lost in thought and had taken too many unnoticed turns; once I did take notice of exactly where I was, I had no clue how I got there. As I wandered further into the density of unrecognized streets, I heard the distant drone of bagpipes. I quickened my pace in the direction of the music, darting in between buildings to reach what I soon realized was a parade. I reached the procession just as the bagpipe band passed, kilts swaying with their stride. Next in the procession, hundreds of men in black suits and bowler hats stepped in perfect unison as if in a funeral mass. "What's the occasion?" I asked an American couple next to me.

"Today is Irish National Day," the husband answered.

I followed the parade around St. James Park and soon it led me into the familiar streets of Buckingham Palace. From this highly touristy point, I was able to navigate myself to the closest tube stop and return home to the study center flats. The delight of walking is while you believe yourself to be lost, you're liable to see sights that you would have missed otherwise.

Finally, I had walked so much that I had exhausted the London encircling my flat, and would take the tube to distant stops like Brixton and Whitehall to wander somewhere new. These distant areas required a different kind of walking. My walks around central London had been susceptible to the larger organism a moving crowd creates, and once I had mastered walking on the British left, I had no choice but to surrender to the motion of the left-oriented. Yet the areas of Brixton and Whitehall were relatively pedestrian-free, compared to the frenzied nature of, for instance, Oxford Street. The open space of these pavements permitted me to meander and stroll, stopping occasionally for a treat or a memento purchase. I walked through Madonna's neighborhood of Notting Hill and the world-famous theatre district, hoping to brush by someone famous, unexpectedly, on the London street.

I walked on the cracked pavement, intoxicated by red double-decker bus fumes, imagining the hundreds of years of history that had laid its foot here in London as well. Part of me walked to escape the small flat where I lived cramped with five other students. Yet more than anything else, I walked because I wanted to feel what London-ness was all about and so that when I left, my feet would be worn down with its realness.

The London pavement has felt the soles of endless numbers of famous figures. Known for his obsessive walking, Charles Dickens would commonly walk extremes of twenty miles. Can we assume that this classic author used these walks to stamp out the madness that might have accompanied his genius?

As long as we're looking at historical proof for the power of walking, let us look all the way back to Aristotle's philosophy. During his lessons, students would walk with him as he taught, creating a method of mobile intellectualism, called "peripateticism." Aristotle must have believed in the connection between stride and clarity of thought.

Certainly, behaviors in everyday life point to the subconscious role walking plays in our mental health. What do expecting fathers do in hospital waiting rooms? They pace. They set their feet in deliberate rhythm, arms clasped at the small of the back, head lowered in thought. There is so much going on inside that they have to express it in an outward action such as walking. With the steady rhythm of footsteps, our minds are inspired to place the chaos of thoughts in order and soon our darting thoughts take linear and understandable direction.

Rebecca Solnit has written an entire book on walking called *Wanderlust: A History of Walking*. In it, she breaks down the connection of mind to feet while taking a stroll. "Thinking is generally thought of as doing nothing in a production-oriented society, and doing nothing is hard to do. It's best done by disguising it as doing something, and the something closest to doing nothing is walking." The United States is a culture that boasts of its world power, suffers the lowest number of allotted vacation days, and whose citizens complain about insufficient time to exercise. Americans figuratively run themselves into the ground with monetary ambition, while remaining sedentary in their seats.

——————— ◆ ———————

I need to push forward as my veins pulse and my mind reels. Let it be written on my headstone that I was a woman of the streets, a roaming nomad, a sauntering pedestrian, a pacing fool, a hiking hermit, a wandering spirit, a watchman on her rounds and so on and on.

Works Cited

Nicholson, Geoff (1997). *Bleeding London*. New York: Overlook Press.

Solnit, Rebecca (2000). *Wanderlust: A History of Walking*. New York: Viking.

Process Narrative for "Memories of Wandering Thoughts"

Once I had completed all the inventions, I still did not feel that I had found a topic interesting enough to inspire ten pages. So I tried to remember times in my life that had meant something to me. The instances when walking was an everyday activity kept surfacing, and I realized that I preached about walking in conversation with friends. Since I was already an advocate, I knew my philosophies of walks could turn into ten good pages and that I could use my personal experiences to illustrate my thoughts.

Now decided on a topic, I typed a page's worth of ideas on the subject, allowing myself to be less concerned with making sense than just getting ideas down on paper. I printed this initial draft and took it outside, where I sat on my front steps and read it. I became aware of what I wanted to express and then spent some time deciding how it could best be expressed. Without referring to this first page, I sat down to write again, this time with the overall plan in mind. I would intermix my personal experiences with walking with my personal opinion about walking and then add in some literary and historical references that furthered my point. My experiences would appear in the paper in chronological order, ending with prospects of my future.

This memory draft was five pages, completed in one session at my computer. For the next workshop, I read the comments my classmates had made on my paper and then reread the paper myself. I marked it up like a teacher grading a test, trying to distance myself from the person who wrote the paper. I read it out loud and looked for places that didn't sound quite right and reworded them until they flowed. I paid specific attention to places that begged for more detail. My next draft was fatter with added images, resulting in around eight pages. My group members read this draft and told me what they wanted to see more of and what to leave out.

For my portfolio draft, I reviewed my classmates' comments and once again reread my paper. This time, I tightened places that seemed unnecessary and tried to emphasize key sections that would lead the reader on to the end.

The challenge in this paper was to keep my "preachiness" in check. I didn't want the reader to feel I was rambling on my soap box. I hope my personal experiences and references made the paper more interesting to read and that they made my view seem less narrow-minded.

Before completing the portfolio draft, I sat with the previous draft that you [teacher] had edited and commented on. I looked for changes I agreed with and instances that you felt could use more description. Sick of sitting at my computer desk, I disassembled my computer and set it up on the coffee table in my living room. This new location refreshed my eye of editing and I went back into "Memories of Wandering Thoughts" and polished it up. I made sure all grammatical errors were corrected. The weeks that had passed from when I last spent time with the paper allowed me to further view it objectively. The weak places stood out and I tried to improve the areas that felt underdeveloped. I added more description about my high school walks. I added more to my walks up and down the hill, trying to bring the reader to see that there was a difference in my attitude from the beginning to the end of my walk home.

Sharing Ideas

- Thia Wolf, in her essay found earlier in this volume, suggested that you write a letter to the future. In what ways is Amanda McCorquodale's essay a letter to the past? Write your own letter of either sort or write an essay exploring the way past events shaped who you are today in a significant way.

- In what ways does Amanda's essay rely on memory work of the sort mentioned in Thia Wolf's essay?

- As Amanda did, make a list of times in your life that meant something to you, and also look for a common element of those times.

- Explore how walking matters in your own life (or doesn't matter). What form of transportation and meditation would you substitute? Some people like to drive long distances and think; for others, different forms of exercise provide meditative space: yoga, tai chi, the gym. In what way would an essay you might write on a similar topic resemble or depart from Amanda's essay?

- Return to a travel journal you've kept and look for a metaphor, image, or other writing prompt that could launch you on a reflective meditation.

Then, look to a Web bookstore to find someone else who has commented on travel in a way you might use in your own essay as Amanda uses the book *Wanderlust: A History of Walking*. If you aren't happy with your journal keeping, write an essay on how to keep a (better) travel journal. As you do this, consider p. 257, *Hint Sheet C, Your Journal* for ideas on journaling.

- Compose your own memory draft of one of your own essays. Read it, set it aside, and write down what you remember. What is most salient and important from the essay or article as you try to recall it? Now, begin a new draft based on those memories. Where does memory take you this time?

- What do you think of the techniques (dialogue, research, and so on) and organization of Amanda's essay (three time periods, four sections, and so on)? What do you find worth borrowing? What might you suggest she do in her next draft? How similar or different is her style of writing, her writing voice, and/or her experiences from your own?

4

Time, Tools, and Talismans

Susan Wyche

Susan Wyche is an Associate Professor in Human Communications at California State University Monterey Bay, where she also directs the University Writing Program. She still struggles with writing, still uses writing rituals to be a productive writer, and sometimes dreams of giving it all up to become a surfer.

Famous writers have been known to do a lot of crazy things to help them write: Dame Edith Sitwell sought inspiration by lying in a coffin. George Sand wrote after making love. Friedrich Schiller sniffed rotten apples stashed under the lid of his desk. A hotel room furnished with a dictionary, a Bible, a deck of cards, and a bottle of sherry suits Maya Angelou. Fugitive writer Salman Rushdie carries a silver map of an unpartitioned India and Pakistan. Charles Dickens traveled with ceramic frogs.

Writers also mention less bizarre practices. They describe eating, drinking, pacing, rocking, sailing, driving a car or riding in a bus or train, taking a hot bath or shower, burning incense, listening to music, staring out windows, cleaning house, or wearing lucky clothes. What do these rituals do for writers? The explanations are as varied as the rituals themselves. Tolstoy believed that "the best thoughts most often come in the morning after waking, while still in bed, or during a walk." Sonia Sanchez says that she works at night because "at that time the house is quiet. The children are asleep. I've prepared for my classes . . . graded papers . . . answered letters. . . . [A]t a quarter to twelve all that stops . . . then my writing starts." Although interpretations differ, one need not read extensively in the journals, letters, essays, and interviews of writers to know that they consider rituals an essential component of their work.

Do these behaviors serve a purpose in the composing process? Are some practices more common than others? Do rituals make for better writers? Until recently, the answer was usually "No," but anthropologists and others who study the subject of consciousness now say that private rituals are used by individuals to selectively and temporarily shut out the daily world. Researchers in psychophysiology have observed that rhythmic activities that can be performed "mindlessly" alter brainwaves into a more relaxed, creative state. Walking, pacing, and some kinds of exercise have this effect. So does staring out windows, which some researchers now believe may actively trigger daydreaming rather than being a symptom of it. Although coffins and frogs are probably effective only in the personal psychology of a Sitwell or a Dickens, scientists at Yale have discovered that rotting applies produce a gas that suppresses panic—a reminder that we should be careful not to scoff too soon at writers' rituals.

I became interested in the subject of rituals after suffering through my master's thesis with a bad case of writer's block. When a counselor asked me to describe my work habits, I became aware of the condition under which I had chosen to work: at school in the afternoon (my worst time of day) in an office where I was constantly interrupted or at home (also in the afternoon) while my husband's band practiced in the living room. I answered the phone, made coffee, and tried to shut out mentally what the walls could not. As Tillie Olsen points out, writing under such conditions produces a "craziness of endurance" that silences the writer. After awhile, even when I wasn't interrupted, I'd create my own distractions by calling friends, scrounging food in the kitchen, or escaping the house to run errands.

At the counselor's prompting, I began looking for a protected place to work—at first in the library and later at coffeeshops, where the conversational buzz and clatter of dishes provided consistent background noise. Somehow the interruptions in these places were less disruptive than those at home. I also began to pay attention to those moments when ideas bubbled up effortlessly, like on my walks to and from the university or while soaking in a hot bath late at night. I realized that ideas had always come in offbeat moments, but I had rarely been able to recapture them at "official" writing times. In the next three years, I gradually revamped my work habits and was able to face writing my doctoral dissertation, not with fear-producing blank pages, but pocketfuls of short passages scribbled in the heat of inspiration.

As a teacher of writing who works with unprepared students who are "at risk" in the university, I began to wonder what they did when they wrote. I knew there were times when they, too, became frustrated, blocked, and turned in work that did not represent their actual abilities. In spring 1990, I conducted a project with two writing classes in the Academic Skills Department at San Diego State University. I wanted to know

What rituals did students practice when they wrote for school?

What explanations would they offer for their practices?

Where did they get their best ideas?

What did they do when they blocked?

Were they aware of habits that sabotaged their composing processes?

Students filled out several pages of a questionnaire on their schedules, their rituals, and the amount of time they allocated for writing school assignments. Afterward, several met with me for follow-up interviews. In the following section, I present edited transcripts of three students who represented the range of responses I received.

Interviews

The first student, Adriana, provides a profile of work habits typical of other students in her class. She takes five classes, works twenty hours each week, and spends six to ten hours per week on homework:

I create a schedule for a day but if there's one particular thing I'm supposed to do, and I fall behind, I just throw it out. Sometimes I call my friends on the phone and tell them what I'm writing about in the essay, and they give me ideas.

Everything has to be clean and neat because if I see my clothes hanging everywhere, I can't study; I can't concentrate. So I have to straighten it up—everything—before I start.

I do most of my writing at night. Last night I stayed up till three o'clock. Before, I used to go to the public library, but it got too loud because of all these high school students jumping around. Now I work primarily at home.

Pacing gives me time to relax and jot down what I'm doing. I can't stay in one place, like for five hours and write a paper. I have to stand up, walk around, watch a little bit of TV and then start again. If my favorite program comes on I just have to watch it. Sometimes it's hard to do both—writing and TV.

To relax, I breathe deeply, stuff like that. I lay in my bed, looking at the ceiling. Nothing special. I work sitting down or lying down. I stare out a window. That's how I get my thoughts all together. I guess it helps, I find myself doing it a lot. I also have this one cassette with all piano solos by George Winston.

At times I put off working on an assignment until it's too late to do my best work, because I work better under pressure. If I start maybe a month before, I won't really concentrate. If I start three days before, then I'll get on it. If I have a month to do a project, and I sit down the week before, I'm not even thinking about it the other three weeks. Sometimes I work when I'm too exhausted, because I have a deadline to make. I've got to do it or fail the class.

I get my ideas sometimes right away, but most of the time it takes an hour to sit and think about it. I also get ideas from reading essays or from the person next to me. I'd ask what they're writing about, and sometimes I get some ideas. When

> I do go blank, I get frustrated—don't even know what I do. I think I just sit there and keep staring at my paper.

Adriana has difficulty creating and following through on self-made schedules. Her problems are further compounded by being unable to concentrate for extended periods of time; instead, she takes numerous breaks, including watching television. By her own account she begins drafts cold, using only the hour prior to drafting to give the paper serious thought.

Given all this, it is surprising to note how many beneficial rituals she practices. She cleans her workspace, paces, and breathes deeply to relax. She stares out windows to gather her thoughts and focuses her attention by listening to instrumental music. However, she mitigates the effect of these practices by placing herself under the pressure of imminent deadlines. It's no wonder that she becomes frustrated when she blocks. She has little time left for delays, and her coping strategy—to sit staring at the blank page—is more likely to create stress than to relieve it. The conditions she chooses would torpedo even a stronger writer's chance for success.

The second student, Marcia, also has five classes, averages eighteen hours each week at a job, and spends sixteen to twenty hours each week (twice as much as Adriana) on homework.

> Usually I study in the evening. I start at seven or eight, and lately I've been finishing about one or two. I talk my paper over with my friends. I ask if it's OK to write on this, or I ask them to read it when I'm finished, to see if it's OK. I usually work in my room, sometimes on my bed or in the living room on the floor. For some reason, I can't do my homework on my desk. When I'm in the family room, I just lie down on the couch, and do my homework with my legs up on the table. I play the radio, sometimes I'll watch TV. If it's an interesting show, I'll continue working during the commercials.
>
> I guess I'm just a procrastinator. I always tend to do my writing assignments at the last minute. Like when they give it to you, and they say, this is due a month later, I'll start on it a week before it's due. Sometimes when I'm thinking about a paper, I think, oh, I could write that in my paper, but when I come to writing it, I forget. I get distracted when I watch TV, or when there's people there and I say, OK, I won't do this now, I'll do it later when I'm by myself. Sometimes I'm on the phone or I go out. Then I end up not doing it, or starting late. When I was doing one assignment, I wrote it in about an hour.
>
> If I block, I put it down for a while, or I ask somebody to read it, or do something else. Then I'll go back to it. When I block, I feel mad, yeah, frustrated. I don't cry. I just think, I hate writing, I hate writing. Why do I have to do this? That kind of stuff. Writing is not my subject.

Marcia writes in the evening, after a full day of work and school. Like Adriana, she describes herself as a procrastinator. She has no designated workspace and often seeks distraction in friends or television. Although Adriana describes using an hour to generate and organize her ideas, Marcia mentions no such practice. She doesn't write down ideas and often doesn't remember them when she is ready to draft the assignment. There are other clues to serious problems. Although help from peers can be useful, she seems overly reliant on her friends for ideas and approval. She looks to them to tell her whether her choice of subject is a good one, to help her when she blocks, and to tell her whether her draft is adequate. She spends very little time on the work and may not even finish if interrupted. Her frustration with writing is obvious; her rituals—what few she practices—sabotage her efforts.

The third student, Sam, represents a highly ritualistic writer. He is enrolled in four classes, works twenty-five hours, and spends six to ten hours on homework.

> I'm really into driving. When I drive I notice everything. Things like, Oh, that billboard wasn't like that yesterday. I notice if my car feels different. I'm constantly looking and thinking. What's going on? And so, when I have time to prepare for my paper, all the thought goes into that, from there.
>
> In high school, my thoughts used to go down on microrecording. But I haven't used it since college. My batteries went dead. I do a little bit of performing stand-up comedy, so now I carry a little book for when I see something funny or some kind of story I want to keep. I've probably been through three of those books. I lose a lot of creative energy when I don't write things down.
>
> My roommates and I lift weights every day. A lot of thoughts come from that. I don't like to sit. When I'm thinking, I pace. I do a lot of what you could call role playing. I think, if I come from here, then I gotta hit the next paragraph this way. I actually look this way, then turn the other way. I really get into my papers, I guess. I'm Italian, I talk with my hands. It's a way to release energy both physically and mentally.
>
> Ideas come at different times. I've been known to write paragraphs on napkins at work. At home, I don't have a desk. I have my computer, which just sits on top of my dresser. I usually sit on my bed. A lot of times I lie down; a lot of times I'll stand up, just depends. I write in the afternoon, I feel a lot better than I do when I write at night. I look out a window and just write. But, when it comes to the mid hours, six o'clock, seven o'clock, there's too many things going on. I'm too jumpy, too hyper to concentrate then.
>
> I'm a very procrastination kind of guy. If I had a paper due in two weeks, there would be a lot of afternoon writing, a lot of jotting down. I'd probably end up pulling it all together late one evening. You never know, that last week, I might come up with something more. But at all times, I'm actively thinking about it.
>
> I never keep working on a problem once I've blocked. I feel this is useless. So, I'll stop, and a half hour later, it'll hit me. If I block at night, I'll stop for the rest of the night. If it's in the day, I'll try to get it again at night. I prefer a sleep period in between. Everybody believes in a fresh new day. A new outlook.

Like Adriana and Marcia, Sam considers himself a procrastinator. But unlike either of them, he actively makes use of the interim between assignments, noting down ideas, even writing entire sections if they take shape in his mind. Because he works better in the afternoon than late at night after he's put in a full day, he tries to schedule his work periods early. He seems to be a kinetic thinker—getting ideas in motion—and he takes advantage of that by allowing himself to pace and act out ideas rather than work at a desk. His interest in stand-up comedy has taught him to pay attention to the world around him, and this has become a source of material for his school assignments. In a way, Sam is always preparing to write. The result? He spends less time on his homework than Marcia and rarely experiences, as Adriana does, the frustration of being blocked.

I appreciated the candor of these and other students in responding to my questions but, as a teacher of writing, I was disheartened by many of the things I learned. Over half of the students surveyed spent fewer than ten hours per week on homework for a full schedule of classes, and three-quarters averaged twice as many hours on the job. The picture that emerged of their composing processes, from both statistics and interviews, was even bleaker. Few practiced rituals to help them write, most wrote under conditions hostile to concentration, and more than two-thirds admitted that procrastination regularly affected the quality of their work.

How Rituals Help

Rituals cannot create meaning where there is none—as anyone knows who has mumbled through prayers thinking of something else. But a knowledge of rituals can make a difference for students who want to make better use of the time they spend on writing. For one thing, rituals help writers pay attention to the conditions under which they choose to work. Some people think, for example, that fifteen minutes spent writing during TV commercial breaks is the equivalent of fifteen minutes of continuous, uninterrupted time. If they knew more about the nature of concentration—such as the destructive effect of interruptions on one's ability to retain and process information—they would recognize the difference. If they knew that language heard externally interferes with tasks requiring the production of inner speech, they would know that instrumental music or white noise (like the hum heard inside a car) might enhance their ability to write but that television or music with lyrics is likely to make work more difficult.

A knowledge of rituals can also encourage more effective use of the time spent on assignments. While many teachers consider two hours of homework a reasonable expectation for each hour in class, the students I talked to spent half that time and projects were typically written in one stressful sitting. Writing teacher Peter Elbow calls this "The Dangerous Method" and warns that it not only increases the pressure but depends for its success on a lack of any mishaps or mental blocks.

The problem with waiting until the last minute to write is that ideas rarely appear on demand. Instead, they come when listening to others, while reading or dreaming, or in the middle of other activities. Certain conditions stimulate their production, such as when a writer is relaxed and the mind is not strongly preoccupied with other matters. These moments may occur at particular periods of the day, for example, during "hypnagogic" states, the stage between waking and dreaming. Automatic, repetitious activity has a similar effect, which may be why writers often mention the benefits of walking, pacing, or exercising of some kind. They learn to make use of those times by noting down ideas or combining naturally productive times with their scheduled writing time.

Having some ideas to start with is an advantage to the writer, but not enough in itself. Ideas seldom occur as full-blown concepts, complete with all of the details, order, and connections that are required for formal writing. More often, they begin as an image, sensation, key word or phrase, or a sketchy sense of shape and structure. Transforming these bits into a full-fledged piece—whether poem, essay, or short story—usually requires one or more periods of concentration. The term *concentration* means "to bring together, to converge, to meet in one point" and in reference to thinking, it refers to keeping one's attention and activity fixed on a single problem, however complex. For the kind of writing required at the college level, concentration is crucial.

Most of us know that it is hard to concentrate when we are tired, when interrupted or preoccupied, ill or under stress—thus we recognize, experientially, that writing requires the concerted effort of mind *and* body. Some people can concentrate under adverse conditions—they could work unfazed in the middle of a hurricane if they wanted to—but most of us aren't like that. Concentration comes naturally to a few things that we like to do or are vitally interested in—music, perhaps, or sports. The rest of the time, we juggle several things at once, like jotting down a shopping list while we watch TV or organizing the day ahead while we take a shower. Switching from this kind of divided or scattered mental activity to a state of concentration often generates resistance, especially when the task is unpleasant or formidable.

Mihaly Csikszentmihalyi (1975), a psychologist at the University of Chicago, refers to this state of intense concentration as "flow," and from interviews with athletes, artists, and various professionals, theorizes that flow can only be achieved when a person is neither bored nor worried, but in control, possessing skills adequate to meet the challenge at hand. The key to achieving and maintaining flow is to balance one's skills against the challenge. "What counts," he says, "is the person's ability to restructure the environment so that it will allow flow to occur" (53).

Although rituals can take a bewildering number of forms, they help writers restructure their environment in one or more ways: clear the deck of competing preoccupations, protect from interruptions, encourage relaxation, reduce anxiety, and provide a structure (through established limitations of time) for dividing projects into manageable increments. This last use is especially important as writing assignments increase in length and complexity. The transition from the shorter assignment that can be completed in the space of two or three hours to an assignment that requires weeks of reading, research, and multiple drafts can be devastating to those who have conditioned themselves to write in only one, high-pressured session. In such cases, the writer needs strategies to help him or her overcome mental resistance and make good use of scheduled work-time.

Using Rituals

Because no two writers are alike, no formula for effective rituals exists. Even the same writer may use different rituals for different projects, or for different stages of a project. One writer may need several rituals involving workspace, time, and repetitive activities; another may need only a favorite pen. Every writer must learn to pay attention to his or her own needs, the demands that must be juggled, the mental and biological rhythms of the day, and the spontaneous moments of inspiration. Here are some suggestions for establishing productive rituals:

1. Consider the times of the day in which you are most and least alert. Most people have two or three cycles each day. Note the times that are your best.

2. Identify those times and activities in which ideas naturally occur. These may include certain times of day (when waking up, for example), during physical activities, or when engaged in repetitive or automatic behaviors (driving a car or washing dishes). Carry a tape recorder, small notebook, or some means of recording your ideas as they occur.

3. Draw up a schedule of a typical week. Mark those hours that are already scheduled. Note those times that are left open that correspond with the times identified in items 1 and 2. These are the most effective times to schedule writing. If possible, plan to do your writing during these times instead of "at the last minute." Each semester, once I know when my classes meet, I draw up such a schedule and post it on my refrigerator. Although I can't always use my writing time to work on writing, the schedule serves as a constant reminder of my priorities.

4. Consider the amount of time that you are normally able to maintain concentration. Even experienced writers tend to work for no more than three or four hours a day. They may spend additional time reading, making notes, or editing a text, but these activities can tolerate more interruptions and can be performed at less-than-peak times. Remember, too, it sometimes takes time to achieve a full state of concentration—an hour may provide only fifteen to twenty minutes of productive time. Writing frequently for short periods of time may be best. Many writers advocate working a little bit every day because the frequency helps lessen the initial resistance to concentration.

5. Consider the conditions under which you work best. Do you need absolute silence or background noise? Does music help you to focus or does it distract you? Do you prefer to work alone or with other people around? Do you prefer certain kinds of pens, inks, or paper, or do you need access to a typewriter or computer? Do you work best when sitting, standing, or lying down? Does it help you to pace or rock in a rocking chair or prepare a pot of coffee? Do you prefer natural, incandescent, or fluorescent light? Is the temperature comfortable? Is this a place you can work without being interrupted? Identify these needs and assemble an environment in which you are most comfortable.

6. Cultivate rituals that help you focus. Many writers use meditational exercises, write personal letters, or read recreationally to relax and prime the inner voice with prose rhythms. Some writers eat and drink so as not to be bothered with physical distractions; others eat or drink while they work because the repetitive activity helps them stay focused. Some writers feel they are more mentally alert if they write when they are slightly hungry. Experiment with different rituals and choose what works best for you.

Once concentration is achieved, writers tend to lose awareness of their rituals, but when concentration lapses or writers become blocked, they may consciously use rituals to avoid frustration and regain concentration as quickly as possible. The rituals vary according to the writer, the situation, the task, and the cause of the interruption or block, but common practices suggest several options:

1. Take a short break from the work and return later. If pushed for time, a short break may be most efficient. The trick is to stay away long enough to let strong feelings that may sabotage the writing subside, without letting one's focus shift too far away from the project overall. This is time to get something to drink, stretch out, or put the clothes in the dryer—activities that don't require one's full attention.

2. Shift attention to a different part of the same task and work on that. If you don't need to take a break, work on a section of the project with which you are not blocked. If you know, for example, that you plan to describe a personal experience later in the draft and you know what you want to say about it (even though you are not yet sure how that experience fits within the overall organization of the piece), go ahead and write it and set it aside for later.

3. Shift attention to a different task and return later. Other tasks can provide a break from the writing and, simultaneously, maintain the feeling of productivity; some professional writers juggle more than one writing project at a time for this very reason.

4. Switch to reading—notes or other texts—to stimulate new ideas and to help regain focus. If you are working from notes or research materials,

sometimes browsing through them will remind you of things you wanted to say. If that doesn't work, try reading materials that are not related to your task. One student told me that he used articles in *Rolling Stone* to help him get into a "voice" that helped him write. If you are working on a computer and have lost your sense of direction ("What should I say next?"), printing out your work and reading that may also help you regain your flow of thoughts.

5. Talk to someone about the problem or, if no one is around, write about it. Writers frequently use a friend or family member to talk through their ideas aloud (notice how often family members are thanked in the acknowledgments of books); reading or talking to someone not only offers a respite, but may result in the needed breakthrough.

6. Take a longer break, one which involves physical activity, a full escape from the task, or a period of sleep. If the block seems impenetrable or if you are so angry and frustrated that a short break won't make any difference, then spend enough time away from the task that you can begin afresh. Get out of your workspace, go for a hike, see a movie, or spend an evening shooting pool. Intense physical workouts can burn off tension created by writing blocks. If you're tired, take a nap. Some people can work well when tired, and pulling an all-nighter is possible for them, but others are far better off sleeping first and working later, even if that means waking up at 3:00 A.M. to write.

Coda

Writing this article has reminded me that knowing about rituals and making use of them are not always the same thing. Parts of this developed easily; others had to be teased out line by line. Ideas came while walking the dog, stoking the woodstove, taking hot baths, and discussing my work with others. After reading the last draft, my husband asked me how I intended to conclude. By discussing X, Y, and Z, I answered. I knew exactly what I wanted to say.

That was several nights ago, and today, I can't for the life of me remember what I said. If only I had thought to write it down.

Annotated Bibliography

The writers' rituals described here were gathered from a variety of sources—interviews, published diaries and letters, biographical and autobiographical materials—but anecdotes about rituals appear almost anytime writers discuss their writing processes. For further reading, see the Paris Review Interviews with Writers series, Tillie Olsen's *Silence*, or *Working It Out: 23 Women Writers, Artists, Scientists, and Scholars Talk About Their Lives and Work*, edited by Sara Ruddick and Pamela Daniels.

For further reading on writing and altered states of consciousness, see Csikszentmihalyi's *Beyond Boredom and Anxiety*, Richard Restak's *The Brain* (based on the PBS television series *The Brain*), and Diane Ackerman's *A Natural History of the Senses*. For an older but excellent introduction to the subject of psychophysiology see *Altered States of Consciousness*, edited by Charles T. Tart.

Although the subject of rituals is not a common one for most teachers of composition, a few have discussed the personal and idiosyncratic needs of writers. See especially several of the self-reflective articles in *Learning by Teaching* by Donald M. Murray, Peter Elbow's *Writing with Power*, and James Moffett's essay, "Writing Inner Speech, and Meditation," in *Coming on Center*.

Work Cited

Csikszentmihalyi, Mihaly (1975). *Beyond Boredom and Anxiety*. New York: Jossey-Bass.

Sharing Ideas

- Describe your best writing conditions and your most effective (even your most secret) writing rituals. For instance, as I write these questions, I have my two cats sleeping behind me, a quiet house, a desk with lots of pencils in a room that is just messy enough (my mess, no one else's), and a mug of coffee. Surely I could write without any of these conditions, but I spent some time arranging the atmosphere I wanted for writing to you.

- Whom do you sympathize with most or view as most like you as a writer: Adriana, Marcia, or Sam?

- What advice would you give each writer for improving his or her writing processes?

- Tell some stories of times when you achieved flow states (as a writer or during other activities, too).

- What would be involved for you in adopting some of Susan Wyche's advice for establishing productive rituals?

- Explore the connection between rituals and inspiration.

- Interview professional or amateur writers of your choice; describe and analyze their writing rituals.

- Use this essay to discuss Joe Quatrone's writing habits as he reports them in his self-analysis in Chapter 24.

5

Putting the Composure in Composing; or, Why I Love My Game Boy

Annelise R. Schantz

Annelise Schantz recently graduated from Columbia University but continues to live in New York City and play Tetris on her purple Game Boy. She is currently employed by a nontraditional foundation that works to end poverty in New York City. In her spare time, she sails competitively and investigates retirement and aging issues, a residual effect of writing her senior thesis on how the gendered nature of retirement will affect the women of the baby boom generation.

OK, it's time to start writing. Do I have to? Could I put it off for another couple of hours? I've had a snack. I've washed my dish and the five other dirty dishes in the sink too. I've piled up all the books I will be using as references. I have a fresh cup of coffee. Ready. No. Still not ready. Do I really have to write this essay? Maybe I should check my e-mail again just in case . . .

In college, I was a dedicated procrastinator. I took a seat-of-the-pants approach to writing papers. If I finished a paper more than ten minutes before it was due . . . well, let's just say that never happened. I often found myself avoiding my initial notes on the assignment as if they were a toxic substance that might poison me: the brussels sprouts and lima beans of my childhood in paper form.

Writing is a skill; so is proper procrastination. Writing is a valuable means of communicating with the rest of humanity and all that other stuff. Procrastinating is a valuable means of catching up with long-lost relatives, high school friends, and your roommate, whether via e-mail, instant messages, the phone, and even snail mail.

Procrastination is not laziness. Procrastination is something writers (like me) do when they are not ready to start writing. But knowing *how* to procrastinate is as important as knowing how to begin a new paragraph.

For example: You find yourself noodling around, doing anything but writing. You might be unsure of what you want to say, what references to consult, or even what you are supposed to write about. As a result, you find yourself too hyper or too distracted by other important demands like Googling the many uses of vinegar or e-mailing your mom with a list of things you would like for your birthday, which is eight months from now.

This type of procrastination, and other related habits such as multitasking, produce adrenaline, which must be dealt with before one can write. While some of you might like that extra boost of adrenaline, it can lead to more bad habits and convoluted sentences than I care to recall. Adrenaline speeds your mind up; it may allow you to write faster, but it can also prevent you from thinking slowly enough to gain clarity. You can jump from this kind of procrastinating right into writing, but I don't recommend it. Your skills will serve you best when your mind is clear and focused. Taking the time to address and purge your frenetic energy before you sit down to write is well worth it, whether you are writing a two-page essay or your senior thesis. This kind of procrastination is a sign that you are not ready to start writing and you need to find a way to compose yourself before you begin.

Think of elite athletes or musicians who frequently must perform under pressure. They arrive at an event with the skills necessary to perform perfectly. It is not raw skill that separates the great from those that falter; it is rather how each performer confronts pressure. While nearly everyone looks jittery and nervous before a big event, great performers know how to transform this energy into composure in the moments before they begin. If you watch a track meet, a baseball game, or a concert and look closely at the players' faces before they begin, you can catch the moment each player converts his or her jumpy adrenaline into focused power. The muscles in their faces slack, their eyes soften, they enter a state of calm before the storm. They are well aware that the better they are able to do this, the better they will perform. Writing is no different.

Converting chaotic procrastination energy into calm, focused writing energy can be conveniently accomplished if you procrastinate *the right way*. Midway through my college career I found my savior, the thing that worked for me. It had a gorgeous purple hue and a lovely color screen. It was a Game Boy, complete with a game cartridge for Tetris. Its ability to focus my adrenaline and calm me before I began writing was amazing. It even worked before big tests and important interviews. This might seem a weird way to compose oneself—in fact, my mother would probably think it was as weird as your mother would—but recently I stumbled upon a scientific study done on methods used to calm children before surgery, and the most effective approach was allowing the kids to play video games.

While I am quite certain that a Game Boy will not be everyone's secret means of instant composure, there is a wealth of other options. Look for a simple activity that you enjoy doing by yourself and requires your entire focus, such as reciting multiplication tables while jumping rope, going for a brisk walk around an obstacle course, shooting hoops, knitting, yoga—anything that requires both your mental and physical attention. It is important that you enjoy this pastime, because in addition to helping you relax and focus, it should serve as a small reward before you start writing.

If your procrastination behavior currently consists of taking out the trash and doing other chores before you start writing, it may be hard to see writing as anything but another type of chore. However, if you begin to associate writing with an enjoyable activity that calms you and provides a sense of composure, it will be much easier to approach writing as simply another interesting pursuit. Having a positive attitude and a cool, collected mindset always pays off.

Once you have achieved your calm and collected mental state, keep it that way. Don't sit in the main room of the library, where your friends are guaranteed to wander over. Search out a rarely used desk in the library or an isolated room in a dorm where your friends won't find you and you are unlikely to know anyone. Don't even think about leaving your cell phone on. Isolate yourself.

If you like to listen to music while you write, don't plan on getting up every time a CD ends; make a mixed CD and put it on repeat. If you want snacks, get them before you start, and avoid foods with tons of sugar, which will give you a temporary sugar high and then cause you to crash. And, unless you desperately need it, stay away from the Internet. Having an instant message program or your e-mail open in the background is a recipe for disaster. Getting rid of the Internet, your phone, and friends can be a daunting task, but shut off from a constant barrage of dings, rings, and hellos, you will quickly find that staying focused is relatively easy.

Lastly, and perhaps most importantly, take yourself seriously. Respect your writing. Have confidence in yourself and take advantage of the skills that you have: brainstorm, write outlines, research. Your writing does matter, and the benefit of focusing on it is that it will be much less painful; you might even enjoy it. So, take five and then let your writing take off.

Sharing Ideas

- Are you a dedicated procrastinator?
- Do you agree with Annelise Schantz that procrastination is a signal to yourself that you are just not ready to start writing yet?

- Annelise believes procrastination can produce adrenaline, which must be dealt with before one can write. Do you agree with this? Have you had similar experiences?

- Do you believe you write best under a deadline? Do you get a writing boost from the adrenaline rush that's produced by waiting until the last minute? Or do you agree that you need your mind to be clear, focused, and relaxed to be ready to write?

- Annelise believes being relaxed and focused after finishing an enjoyable prewriting activity (like a Game Boy workout) and having a respectful, positive attitude about your writing are two important secrets to making writing an enjoyable activity. Do you agree? What else can make writing enjoyable?

- Do you go through a routine before you begin to write? What is it about the routine that helps you prepare to write?

- Do you agree that it is as important to prepare yourself mentally as it is to prepare your research and notes before you begin writing?

- What other types of situations also cause you to procrastinate? Is there a connection between your feelings toward these situations and your feelings about writing?

- Some people would say that procrastinating is actually a form of prewriting, a way of working on a paper before you actually start writing anything. What do you think of this idea? If this is true, then how do you think your writing process would be affected if you talked to someone about your paper while you were still procrastinating?

- Annelise uses a lot of humor in her chapter. Does this add to her argument or detract from it? How? Think of a paper you've recently written. What's one way you could add humor to the paper? How effective do you think the addition of humor would be?

- Annelise says writing is a lot like playing sports: you have to get into the right mindset or zone. At the end of her chapter, she suggests avoiding distractions to help you stay in that writing zone. What else can you do to help you stay in the zone of a paper you are writing? To extend the sports metaphor just a bit further, how could you stretch and limber up to prepare yourself for a writing session?

6

Invention Throughout the Writing Process

Amy Hodges

Amy Hodges studies rhetoric and composition at Florida State University, where she is a graduate teaching assistant. She is amazed by her students, their writing, and the stories they share. The focus of much of her work is on letter writing and writing about personal experience.

Invention never stops.

—Kate Brown, writing teacher

Are you staring at your computer screen? Is it blank or filled with text you don't know how to revise? I am, too. Getting started again and again with an essay draft is difficult. The act of writing well is based on a process that begins and ends with invention.

Let's investigate the truth of this claim by considering possible invention tools we can use to get started without getting frustrated. Remember that the main point of invention is to generate ideas and then move those ideas onto paper. While invention allows you to create and then re-create your text, invention for getting started on a draft is most often the place where writers get stuck. Many beginning writers are afraid to share ideas for fear that their topic will prove less effective than topics their classmates generate. In order to begin writing, you have to let go of that fear, which every writer experiences. To do this, make a list of five things you have successfully written, and make that list visible in order to explore possibilities. Here is my list:

1. a letter to my ex-boyfriend

2. a Classical Rhetoric paper

3. grocery lists

4. a personal experience essay to my dad

5. thank-you notes

Don't compare yourself with other writers, published or unpublished. Just allow yourself to experiment with ideas, topics, and words. Since it's not that easy to begin experimenting when you've been staring at a blank sheet of paper far too long, here are several invention-based steps to consider when starting to write.

Part I: Invention for Generating Ideas and Drafts
Discovering a Topic

The most effective topic will be the topic that interests you most. Generally, if you are interested in your topic, you will capture your reader's interest as well. Think briefly about your interests, passions, and curiosities. What would you like to explore? Are you really into fashion, sports, women's rights, toxic waste issues? Start by quickly making a list of at least ten ideas and topics that genuinely interest you, and don't analyze what pops into your head for effectiveness or information; just focus on listing at this point. Here is a student's initial topic list, composed to help her generate an essay focused on personal experience.

Pam's List
1. the first time I skipped school

2. breaking up with Rob

3. Mom didn't show up for my dance recital

4. Peter's rejection

5. Dad and my homecoming dress

6. Matthew on the other side of the twin beds

7. Danielle's breakup with Tom

8. fight with Mom over Uncle Mike

9. Shannon's suicide attempt

10. the peanut butter incident

As you can see, Pam's list is somewhat haphazard and your list should be, too. Now, read back through your list at least three times, jotting down ideas for elaboration beside each topic. After you have generated specific ideas that could move each topic into an essay, go back through and mark off the topics that seem limited or ridiculous (Pam marked off #10). Next, find the boring or general topics and mark them off the list (Pam marked off #7 and #2). Read back through your remaining topics and circle the topic that you can't seem to cut from the list.

Talk It Out

Still having trouble narrowing your topics list? Because writing can seem so solitary, sometimes vocalizing your essay ideas can be an effective invention tool. Try talking with a classmate, roommate, or friend about your topic choices and watch which topics they respond to and which make your interest level rise. Notice, too, which topic you spend the most time explaining—you can use your existing knowledge of the topic to build on in your writing. As writing teacher Nancie Atwell suggests, try to write down the ideas you share during the conversation for future reference. Also, encourage your conversation partner to ask questions about your possible topics. Allow him or her to tell you which idea seems the most interesting, and which topic seems limited or even impossible. Simply tell the story, describe the experience, or share the facts in conversation and see which topic wins your audience.

Just Write

Now that you have a tentative topic, begin writing. One of the most effective invention techniques is freewriting. Freewriting can help you continue thinking about the beginning stages of your writing process. Peter Elbow popularized this technique in *Writing Without Teachers* and suggests that freewriting helps writers escape from their self-consciousness and invites the mind to discover ideas and words, which, in turn, helps generate drafts. To begin this exercise, write your topic at the top of a blank sheet of paper or computer screen. Then just begin writing about your chosen topic and continue writing for twenty minutes without stopping your pen or your typing. Make sure you don't edit too soon, and allow yourself to simply write without distraction or proofing. The following freewrite was written during Lauren's invention stage of a personal experience essay:

> Brad gets here in two days. YIKES! I am excited, but I've noticed that I'm getting used to our long-distance routine. The elation at seeing each other after two or three months apart, the whirlwind ten days together, a teary public good-bye right in front of the security checkpoint at the airport, and then two or three more months of waiting. But, as predictable as it is, I wouldn't give it up for anything. Those ten days make up for all of the waiting and daydreaming and long distance phone calls.
>
> And I'm not doing this all for fun. Someday I want us to be together. I wonder what that would be like. Will we be completely happy and in love, or will we annoy each other to death and go our separate ways, disappointed and heartbroken?

I have no reason to believe that we will be anything but happy and in love, but years of bad relationships have conditioned me to expect the worst.

Unfortunately, it is not my nature to let things be. I want a part in it. I am 21 years old, about to graduate from college in two months, and one week ago I decided that I want to be a lawyer, too bad I have been training to be a reporter for the past year. I have even sent out tapes to get a reporting job and gone on an interview in Panama City . . . (YUCK). I think I always knew that it wasn't right for me. I mean, isn't it kind of a bad sign when you send away for a job and secretly hope that you don't get an offer? Yeah, that was a big clue. Hello. Big clue. Big . . .

Did you notice how Lauren was working to find meaning, reflectively and associatively? Finding possibility is the goal of freewriting, not perfectly worded sentences. Like Lauren's freewrite, your writing is rich with possibility. Go back through your freewrite and mark places, words, or ideas that you think could readily be shaped into an essay.

Question Yourself

Are you wondering how Lauren moved her freewrite and discovery into an essay based on personal experience? She explained in her process memo that "the freewrite exercise helped me realize I wanted my readers to understand the scattered emotions that were caused by making a career change so late in my academic studies." Rediscovering personal and professional goals became the focus of Lauren's essay. How can your inventive writing lead you toward a draft? Once again, read through your freewrite and this time apply the reporter's formula to what you've just written; that is, ask: Who? What? When? Where? and Why?

Lauren's Answers

Who? myself, Brad, school

What? making a hard decision

When? two months and one week before graduation

Where? school, my house

Why? this experience is happening right now and it is powerful

These W questions, often used in journalistic writing, can help you decide *who* your audience should be and/or *who* will be involved in the essay, *what* your essay will focus on, *when* the event or facts took place, *where* the experience, setting, or argument was brought to fruition, and *why* this is an important essay either for you or for your audience.

Questioning should not stop here; in fact, continue asking questions about your text and topic throughout your drafting sequence. Remember, the more questions you ask, the more information you generate. Some questions you might ask include the following:

- What claim will you make about this topic?
- What is the scope of the overall topic?
- How will you focus?
- What knowledge must you provide to readers?
- How can this information lead to an effectively organized essay?
- Who is the audience for this essay?

After reading Bobby's list, create a list of specific questions you plan to answer through your essay.

Bobby's List on Bullying in Schools
A. Why do kids kill in schools?
B. Is bullying a universal experience for all kids?
C. Are there organizations that support tolerance among children?
D. How can I make my reader feel alienated, too?
E. Can I share my experience without seeming like a loser?

5. Moving Toward Drafting

As you consider your chosen topic, think about its significance in your life, whether it is an argumentative essay on a controversial topic like marijuana legalization or a sensory observation exercise for a Psychology 101 class. Now we will work through some prompts that can help a writer get ready to write an initial draft of a personal experience essay. If you fully elaborate on each response, Q-and-A prompting like this can be a very effective invention tool. In the following examples, Brian investigates his relationship to music. After you read Brian's responses, try the prompts using your topic.

Writing Prompts
A. When did you discover your interest or love for your topic?

Brian's response: Music has always been a strong part of my life. At first, I thought I would focus on how music has touched my life in this essay, but I think I will now focus on the music and how it is part of me.

B. Name the people, books, or events that have been influential in generating your interest in your topic.

Brian's response: My mother enrolled me in a group piano class at five, probably because that is the age Parents Magazine *suggested was most appropriate for that sort of thing. Also, I have Anthony to thank. He was into music and we began playing together as kids. And my saxophone. And all of the countless bands I followed, their lyrics, the way their music brought me energy.*

C. Explain how you are involved with your topic. How long have you been involved?

Brian's response: Music has really shielded me through life, through my social inadequacies. I was safe from childhood games because I was always in a practice room and always got to play the hero on stage. Now when my music causes a strong audience reaction, I am surprised that what I love, others love.

D. Take ten minutes and write whatever you know about your concept or topic at this point. Write quickly, without planning or organizing.

Brian's response: "Why don't you stop practicing, so we can hear the television?" It was never a question. They didn't understand, and I guess I couldn't have expected them to. After all, I have no better response than "Amanda Simpson" when people inquire about the source of my desire to learn the guitar. My intent wasn't so much to woo her with my jazzy melodies as much as it was to sit next to her in fourth-grade band class. In one of several attempts at winning the attention of my prepubescent dream girl, I chose the saxophone in the fourth grade band before the school ever did any of those tests to see which instrument was right for me. When I moved away a year later, I took with me the only thing that has lasted.

E. What possibilities are there for engaging the reader's interest?

Brian's response: The passion that accompanies my love for music should interest my readers. Music drove me to spend more money than I possessed on a plane ticket to Philadelphia to see Sigur Ros in concert. For two and a half hours, I listened to music about my own humanity, love, death, and beauty in language I didn't understand. Enlightened, humbled, and inspired . . . that's how I want to leave my readers.

After you have worked through these prompts, you have the makings of an essay. We will worry about sentence-level revision and snappy introductions and conclusions in a bit; for now, focus on writing an initial draft.

6. Developing the Body

You should now be ready to decide where you want your essay to go, how to start giving it life and shape. You may find yourself focused on developing the main part of the text, which is referred to as the *body*. Remember that the body of your essay will develop your writing plan.

When deciding how to present details to support your focus, you have many options. When you are writing from personal experience, readers expect you to employ concrete sensory details—recapture bright or dull colors, eerie sounds, pungent smells, images of soft touch, and bitter or sweet tastes that will make the experience real to your readers. Remember, sensory imagery is effective whether your essay is informative or expository. Here is an example of sensory imagery from Ruth's essay:

> As I sit under a large shade tree, waiting for my next class, my eyes wander aimlessly about me. An occasional breeze passes by, as an attempt to apologize for such a dreadfully sticky day. I hear the never-ending traffic not too far away, and the unexplainably annoying crosswalk buzzer that screeches at the pedestrians every four minutes or so. A maintenance man picks up papers that have been scattered on the ground. I glance over and smile at him halfheartedly, so I don't come off as a snob. He notices but goes on with his task almost as halfheartedly as my smile. My stomach begins to growl, and I can smell food coming from somewhere. I'm nowhere near the cafeteria so I'm afraid it's all in my head. I chew a piece of Big Red in an attempt to calm my hunger. The sharp taste just makes me hungrier and now I'm out of gum.

Now revise one of your paragraphs to increase the sensory imagery.

If your essay is mainly based on factual evidence, it is important to draw on data to support your claims. Be sure to find statistics, facts, and cases that demonstrate your thesis or main point explicitly. Research is a technique you can use to create a new, richer version of your draft. For example, if you are writing an essay on the importance of driver's education courses, you might find a study that illustrates the drastic decline in teen driving accidents in cities where driver's ed courses are enforced. You also may consider using experts to help support your argument. In the driver's education essay, you could interview an expert with the department of transportation or state highway patrol. In a personal experience essay about your birth, the expert may be your mother. Depending on your topic, you will find a range of experts to use in support of the issue you are presenting.

Also, try to go beyond human experts when thinking of ways to support your essay's focus—think about the books and magazines you read, CDs and radio stations you listen to, the TV shows you watch, the classes you attend. You will add validity to your argument when you are able to present a well-developed, well-supported essay. Read the following data Evan used from a television documentary to support his essay on child abuse awareness:

> It is startling how many children in the U.S. are abused within a twenty-four-hour period. On February 7th, in House Springs, Montana, a nineteen-year-old mother broke her five-month-old son's ribs in order to get him to stop crying. In Illinois, a twenty-one-year-old mother and her boyfriend forced her daughter to sleep in the shower after beating the child with a belt and a wooden cutting board for wetting the bed. While this abuse took place, a twenty-seven-year-old mother starved her five-year-old son in New York, shortly before tying him to a chair and beating him to death with a wooden handle. These are publicly known cases, but what happens to the 969,000 cases that don't make headlines?

Now I invite you to consult one or more sources and use data to rewrite a section of your current draft.

Collaborative Invention

Now that your essay is taking shape, you may find sharing your writing with fellow writers a very effective tool. Peer reviewing (having fellow writers read and critique your essay) can be a great way to invent new possibilities for your essay. Be sure to arrive at the workshop prepared with specific questions about your text. You should deal with large concerns like the essay's focus and development at the workshop. Many composition teachers will incorporate peer review workshops into the writing classroom, but here are a few important questions to ask your reviewers if you consult with them outside of class:

- What part of the essay do you want to know more about?
- What do you wish I would leave out in the next draft?
- If this were your essay, what would you do to revise?
- Invent four questions specific to your essay.

After you workshop your essay, you should return to the text and revise it in light of the suggestions your fellow writers provided. Like research, peer review is a form of collaborative invention that helps you continue experimenting with your focus, drafts, and ideas.

Part II: Inventing Drafts and Revision

Most textbooks focus on invention of ideas and topics in the initial writing stages, but invention is rarely mentioned in connection with the drafting and revising stages of writing. Does invention stop with the creation of an idea or a first draft? It shouldn't. Remember the quote from the writing teacher that opens this chapter? "Invention never stops." Creating and re-creating your text throughout the writing process will help you produce a stronger final text. The majority of writers depend on rewriting to compose well. It is very seldom that even the most successful writer simply writes one brilliant, thorough essay draft. Try to think of drafting as constant invention and revision. Now, let's consider some writing options. Are you having trouble inventing your introduction or conclusion? Are you having trouble moving from writing to editing? Try some of the following options.

Inventing Opening Ideas

Invention should not stop now that you have a draft. As you write and rewrite your essay, continue narrowing and elaborating on your focus. If you can't find a focus, think about the following options to help you create an effective introduction.

Remember that many writers use introductory paragraphs to trigger a start, while others wait and develop their introductions after half of the essay is complete, or come back to create the introduction after the rest of the essay has been written. As you think of possible openings, keep in mind that choosing your focus may be the most crucial element in the inventing process.

When considering the most effective way to introduce your essay, think back to your interest in the subject. There are many ways to invent an introduction; consider the following options:

1. Try using an example from a published source or from a dramatic anecdote or an example from your own life. Here is an excerpt from Evan's introduction:

   Whap! I can still remember the gust of breeze that would be taken away and then pushed down onto my bottom as I leaned over my mother or father's knees, waiting in apprehension for the next sting to take place. Wham! And that was only the beginning.

2. You may also start by providing background information for the reader. You may need to set up the concept, describe a situation, or set up a scene for what is to come in the essay. Now, read Bill's opening, and try this yourself.

   I remember watching classic television western shows like The Lone Ranger, Have Gun Will Travel, The Rifleman, *and my all-time favorite,* Roy Rogers. *Besides being filmed in black and white, these great shows all had two things in common; in the end the good guys always got the bad guys, and the star would always return ready for a new adventure in the next episode. It always impressed me how those rugged cowboys survived hardships such as fistfights, desert thirst, snakebites, and the ever-suspenseful gunfight always ready for the next adventure. I do not remember ever seeing blood from the wounds of a dying bad guy. Nor did the good guys ever seem to show remorse or any psychological trauma after killing a bad guy. Clean and easy, just like the movies, became my youthful and innocent understanding of death.*

3. You may also begin with a question or problem that will engage your readers in your topic. Lucy's opening is vivid:

   The year was 1968. Karen Hubbard, a twenty-two-year-old woman from Miami, Florida, with grassy green eyes was approaching her third year and final stint in the United States Air Force, but was faced with nowhere to transfer. Except Vietnam. The war was increasing its strength, but with faith in her abilities as a nurse, Karen transferred to Cam Ranh Bay, Vietnam.

Inventing the End

Does your conclusion seem like a rerun of what you've already written? Are you out of ideas? You aren't alone in your frustration. For many writers, writing a conclusion is the most difficult step in the drafting process. Your conclusion may be the first section you write, or it may come to you after multiple drafts and collaborative consultations, or perhaps after a writing conference with your teacher. Regardless of how you find your conclusion, try to keep in mind that your reader just read your entire essay, so there is no need to summarize all of your main points in the conclusion, and most writers advise against opening up too many new doors. Instead readers seek some closure, a sense of review, connection, or resonance in the conclusion.

The ideas below should help you avoid the predictable "In this paper, I discussed Point A, Point B, and Point C." Experiment with the following possibilities if you are having trouble inventing a conclusion on your own:

1. Encourage your reader to become involved in the broader context of issues you are presenting. You may also end with a call for action. The following conclusion comes from Evan's essay on child abuse:

   Acknowledgment by society, by you, that the problem of child abuse and neglect does exist and is on the increase might help save a child's life. There are many organizations like Our Kids, Inc. and Guardian Ad Litem that are in need of volunteers to help in child protection. On May 1st, a woman was sentenced to a twenty-five-year prison term for beating her malnourished grandson to death with a cutting board after catching him looking in the pantry. The child weighed twenty-eight pounds and was severely scarred from belt and electrical whippings when his body was found. The boy was removed from his mother and placed with his grandmother, even though he begged not to be sent with his grandmother. If nothing else, always be ready to listen to a child.

2. Share an anecdote or illustration that will cause your reader to continue thinking about the subject you are presenting. You may want to revisit images you have used throughout the essay or even repeat wording used earlier in your text. The following is the conclusion to Bill's essay:

   I stayed with Dooly as the other guys milled around the wrecked car looking at all the damage. I watched as Dooly opened his eyes again, looked around, exhaled his last breath, dropped his head to one side, closed his eyes, and died. It was that fast. "Clean and easy, just like the movies," I thought. . . . Then it hit me. This was not the movies. This man would not be back next week for a new adventure. There would be no sequel movie, Vehicle Accident, Part II. *There was no director to shout, "Cut! That's a wrap, Dooly. You can go home now." There in the cold, I finally felt the sting of death. I realized for Dooly, this truly was THE END.*

3. You may want to end with a question, a quote that is especially compelling, or a prediction. Notice how Karen's use of a quotation carries her conclusion:

"The first step toward healing is learning who Vietnam Veterans are," Gail said. I learned who Vietnam Veterans are. I learned they are men and women. They are dead and alive, whole or maimed, sane or haunted. They grew from their experiences or were destroyed by them. They were the Army, Navy, Marines, Air Force, Red Cross, and civilians. Some enlisted to fight for our country. Some volunteered. Others were drafted. They drove Jeeps, operated bulldozers, built bridges. They spent their time in high mountains drenched by monsoon rain or the dry plains or in hospital wards or at the most beautiful beaches in the world. They got vaccines constantly, but have diseases no one can diagnose. They feared they would die or they feared they would kill. They feared they would keep the wrong one alive. They simply feared. Do they still?

Part III: Inventing the Final Draft: The Process of Revision

After you have written a complete essay, it is important to get away from it. You may not be able to budget a large chunk of downtime in your schedule, but try to at least put the essay aside and have dinner or take a walk. Unless you divorce yourself from your text, you will be unable to invent new ideas. Without distance from the text, you may only see what you intended to be on the page, not what actually *is* on the page. When you do return to the essay, reinvent yourself as a reader or analyzer; distance yourself from your writer role. One more thing: Don't be afraid to make major changes to your essay in the final revision stage of the writing process. You may decide to change your introduction and open with a letter or a recipe rather than the standard opening you have in front of you. You may choose to move the conclusion paragraph up to paragraph 2. Allow yourself to experiment, delete, and add information and ideas, up until the last print job.

1. Altering the Big Picture: The Second-to-Last Look

Read through the complete essay, noting gaps in detail or uneven transitions between paragraphs. To begin revision, print out a draft of your essay and read it aloud like you would a short story or a movie script. Once you've read through the draft, write down at least three details that are missing from the text. Here is what Lucy thought was missing from her survival guide for women living alone for the first time after college:

1. safety concerns
2. how to cook for one
3. meeting the neighbors/socializing

Now go back through your entire draft again with a pen, making note of places that need further elaboration and where you will include your newly developed ideas. Then, mark the sections that need to be cut from the essay entirely. Also, you may choose at this final stage of the writing process to rejoin your workshop group for one final review of your essay.

2. Final Touches: The Last Look

Sentence-level invention takes place last, after you have filled in all of the gaps and feel confident in your paper overall. When editing or proofreading your essay, try new ways to look at your text; for example, you may read your essay backward (last sentence first) to catch sentence problems like fragments or comma splices. As you review each sentence, make sure that you have chosen the clearest wording. Many readers base clarity on sentence structure so if a sentence seems awkward, change it. If you are struggling with how to best state an idea, try writing at least five variations of the same sentence and then choose the most effective sentence. The following list shows five variations of a sentence from Meg's personal experience essay on her decision to attend medical school:

1. My love of science was fostered by my second-grade teacher.
2. I have loved science since the second grade.
3. My second-grade teacher fostered my love for science.
4. Mrs. Scott, my second-grade teacher, fostered my love for science.
5. I love science, which began in Mrs. Scott's second-grade class.

It is also important to consider the effectiveness of your focus throughout the essay. I invite my students to write the main idea of each paragraph in the margin of their draft, and then I ask them to underline the sentences that support that focus. Read Lee's example and then complete this exercise with your own essay.

> In the huddle of two parents, three older sisters, two dogs, three cats, five houses, four towns, one church, four schools, one bankruptcy, and twenty-two birthdays, it is important to remember the growth—the good with the bad—because the past becomes inconsequential. A family's love forgets the discouragement, mistakes, and disappointments. As a member, it becomes a duty to encourage, forgive, and most of all, move on. I barely recall my childhood with two older sisters. The youngest of them has a nine year seniority on Colleen and me.

Lee's last two sentences do not belong in this paragraph. What did Lee do with those last two sentences? He moved them into another paragraph and invented new sentences to support the paragraph on his relationship with his sisters. You, too, may need to invent new words, sentences, or paragraphs even during final editing. Here's a useful checklist to use at this point:

1. Do you have repetitive sentences, words, or details?

2. Can you find fragments or places where commas are needed? Do you have any run-on sentences?

3. Are your paragraphs in the most effective order? Do you need to rearrange the order of your essay?

4. Where do you need to add sentences? Is your verb tense consistent?

5. List one thing you wish you could include to make your essay complete. Is it information necessary to the final essay? Invent a way to include it.

This checklist suggests the many ways that writers continue revising and inventing all the way to the final print job of the final draft. Remember, invention never stops.

Works Cited

Atwell, Nancie (1998). *In the Middle: New Understandings About Writing, Reading, and Learning.* Portsmouth, NH: Heinemann.

Elbow, Peter (1973). *Writing Without Teachers.* New York: Oxford University Press.

Sharing Ideas

- Amy Hodges' advice in this chapter intersects with advice found in several other chapters in this book. How does advice from these authors contradict, enrich, add to Amy's observations about invention? Explain. Freewrite on any two of her observations that struck you as new or unusual.

- Highlight the practices in this chapter that you have never followed, always followed, regularly follow. In a group, compare your lists. Make an effort to try several of the practices in your "never" column on your next paper.

- Take a paper you finished some time ago (for another class, a year ago, earlier this term) and invent some new directions you could take if you had one hour, one week, one month, or one year to expand this paper. What could and would you do?

- Speculate on published authors' writing lives. Do you think invention stops for them? Find two versions of a published story and compare the changes the author made. (Hint: Raymond Carver's "The Bath" and "A Small Good Thing" are examples that might come to hand fairly easily. Or, look up a variorum edition of an author's work and study early and later drafts; for example, look at the two drafts of a W. B. Yeats poem.) How did invention during revision seem to take place?

- Interview campus authors in order to discover if it is common for them to revise previously published work. Do they consider that they're reinventing their work along the lines suggested in this chapter?

- Look at two drafts of a peer essay (or one of your own earlier essays). What changes were made? Were they mechanical (technical, editorial) or did the writer invent new directions, ideas, and material? Characterize what you find.

- What are the perils and pleasures (as you've experienced them) of using Web research to invent a next draft? How reliable are the sites that may be sparking your ideas? What about the problems of borrowing too freely? When does invention turn to theft? Tell some stories of Web- and non-Web-related plagiarism. As a class, discuss the ways writers acknowledge influence yet also use it to good effect in their writings.

Part II

Choices Writers Make About Style, Voice, and Genre

Using a computer will change the way you write. I would like to be able to say that using word processing will transform your writing into prize-winning prose, or at least grade-A material. But I cannot. I can tell you that your writing will be different because my students tell me that the computer changed how they write. It didn't make them better writers; it made them different writers. Maybe that's not so bad. Changing old habits may allow us to examine the way we write, thereby prompting us to learn new strategies as we become different writers.

—James Strickland, writing teacher

I want student writers to show themselves to me in what they write, to give themselves to me, as I try to show and to give myself back to them in what I write. I want them to remember their lives, their histories, the particularities of their existence, and to show them to me. I want to know what they think and how they think and why they think that way, and I want to know the particular experiences that count to them.

—Jim Corder, writing teacher

My voice isn't exactly what I want it to be. When my writing is working for me, I'm clear and conversational. . . . Now I'm at the point where my voice is finally becoming less self-conscious, perhaps consciously less self-conscious. The talky stuff seems to work better for me than the attempts I made at being a high-brow artiste. So that's what I'm concentrating on—just talking.

—Brad Usatch, writing student

Writing is not a gift of the muse nor a mysterious process you cannot understand. Nor is it a simple one, two, three process. Writing involves going backward—to the internal mental text—as well as going forward—to the external physical text. By understanding the process by which writers and readers construct texts, you will become a better writer and reader.

—Jeanette Harris, writing teacher

7

Don't Tell Me What to Write
An Expressive Approach to Writing
Joe Antinarella

Joe Antinarella is an Assistant Professor of English at Tidewater Community College in Chesapeake, Virginia, where he teaches courses in writing, world literature, and reading and writing across the disciplines. With three children recently graduated from university, he should find more time and money to travel the world with his wife. He is passionate about photography, music, and coaching youth soccer. He has made recent trips to England, Italy, and Russia in search of the perfect soccer match.

Early every semester, I ask my first-year writing students to answer two questions anonymously: *Why write?* and *What is a writing complaint you have?* I generally receive the usual responses to the first question, such as, "I write because . . . it's required" and "I want to express myself." Some say they "need good communication skills" and others want to be able to "pass tests." But categorically, students' responses to the second question are always more interesting and revealing, and the most recent occasion was no different. In addition to the answers such as "I don't like writing because . . . it has to be perfect," or "teachers are too critical," or "words limit my true expression of feelings," I received this one: "I never know what to write about. I also hate being given a topic to write about, which is kind of funny I guess. I was never given [a topic] that personally interested me." The more I began to reflect upon this student's comment, the more this paradox resonated with me as a recurring defining point inherent in the way student writers approach writing. Students don't

63

want to be told *what* to write, but they sometimes struggle to come up with their own ideas. A contradiction, yes . . . but one that makes sense to me.

The questions I ask my students are like those posed by James Britton almost thirty years ago in England. Britton and his research team visited schools and classrooms throughout England, gathering information and making inquiries to find out why a majority of students were graduating from schools in England with unsatisfactory writing skills and why so many students had a negative attitude about writing. Once he determined the reasons, Britton made some powerful recommendations to help students make their writing better and improve their attitude about writing. Underlying these recommendations, I detect the origin of my student's complaint.

Britton discovered three types of writing occurring in schools: expressive, poetic, and transactional writing. He defined *expressive* writing, the most personal type of writing, as the closest to "inner speech" and the thinking process itself. This kind of writing emanates from personal discovery, a desire to share feelings, explain thoughts, and understand experiences. At times, this writing can be informal, incomplete, exploratory, and purely subjective. Britton described *poetic* writing as writing that is personal, creative, and focused on relating feelings; it is often the kind of writing that is published and intended for a wide and perhaps unknown audience. He defined *transactional* writing as writing to communicate information; it's factual, formal, and often written for a narrowly defined audience, like a teacher. It tends to lack a spirited personal voice while presenting objective ideas and adhering to a stylized format. His conclusions, in a nutshell, were these:

- Clearly, *transactional* writing was then (and often still is) the dominant mode valued and practiced in school—64 percent to 85 percent of writing done in schools with students ages 11 to 18.

- Personal *expressive* and *poetic* writing was practiced little and valued less in school—only 10 percent and 5 percent of the writing, respectively, and these numbers declined as students advanced in their schooling.

If we also consider the research Arthur Applebee conducted in our own country, we find similar results and a new category—*mechanical* writing. This kind of routinized writing, identified as copying, note taking, recording, and filling in blanks, constitutes, in some cases, almost 24 percent of the writing students do in American schools.

Based on these findings and recommendations for fundamentally changing our approach to a writing task, it's crucial that transactional and mechanical writing not dominate the way in which students write because when that happens, students get little opportunity to see the craft of writing as a powerful art form that can have boundless outcomes. And, Britton argues, since expressive writing is the "matrix," or heart, from which the other kinds of writing develop, students need to devote increased time to this kind of writing in all schools and at every age. If students are immersed in personal expressive writing when they are very young, or even when they enter a college-level composition course, it will not only enhance their writing skills and positively affect attitudes but also improve student writing in all modes, including transactional pieces, ironically enough.

Well, if you've had teachers who were current and informed, this may not be news to you—certainly not a radical change in your standard operating procedure—but far too many middle, secondary, and postsecondary schoolteachers have not embraced this shift, so you may unfortunately have instructors who still emphasize predominantly transactional writing. Many administrators, educators, and textbook developers are still disturbed by the suggestion to deemphasize transactional writing assignments, such as reports, research papers, business letters, and formal expository essays. They claim that personal expressive writing, a *soft* kind of writing in their view, will not prepare students for the real world—one in which they will find themselves working and being productive citizens. They argue that the real world cares mostly for informative, formal, and transactional kinds of writing (and at times this is absolutely true). They believe that an extensive background in this kind of writing will more likely guarantee success in higher education, in business, and in life. They not only lobby, often vehemently, for continuing to emphasize transactional writing but even advocate a more intense focus on these kinds of assignments. This thinking is supported widely by many concerned parents, traditional academicians, and educational administrators who are loathe to change what they trust to be true. And it's not that they care little that students don't like writing—perhaps an unfortunate condition or a necessary evil in their minds—but they perceive writing as a tool for formal communication that must be taught uniformly and systematically, with a focus on transferring information and on a strict adherence to correctness. So this is what you are up against.

With this widespread view, it's no wonder that Britton's proposal that teachers revamp their writing assignments and allow students to focus on personal expressive writing was not well received and, in some cases, totally rejected; it still encounters resistance in too many schools today. Accepting his methodology requires a fundamental change in the way many teachers approach writing, including professors in college who require traditional research papers, book reports, scientific write-ups, formal analysis essays, essay tests, and so on. They claim there is no time in the curriculum for writing about feelings or writing personal exploratory pieces, but mostly they fundamentally distrust this new method and don't believe it will produce competent writers who could *like* writing *and* write successfully in many situations. And so the debate continues.

But there is good news. Even though the division in beliefs about teaching writing exists, you should know that many effective and reputable educators have adopted Britton's suggestions for change. And while it has, in some instances, taken more than twenty-five years for this approach to writing to become classroom practice, an ever increasing number of students are experiencing this refreshing change in their classrooms and the incredible impact of this approach on writing. And they continue to witness the tangible success of Britton's proposal in their own writing. Many students have improved how they write and how they feel about writing and are emerging as effective, confident writers because of this shift in approach. You can, too.

But the best news is this: Even if you have been steeped in transactional writing, it doesn't take long at all to see the results of a slight shift to personal expressive writing, nor are you ever too old to reap its benefits. A willingness to embrace this method will rapidly transform your writing on many levels. It will not only change your deep-rooted notions about the writing process but also make extraordinary improvements in how you write.

Need more proof? Let me take you back in time to when I was a student. Consider this scenario, perhaps reminiscent of an experience you may have had:

I distinctly remember a teacher who assigned everyone a one-page report to write for homework. She randomly distributed what she thought to be a diverse and interesting array of topics during class: freedom of speech, Egypt, Thomas Edison, the Boxer rebellion, loyalty, and so on. I was assigned the Boxer rebellion. I was not at all familiar with this event in history or its importance (I had never even heard of it), but I had to write a report about it for homework.

Many students today might immediately engage their favorite search engine on the Internet to find comprehensive information on this topic, but only a few years ago, I, like many of my classmates, went to the library to do my research in the trustworthy *Encyclopaedia Britannica*. Like most student writers who were handed a topic, I paid strict attention to the parameters we received for the one-page report (name in the upper right corner, neat penmanship, no cross-outs, no misspelled words, no writing on the back of the paper—just to name few), and I assumed that I should write a summary explaining, describing, or defining my topic. I could accomplish this by pretty much copying information from the encyclopedia and, to show my cleverness and academic prowess, changing a few of the big words to make the report sound more like my writing. In parts though, I just copied the encyclopedia verbatim, not intending to plagiarize, just trying to get the information correct and the assignment done. I had quite successfully used the same technique for a social studies report on the battle of Manassas. So I wrote my transactional piece, void of personal thought and feelings.

And relying on my youthful dedication to homework execution and given the one-night time limitation, I produced (mostly copied) exactly one page about the Boxer rebellion (a political uprising of men in China in 1900 who might by today's definition be described as martial arts experts or even ninjas). Most of us thought we might get a little better grade if we added a picture (you call them graphics today), so I included a colorful map of China on the cover and also included a list of references about the Boxer rebellion (not necessarily books I used, but three book titles that I found in the card catalog in the library). In addition to the cover, I included several pictures of Chinese men carrying signs, cut out from *National Geographic*. I felt confident that my report more than met the requirements of the assignment. In fact, I thought, maybe a bit smugly, that I had included the little extras teachers love. I felt good about what I had done.

Many of my diligent classmates were following a similar procedure with their assigned topics of Egypt, Thomas Edison, and so on, and once everyone handed in the written reports, the transaction was almost complete. When the reports were returned, we eagerly scanned the pages, turning to the last page to find the mark that would complete the transaction: a letter grade or a number. Game over! Sad or happy, fulfilled or indifferent, thankful or resentful, content or angry, we moved on to the next task.

Does this experience sound familiar? My guess is that, even so many years later, this writing scenario occurs fairly regularly in many classrooms and in many schools. And something else plays out rather consistently: any digression from the standard transactional report is regarded at best as a cute diversion from the "real" assignment, and at worst as unacceptable and unworthy of credit. For example, imagine a student in today's classroom who naturally thinks beyond the parameters of a prescribed writing assignment and who decides not to research the Boxer rebellion in an encyclopedia or on the Internet, but rather to write a personal expressive piece, using her imagination, about a place in which dogs, led by a powerful group of boxers, unite to overthrow their cruel human masters. Or consider another student who chooses to write about his quirky family, specifically a brother who openly refuses to wear boxers anymore! And imagine another student who actually does research the Boxer rebellion and is intrigued by these martial-arts-trained Chinese rebels, who were dubbed Boxers by foreigners but called themselves the Fists of Righteous Harmony. She decides to write her feelings and thoughts about how these Boxers are similar to another rebellious group in our own country—the Sons of Liberty in the American Revolution! How would these decisions be received by transactionally oriented teachers intent on achieving formulaic answers or adhering to a rigid curriculum? You know the answer.

Personal expressive writing requires you to think, to question, to view and review, and then to experiment with language, by choosing the right words, to express ideas in just the right way. This writing is ultimately more time-consuming but intellectually more stimulating than transactional writing; it's difficult and at times messy, but more importantly for you as a writer, it's more valuable in the long run. Communicating your thoughts and feelings to readers becomes the focus, not mechanical recording or copying. Imagine a classroom in which you are eager to sit with a small peer group and share what you have written and then hear the reactions of others to your writing. This kind of experience teaches you how to communicate your thoughts, how to approach future writing tasks, and how to revise your existing writing for maximum effect on an audience. These were never pressing considerations or concerns in my transactional writing experience about the Boxer rebellion.

So what does all this mean for you? Simply this: If you want to develop powerful abilities to communicate in writing, begin with personal expressive writing and focus on vital ideas, places, people, experiences, and concerns that you know about and which have some driving personal investment for you. Finding instructors who have adopted this philosophy and will allow you this real freedom, of course, makes this easier to do. But you can always take the initiative and try out personal expressive writing on your instructors; ask for feedback.

With this alternative approach in mind, the focus shifts to a technique all effective writers consider imperative: appealing to readers' hearts rather than appealing only to their intellects. Successful writers allow readers to really know or understand an experience by choosing words that touch readers' many sensibilities. And you can infuse this quality in *all* writing tasks, even the most transactional ones. Writing teachers who encourage students to *show* what they mean rather than *tell* what they mean (a subtle but significant distinction) know that *showing* is at the center of personal expressive writing and informs the choices writers make and the sensory details they choose to share. (See "6. Developing the Body" in Chapter 6 of this book for more on writing with sensory details.) The more you attend to this in *all* your writing assignments, the more success you will see in the reactions readers have to your writing. So even if you have the most transactional of instructors, you have the power to apply personal expressive techniques to the kinds of assignments given to you. For example, spend some time considering your word choices— especially your verbs—and examine the effect this has on readers.

Although I give my own students freedom to frame pieces of writing and choice in what approach to take, students who are not confident in making their own decisions (largely because they haven't had much practice in school) sometimes have problems with a typical personal expressive assignment that I use. The assignment: *Recall and write about a person in your life, past or present, who somehow changed you or taught you about the world or yourself.* One student, Jim Moran, preparing to write a meaningful personal essay about a coach he had as a boy, found himself wondering: "Do I have to stick with the truth, or can I use my memory and imagination, too?" Jim used sensory details, concrete images, and quoted lines to appeal to readers' sensibilities. Energized by this open-ended personal expressive writing task, Jim, rather than being overly concerned about facts, chose to share the vivid memories, thoughts and feelings he had about his swim coach. The following excerpts from his essay show what I mean.

Back in the USSR

Although I have never taken the time to extensively research the matter, I am confident that somewhere, perhaps buried beneath layers of dust and confusing legalese, there exists a law against making eight year old children swim six thousand yards at five o'clock in the morning. Such strenuous practice schedules defy common sense. They make parents in charge of the carpool cringe at the very thought of waking up to find the alarm clock displaying four thirty and the thermometer displaying temperatures more aptly suited to a tundra ecosystem. They make most eight year olds want to roll over and go back to sleep, willing to sacrifice all vague notions of Olympic eligibility for those few precious hours of early morning slumber. I, however, found myself sluggishly walking onto that pool deck morning after morning, swimming endless laps, perfecting the elusive flip turn that would shave precious seconds off my time.

Jim's opening is vivid, a bit sarcastic, and full of sensory details to which readers can relate their own experiences with doing any activity that seemed extreme and forced. It hooks us into reading more.

After this engaging opening, Jim decided to further describe his coach, the architect of his memorable experience:

Alex Boutov was once the darling of the Soviet Olympic Swim Team, and his regime centered on fear and intimidation. He did not merely stand at the edge of the pool, he loomed. To this day, I still consider him to be the tallest man in the world. Staring up at him from the swimming pool, my exhausted fingers gripping the ledge, he seemed to be at least eight feet tall. His thickly muscled body filled the entire room. He would glare down at us, his enormous swimmer's shoulders eclipsing the overhead lights, and point at the stopwatch with disgust. In his thickly accented English, he would tell us our times were too slow, our turns too sloppy, our hands slapped the water too frequently, or any one of a million grievances he could find with our performance. I remember him as a hulking, shadowy figure poolside, lips curled around a whistle, glancing from his stopwatch to the water screaming, "Faster, faster, you must swim faster." Even during meets, when all the ambient noise melts into one dull roar as you tipped your head up for breath, I could always hear his voice distinctly. The water aborted his words, distorted his message, but it was already so ingrained in every swimmer he need not say it at all. We had to swim faster.

Jim includes slightly exaggerated sensory images so readers can see, feel, hear, and experience what it was like in that pool, swimming for this coach. The simple line uttered by his coach, especially the sound of his clipped Russian accent, helps us form a total picture here.

Jim ended his essay with personal meaning—an insightful reflection and unexpected admission about this man and his feelings toward him:

I still imagine today that if I were to return to that YMCA at five A.M., I would find him exactly where I left him, pacing up and down a twenty-five meter pool, his knuckles growing white around a stopwatch. He would not have aged at all, for people like him are frozen in time. They die at obscenely old ages with four percent body fat, their shoulders and backs just enormous packs of ropey muscle. I can hear him even now, his accent as thick as always, as though he arrived from Russia only weeks previously. He would tower over me just as I remember, and, just as I remember, I would secretly thank him for his harsh words and constant vigilance. As always, I would leave wondering, hoping, if maybe, just maybe (even though he would never admit it to me) just one time, I had swum fast enough for him.

One strength of this writing is Jim's personal decision to show how this experience made him feel then and now. He reveals, quite honestly, that his feelings are complicated. He neither totally fears, hates, loves, nor appreciates what this coach did, and he openly shares his conflicting feelings. As you might imagine, peer responses to his essay were favorable as students noted many attributes of his writing, especially his word choices and exaggerations for effect. Yet one question still lingered for several students: "How did you remember all the exact details of a person and an experience from so long ago?" It's a good question.

To respond, let me pose my own question to you, as I did for my students: Does faithful accuracy matter in this personal essay, or is it more important to share a personal perception of the memory of a person and an experience? Part of the freedom you have in writing a personal expressive essay is blending a memory with what you think and how you feel *now*. There's no foul here; it's legal. You can imagine, though, how students accustomed primarily to transactional writing would respond to the question—believing, of course, that accuracy and facts are of utmost importance in writing. But many of us who are not so concerned with facts love Jim's piece because through it we can recall similar people, experiences, and emotions in our own lives; we recognize the universal element this essay presents: pleasing someone we respect, love . . . or even fear! So who's right? Well, American poet Richard Hugo, in his book *The Triggering Town,* asserted that you owe the facts nothing when you're writing, but you owe the truth about your feelings everything. Hugo suggests that the purpose for using sensory details is to share your true feelings and evoke true emotions in readers; writers often must use their imaginations for what they have forgotten. Again, no foul; it's legal. A quote from Mark Twain also gets at the heart of the controversy: "If you tell the truth you don't have to remember anything." Jim provoked us to remember, to think, to feel.

Good writing that touches readers is personally revealing, is not always accurate, and is driven by your need to make meaning out of life's experiences. Maintaining these fundamental qualities of good writing may help you uncover a deep-rooted talent that you possess. Allowing yourself to embrace personal expressive writing as an approach can energize *all* your writing tasks. It's worth a try.

Sharing Ideas

- Tim O'Brien, an American writer, once said that there's story truth and there's happening truth, and he believed that the truth told in stories is more powerful than what actually happened in real life. What do you think, based on what Joe Antinarella shared?

- What kind of writing—transactional, expressive, or poetic—do you remember doing in school? Tell stories about specific assignments you remember.

- Thia Wolf, in Chapter 1, speaks of the inherent inaccuracy of memory and she seems to say that the factual accuracy of what you remember isn't nearly as important as what you understand about the memory. What is your position on the relative importance of remembering versus understanding?

- What qualities of personal expressive writing make this kind of writing more attractive and alluring to readers than transactional writing?

- Consider focusing a piece of personal writing under these subheadings: a person, a place, and an experience. Create a short list of topics that you've always wanted to write about in each. What motivates you to write on one or all of these?

- Take an actual piece of transactional writing that you did in the past and play with it—revise it, taking word choice and stylistic considerations into account, to make it more expressive. Did doing this help you end up owning the topic, even though a teacher assigned it to you?

8

Writing Stories in College

Gian S. Pagnucci

Gian S. Pagnucci is a Professor of English at Indiana University of Pennsylvania. He loves doing and teaching all types of writing, from stories to essays to computer manuals. But even more than writing, he loves football and the Green Bay Packers. Gian is often running late, a fact that never fails to exasperate his very punctual wife. She promises that their two young sons will learn to be on time!

The day started like most of my days in college: I was *late* for class. Getting up early for classes in high school had never been a problem for me. But now, morning just seemed to come way too fast.

I had Boston's "More Than a Feeling" blaring on my stereo as I dried my hair and tried to find a sweatshirt that looked reasonably clean.

"Do you have to play that song *every* single morning?" asked my roommate, Mike, from his bunk bed.

"No," I said. "Just the mornings I'm late."

"Terrific," he said and pulled a pillow over his head.

I tossed a notebook and a used copy of Jay McInerney's *Bright Lights, Big City* into my backpack, spent a few minutes madly searching for my watch (which was conveniently sitting amid a pile of tapes and CDs), and then dashed out the door. Since Mike was almost back asleep, I gave the door a good, solid *bang* on the way out to make sure it closed securely. That's what friends are for! Mike's shouted commentary at my exit hung in the air behind me as I ran down the hall. It's probably better left unprinted.

———— ◆ ————

Lesson One: Get off to a good start. (Try not to be late!)

This is a story about telling stories. Like the other authors in this book, I want to help you write better papers for college. But, more importantly, I also want to help you tap into one of the greatest abilities you possess: your power to tell stories.

Humans are born storytellers. Stories permeate every facet of our lives. Each day, in our heads, we tell ourselves stories: I was there; I did this; tomorrow I'll go there; tomorrow I'll do that. Psychologist Jerome Bruner argues that one of the most basic ways we understand the world around us is through stories.

Our greatest literature, from the plays of Shakespeare to the novels of Toni Morrison, is stories. We also read news *stories*, place world events into hi*stories*, and watch television shows that are the stories of other people's lives, either real, imagined, or sort of real (like most "reality" shows). Even as children, the games we play are mostly stories: You be the good guy and I'll be the bad guy and we'll see who wins.

Unfortunately, because stories are so natural and such a big part of our childhood, the art of storytelling often gets overlooked in school. Teachers generally confine storytelling to reading fairy tale books in preschool, or they ignore stories in favor of more objective, scientific facts. Of course, when we try to figure out what those facts mean by interpreting them based on our experiences, we are actually using the stories of our lives to explain the world in which we live.

Since storytelling is such an important skill, I'm going to try to help you with three types of storytelling:

- writing literary stories (like the type with which I opened this chapter)
- using story elements in other types of papers (like essays or scientific reports)
- using stories as a tool for personal growth and learning (like reminding you that you should avoid being late for class)

I'm going to discuss these different aspects of storytelling as lessons that came up during the course of the story with which I began this chapter, about what happened to me one day when I left late for my English class. Hopefully the story will make the lessons clearer. Even if the lessons don't help you too much, though, at least you'll have a story to keep you entertained. So, for instance, I could have started out by telling you that every paper you write should have a clever introduction that gets your reader interested in the topic. But, instead, I opened with a story about something to which most people can relate: being late.

I also put some very specific details into my opening story. Again, this is a key to effective story writing. For instance, I didn't just say I put a book into my backpack, I said I put *Bright Lights, Big City* into the pack. Some readers (not all, true, but some) may be interested in why I mentioned that book. A more clever detail I included was the song I was listening to on my stereo that morning: Boston's "More Than a Feeling." Certainly at least one rock aficionado in your class will know who the group Boston was and perhaps that "More Than a Feeling" is ranked eighty-fourth on VH1's list of the top one hundred rock songs of all time. Of course, you'll have to actually listen to the song to find out why it is such a great wake-up tune. Both the song and the book also help establish the time period of the story.

All right, enough with the lessons. Let's get back to the story. As you might recall, I was late for class . . .

———— ◆ ————

Mike and I lived on the fifth floor of Ogg Hall, so it was faster to jog down the stairs than wait for the elevator. Outside it was still a cool Wisconsin morning, and the sun was glinting off the white concrete stones around the dining hall. I was going to miss breakfast. Again. I really needed to start using my Thursday nights for studying and getting to bed early. *Next week,* I promised myself.

The University of Wisconsin is a big place: almost a thousand acres to be exact. So naturally my English class was miles away. Well, it seemed like miles whenever I was late. In this case, my class was in Bascom Hall, which meant climbing the big hill at the center of campus. The student government had told the administration we needed a ski lift for that hill, but the request just hadn't gone anywhere yet.

Anyway, time was running short, so I took off at a good clip. I got over to University Avenue and turned left. For once, traffic was pretty light. I looked at my watch and saw that I was making decent time.

Now, the University of Wisconsin, like most campuses, is crawling with students. Actually, there are 41,588 according to the university's "Campus in Profile" website. That's a lot of students, more than the populations of some small American towns. In fact, there are so many students walking around the University of Wisconsin campus that they can stop traffic when they want to. On football-game days, for instance, a crowd of students will often just step into the street and make the oncoming traffic wait until the crowd crosses, usually banging on a few car hoods along the way. Even without big crowds, pedestrians rule the land, and no one ever worries about jaywalking or crossing against a light.

———— ◆ ————

Lesson Two: A good story can make sense of the facts and support an argument (and even get a few tears flowing).

In most of the papers you'll write for college, you'll be trying to convince someone to agree with your argument. You might be trying to make someone believe the death penalty is wrong or abortions are justifiable under certain circumstances or the war in Iraq was really about oil interests or the United States Constitution protects a student's right to pray in school. As you write your paper, you'll be trying to marshal all the reasons you can find that prove your view is correct.

Sometimes the most powerful way to make your argument is to tell a story. People naturally relate to stories. When we hear a story, it makes us think about similar stories we've heard and similar experiences we've had. We do this automatically. If I tell you today is my birthday, you'll probably start thinking about the last time you had a birthday. Stories are one of the main ways we process information.

This makes stories an extremely powerful tool for writing. So let me give you an example. Suppose I'm writing a paper about abortion and in the paper I want to prove that abortion is a bad thing and should be outlawed. I might try to prove this argument statistically. For instance, the Center for Bio-Ethical Reform has calculated that 3,700 abortions take place every day in the United States, for a total of about 1.37 million abortions annually. Even most wars don't take so many lives.

The problem is, it's hard to relate to statistics. Numbers are sort of cold. Just how many people is thirty-seven hundred? What does that look like? We know it's a lot. But it's also just a number. We can look at the number, say, "That's sad," and forget about it. Tomorrow, we might remember only that there are a lot of abortions. We might also say, "Maybe those numbers aren't accurate," or "Maybe the Center for Bio-Ethical Reform is biased; how do we know it isn't lying or distorting the numbers?"

So the numbers might help me make my argument about why abortion should be banned, but they probably aren't enough to win the argument on their own. To make those abstract numbers more concrete, I could add a story about someone I knew who actually had an abortion. I might talk about how once when I was a resident assistant in the dorms at the University of Wisconsin, I found a young woman who was crying, shouting, and throwing things all over her dorm room. She was angry and drunk, and her terrified roommate had come to me for help. When I finally got the woman to sit down so we could talk about what was happening, she burst into tears again and told me she had had an abortion three weeks earlier because she was too young to have a baby, but now she couldn't stop thinking about what she had done. And all I could do was sit there holding her as she cried.

Now the truth is, with a controversial issue like abortion, you can never convince everyone that your side of the argument is correct. People will say that a mother has a right to choose, or a teen mother's parents have a right to know, or a mother should not be endangered by a problem birth, or that God says abortion is wrong, or that God gave us minds to decide for ourselves what is best. If you give statistics about how many babies die from abortions, someone else will point out how many women in third-world countries die in childbirth each year.

What a story does, though, is help your reader to feel. Even if you're pro-choice, you can still feel the pain of the woman in my story. You might think of someone you know who has had an abortion, or you might imagine what it would be like to face that kind of decision yourself or with someone you love. It's hard to win the debate over abortion, which is why people are still fighting about it. But a story can help show how an abstract issue affects real people. A story can show, in a way that numbers never can, why things like abortion and war and illness and even love matter so much to us.

Since I was running late, I figured I'd have to make a fast dash across Park Street and then cut up past Lathrop Hall. I thought there was even an outside chance I could get to class on time if things went my way. It was looking like a fine morning after all.

The trouble is that you always end up having an unexpected problem when you are late and time is the most critical.

That morning, just as I picked up my pace, hoping to gain a little more time, my backpack strap broke. I always carried my backpack slung over one shoulder whenever I walked to class. That was the cool way to do it. A broken strap would have been a minor problem, except that at the time I didn't have a hand on the backpack. The strap broke near the top, so the backpack tumbled off my back and hit me on the left foot as it fell to the ground. I lurched sideways, caught my foot on a black plastic chain-link fence, and landed with a thud next to a "Keep Off the Grass" sign.

Several feet away, a young woman giggled for a moment and then called over to me, "Are you all right?"

"Fine," I said.

She nodded and then turned and began walking in the other direction.

"Ugh," I groaned. I pulled myself into a sitting position, rubbed at a new dirt stain on my right knee, and then rose to my feet. Why did my efforts to look cool always seem to end up with some girl laughing at me?

"Piece of shit," I cursed the backpack under my breath as I gave it a small kick. Then I bent over and picked it up, inspecting the broken strap. The stitching on the seam had come apart.

I sighed. "Cheap junk," I said and resolved not to buy any more clearance items. I pulled on the other strap. It seemed to be holding up fine. I slung the pack over my other shoulder, pulled the little chain fence back into a standing position, and took off again for my class, later than ever.

Lesson Three: Don't be afraid of words (even swear words).

Your mother probably taught you never to swear in public (still a good rule to follow most of the time), but sometimes you may want or even need to use a swear word in a paper. You might, for instance, need to shock your reader awake or incite anger about some sort of injustice. Sometimes you need to tell a graphic story, complete with curses.

If you decide to swear in a paper, though, keep in mind another important lesson: all things in moderation. Less is generally more, and this is especially true with swear words. One colorful word might be exactly what is needed to accurately describe some situation, but if you use swear word after swear word, you start to lose the effect. You might remember I told you at the beginning of my story that my roommate swore at me but I didn't tell you what he said. One obscenity can be shocking, but five in a row may bore or even annoy your reader.

The same thing is true for other words as well. Some students, in an attempt to impress their writing teachers, use the thesaurus to find as many big words as they can, words that sound impressive or even august, words that the students hope will make them appear intelligent or even sagacious. Now, as with swear words, a complex word used at just the right moment can, indeed, impress your reader. But overuse of voluminous words can start to make your writing odious to read.

One of the best writing techniques is to aim for variety. Use simple and complex words, short and long sentences, facts and stories. Mix it up. Try a little of this and a little of that. If, for instance, you've just discussed a complex theoretical idea, summarize that thought into a simpler statement. Remember, readers get bored easily, so you have to keep working hard to maintain their interest. In fact, you're probably bored with this lesson by now, so let's get back to that story.

———— ◆ ————

But then, just as I got near Park Street, I saw that there was a lengthy procession of little kids ahead of me. The kids were in a long line, standing two by two, each child tightly gripping the hand of a walking buddy. They were marching along in tiny baseball caps and tennis shoes, little blue jeans and T-shirts. Every kid was lugging a backpack that looked almost twice his or her weight. It was like a miniature army. There must have been thirty kids, plus a couple of teachers.

I swung out to the left to get around the group, figuring I could dash ahead of them at the light. They weren't exactly in a hurry. As I moved up alongside them, I could see that what I first took to be neat ranks of students was actually a wild mass of shoving, talking, jumping, laughing kid energy.

When I got closer to the head of the line, I could see Park Street and started looking for a break in the traffic. It's three lanes there, and the cars move pretty fast, but you can get across if you keep your eyes open.

The teacher at the front of the line looked a little frazzled. But she was cute. She had her hair in a ponytail, pulled back through a red Badgers cap.

———— ◆ ————

Lesson Four: Tell a story that is important to you (you'll learn something from it, no matter who else does).

Don't despair. Even if you get robbed and your boyfriend dumps you and your apartment burns down and your dog dies, you'll still have one thing no one can take away from you: your stories.

Stories are the greatest treasure we have. They link us to the past and prepare us for the future. Stories bind us to our friends and family. Stories help us preserve the good times and survive the bad times. Most importantly, stories can help us discover who we really are.

If you look back at your life, what you will find are stories: stories of childhood games, family holidays, romance and heartache, silliness and friendship. Writing about these experiences, good and bad, can help you understand why you think the way you do and why you act the way you act. But too often, students choose to tell stories that they already understand— about meeting their first love, or winning the big game, or losing a dear relative. These are important stories, yes, but because they are so important, we've already spent a lot of time pondering their significance to our lives. That's why, when you are asked to write a story, you should pick an experience whose importance is not entirely clear to you. Try writing about something you and your brother always did together. Try writing about a time you helped a stranger. Try writing about an afternoon when you took a walk for no reason at all.

Now I should warn you, though: Writing this type of story won't be easy, because you won't know ahead of time what the point of the story is. You'll have to figure that out as you go. But that's also the beauty of this type of writing. As you write, you'll be able to learn something new about who you are and why you believe what you believe. Pick an event from your past and describe, in as much detail as you can, what happened to you. Almost always, there's a reason that event has lingered in your mind. Writing that story will help you discover something about yourself.

Maybe you'll end up telling a really interesting story or maybe your story won't make much sense. Maybe you'll discover a key to your philosophy of life or maybe you'll just discover something simple, like taking walks makes you happy. It doesn't matter. Even the grade you'll get for this story won't matter. What will matter is this: If you can write a story that helps you discover something about yourself, then you will have learned why writing is so important. And you will never be quite the same again.

But you have to learn this on your own. That's why the grade you get on the story truly doesn't matter (but, as a backup, *please* promise me you'll work really, really hard on all your other papers too!). When you write a story, or any paper, that teaches you something, you are no longer just a student writing a paper for a class: you've become a real writer. And no one can ever take that away from you, no matter what grade the paper gets.

——— ◆ ———

I had almost gotten past the army of kids and the cute teacher. But then, just as I was reaching the front of the group, I caught the tail end of the teacher's speech to her students:

"And that's why we have to look carefully whenever we cross the street. We only cross when we see the green light with the little man who is walking. Otherwise, we have to wait."

Even as she said it, I watched the stoplight on Park Street click from green to red. My foot hung in the air, locked in midstride where I had been gathering myself for a quick run ahead of any traffic.

Then I felt lots of tiny eyes land on my back and I lowered my foot to the ground. I looked at my watch. Two cars rolled through the intersection. Then, naturally, there was a gap in the traffic. I looked at a blank section of street that I could have walked across with my eyes closed.

"Very good, boys and girls," I heard. "Make sure you have your partner's hand. Watch for the walk signal. And stay in the crosswalk. See those white lines in the street? That tells you where you have to cross."

The Don't Walk signal was still glowing red. It was the slowest light I had ever seen. I wondered, looking at my watch again, if perhaps it had gotten stuck. I pictured myself standing for hours with those kids, modeling proper street-crossing etiquette. What else could I do?

——— ◆ ———

Lesson Five: You never know where a good story will finish (and you also shouldn't forget where your starting point was).

Most people don't know when to quit. They keep talking or writing, going on and on until their audience can barely sit still. Don't make that mistake. I find that many times, when I'm writing a story, I say far too much. What I have to do then is go backward and look for the real ending. The trick is looking for a meaningful place to stop. Many times, if I cut the last few paragraphs of my writing, I'll find a more interesting finishing point. Usually a character says something interesting or there's some sort of simple image that helps capture the main focus of the story.

What I usually end up cutting are all the statements I put into the story about what it meant and why I was writing it. Readers aren't stupid. You don't have to tell them this is a story about love or this is a story about why war is bad. Most readers can figure that out. And if you've written a story about why your grandmother was such a wonderful person, you probably don't have to end your story by *explicitly* telling your reader that your grandmother was a wonderful person. If you've done a good job with the story, your reader should be able to figure that out. Instead, you probably want to end the story with something your grandmother said or maybe with an image of some item, a ring or a shawl, that meant a lot to her.

The other key to a good conclusion is what's known as coming full circle. Readers often enjoy it when a story ends in a way that reminds them of where the story started. So, if you began your story about your grandmother by describing her wedding ring, which she gave to you on your sixteenth birthday, you might want to end your story by talking about the ring again, perhaps by describing how the ring feels when you place it on your finger. If you are writing an argumentative essay rather than a story, you can still come full circle. In an effective conclusion for an essay, you should first summarize the main points of your paper. This will help to make sure your readers haven't forgotten any of your major arguments, and it will help further persuade the reader that you've argued a strong case. But then, after providing that summary, you might want to return to the statistics or quotation or story with which you began the essay. Remind your reader, for example, that you began your essay by pointing out the rising death toll in the United States from crimes involving automatic weapons. You might then offer one more grisly statistic, perhaps the number of terrorists estimated to possess automatic weapons, as a way to bring home both sets of statistics and your overall argument.

Starting and finishing a paper on the same terrain can help establish a clear, central theme for your reader.

It was definitely the longest light on earth. Next to me, a small boy in a Teenage Mutant Ninja Turtles jacket raised his hand.

"Yes, Patrick?" said the teacher, whom I was beginning to find more irritating than cute.

"Can we write about crossing the street in our notebooks?"

"That's a good idea, Patrick. OK, class," she said. "Everyone get out your notebook for a minute. Since we have to wait for the light to change, we can all look around and see what there is to write about."

"I'm going to write about that funny-looking building," one boy said.

"Me too," said another boy.

"I'm tired of walking," one kid said.

"I'm going to write about the sunshine."

"I'm going to write about that eagle."

"Where?"

"That's not an eagle."

"It is too."

"It's a crow."

"Well, I'm still going to write about it anyway."

One by one, the students opened up their backpacks and got out their notebooks and sat down on the sidewalk to begin writing.

As I turned to watch them, the stoplight behind me went from red to green to red again. I stood there, staring, while the kids began busily writing in their notebooks. I was always nervous when I started a paper, but these kids seemed to think writing was fun. I looked around slowly, trying to see the dazzling world that they could see. My own English class could wait, I decided. After all, I was late anyway.

———— ◆ ————

The Final Lesson: Stop reading my story and start writing your own. (Your stories are the ones most worth telling.)

Sharing Ideas

- One of the keys to effective writing is using specific details, a lesson Gian Pagnucci says you can learn from writing stories. Look at a recent piece of writing you've done and analyze your use of specific details, the kind you find in stories.

- What are some of the most common stories we encounter on a regular basis? Where do these stories come from and why are they important? How do we use stories in everyday life?

- Gian claims that stories are more powerful than numbers and isolated facts. Is he right? Under what circumstances might a story be the most persuasive argument? When might a story be insufficient to win an argument?

- What was your reaction to the vulgarity Gian used in recounting the story of his broken backpack strap? Were you shocked? Did it give the story veracity?

- Gian believes most people don't know when to end their stories. How do you determine when to stop? Do you use page requirements as your guide? Do you have a point in mind that you're writing toward? Do you write and write until you're too tired to go on?

- Gian switches between his story of being late for class and some suggestions for how to write stories. It's almost as though his chapter contains two different papers and arguments: the story and the directions. What do you think of this approach? Think of a paper you've recently written. How could you revise the paper so that it had a second line of thought? What sort of story could you weave around your argument? How do you think this sort of revision would impact your paper?

- Are bad stories worth remembering? Do they serve any purpose? Why or why not? What's a story, good or bad, that you can't seem to forget? Why do you think that story has stuck with you? If you were going to write the story down, where would you start?

9

Hearing Voices:
Yours, Mine, Others

Jay Szczepanski

While working on his master's degrees in rhetoric and composition (with an emphasis on voice) and American studies (with emphases on Southern history and literature), Jay Szczepanski teaches first-year writing courses at Florida State University with wild titles like Digital Discourse, Writing About the American South, and Controversial Social Issues. He received his B.A. from Flagler College in St. Augustine, Florida, in 2001.

You may have heard one of your instructors tell you that a certain piece of your writing had a "good voice," or a "distinct voice," or a "conversational tone," or any one of a number of expressions. Voice, style, tone, affect, effect—it's a long list. As a term in composition, voice has a long history. So, what is it (exactly), and more importantly, how do you get it?

To begin, you have to start writing, which seems obvious. And it doesn't necessarily matter what you write, either. There's voice in almost every type of writing. Take, for instance, what I'm writing now. I'm conscious of the voice I'm using to address you, a student in a composition classroom. I'm trying to have a conversation with you (admittedly, it's a bit one-sided). I'm trying not to scare you off or intimidate you. I want you to read whatever it is I end up with so that you say to yourself, "Damn. I understand this."

This might be more easily said than done, but it's what I'm getting at, in any case.

So, again, what is it? There are quite a few different interpretations of voice. While not everyone will agree with the definitions that I give below, there's enough agreement among composition instructors to make them worth considering. And remember: This is only a short list. We can break voice down into smaller and smaller parts (for more on this notion, see the last section below, "Other Voices").

Some Working Definitions

Authentic Voice

In a nutshell, authentic voice is the voice that you, as the writer, innately have; that is, authentic voice is the one that you own that is distinctly yours: no other writer has it, and no other writer can reproduce it—exactly. Think in terms of fingerprints. You have a unique set that no one else has or will have. Apply that principle to your writing: someone can read whatever it is you have written and know (maybe not immediately, but with a closer look) that you are the person who wrote it based on your voiceprint.

Academic Voice

Academic voice is trickier. Generally, academic voice is the voice we use in the university and in the professions. It adheres to what's called Standard Written English (SWE for short). SWE includes areas like proper or formal grammar, mechanics, standard punctuation, and appropriate degrees of slang and nonstandard language usage. Consider questions like the following: Should you end a sentence with a preposition? What's the impact or consequence of using the second person ("you")? What about slang terms? Faulty or elaborate sentence parallelism? It's usually not a good idea, when writing formally, to break away from SWE.

Personal (Private) Voice

Personal voice reminds me of journals or diaries. It's the voice you're most comfortable with, and possibly one that you write with when you're sure no one else will see it. The personal voice makes me vulnerable and shows my insecurities. For me, it's different from authentic voice because the personal voice isn't a public one like authentic is. When I write personally, I know that I can tell myself the absolute truth and then throw it away because no one will ever see it. And that brings us to . . .

Public Voice

Your public voice is the one that you let everyone hear. It could be how you write some college papers, when you give a speech, or even when you're sharing your writing with only one other person. Drafts of papers that you workshop in class are a good example because they're the ones that you directly aim to an audience (or peers, the teacher, your friends). I think of it as if I were speaking out loud—whenever there is someone to hear me, I feel as if I'm in the public realm.

Other Voices

Subcategories can include voices of power and authority, such as an oppressor and the oppressed, minority and women's voices such as gay/lesbian, African American, immigrant (these voices are related to voices of power, too), children's voices, voices of spirituality, voices of the mass media/nation groups, and the postmodern "global" voice that makes cultures and values collide.

Situations

You have to write a research paper. You have to compile data for an experiment you completed in last week's chemistry lab. You have to ask Mom for more money. How will you write each of these, and what is it that helps you decide? Well, whenever I want to figure out the voice I should use, two issues immediately jump to mind: audience and rhetorical sensitivity (and all that rhetorical sensitivity really means is context). For this essay, you, a composition student, probably a freshman, are my audience. I imagine that you're probably eighteen or nineteen, that you were admitted into college, and that you're no slouch. I also envision that you're probably tired of reading dry essays (I am too), and you want something a little more engaging, a little more conversational—something that doesn't demean your intelligence.

When you choose one form of writing over another and consider how reader and writer and subject and text interact, you're considering the rhetorical situation.

You consider the rhetorical situation every time you write. You choose one form of writing over another and consider how context shapes what you have to say.

My rhetorical situation is this: I have to look at the assignment my editor has given me (write an essay that addresses the issue of voice in composition for students like those I teach), consider what I want to accomplish (to give my audience a quick overview of what voice is, ways to develop it, and times when different voices are appropriate), and choose the best way to address the already envisioned audience (straightforward language, questions to engage you in order to make you grapple with the text and issues, respect for whoever reads this).

How am I doing?

Some Examples

Definitions are good, but examples are better. Look at the list of writing tasks and types below, and think about what sort of voice you would use in writing to the audience who would read each text. In your head, assign each one a level of formality, where 10 is completely formal and 0 is the most informal. Add your own tasks to the list.

1. a letter to your parents asking for more money

2. a scientific research project where details are important

3. a paper for this composition class

4. an e-mail to an old friend

5. a letter to an aunt whom you rarely see

6. an instant message conversation

7. a memo to yourself

8. an entry in your diary/journal

9. a general news article

10. a newspaper sports article

11. ad copy for a radio advertisement

12. advertisement for perfume in a women's magazine

Perhaps all you can really say for each task is "formal, informal, very formal, very informal, in-between," and the exercise doesn't really get you anywhere—yet. Still, you already knew without having to think for most of these writing tasks which number or term you would pick. But now the question to ask yourself is, "What is it that makes these writing situations and genres, or types, of writing formal or informal or personal or public?"

Let's examine a few of these examples in a little more detail, starting with #4: an e-mail to an old friend. For the sake of argument, let's assume that the person you choose to write to is your best friend (or a good friend) who does not attend the same school you do. How are you going to address him or her? Take a sheet of paper and jot down a few of last week's experiences that you want to tell your friend about. Is there a person or situation who is really irritating you (say, a few too many parking tickets or terrible food in the cafeteria)? The first frat party you went to—what happened? What time did you get home last night? New love interests? On a separate sheet, go ahead and write the letter with your friend as the audience. Then set it aside; we'll refer to it in a little bit.

Now, take a look at #5: a letter to the aunt whom you rarely see. What would happen if you used the same letter and sent it to her? There's a big difference here. You might not want to be so loose with the details with your aunt (then again, who knows—maybe she's the liberal one in the family). For perspective, take yet another sheet of paper and write a letter to your aunt that uses all of the same details that you gave to your friend. Don't lie, but think about creative slants that may allow you to bend the truth a little. When you're done, think about the ways the actual language that you used changed.

For ideas, consider these excerpted examples of voice writing that two of my students have done. Talking to her friend, a writer says:

> . . . Living in a dorm is a totally different thing than living at home. I like the fact that I'm on my own, and doing stuff for myself instead of depending on everyone else to do stuff for me. . . . Parties are everywhere, and everyone is invited. Not just the so-called "cool" people. There's at least one on our floor every night. I like how you can go dressed in pajamas if you want to class, or whatever else you want to wear. Anything goes basically, and I like that.

Talking to her grandmother, she changes her voice:

> I like living in the dorm too. I'm glad I'm rooming with a friend because I've had someone to hang out with the whole time.

Writing to a friend who went into the Air Force, another writer says:

> As for college, I've been having a heck of a time trying to figure this place out; I have pretty much mapped out the entire city in my head by now. (I've been spending a lot of time this week going out of my way to explore.) Classes are okay, most of them easy, but my English class seems as if it's going to be a lot of work.

Sharing with his mom, he says:

> As for college, I think I have the city pretty well known by now. . . . I have spent several hours this week just driving around exploring. Classes are easy, except for English, that is a tough class. Well correction, the content is easy, but it is time consuming.

Finding Your Own Voice

You have your own voice. You've been developing it all of your life through the writing that you do. Chances are, the development has been unconscious. I'll bet that, from time to time, you've written something that you thought was excellent, and you said to yourself, "I'll have to remember that." Maybe voice is a technique: When you write something you know works, you file it away somewhere in your mind, and you refer to it later when writing in the same manner seems appropriate or effective.

Now, if you have a good many techniques filed away, how do you know when (or if) to use them? That is, if it's not in sight, how do you find it? More importantly, once you find it, what do you do with it?

While the examples above are useful for illustrating to us the different ways to use language when we write in different situations, chances are that one of the examples is more closely associated with the way you really write than are the others—and I'm willing to bet that it's the letter to an old friend.

Think of voice as if it were a suit of clothes. You have your fancy dress pants, long-sleeved dress shirt, tie, and jacket (sometimes a tie clip or cuff links). Or, maybe it's a matched two-piece suit—whatever the case, these are your formal clothes. They might be a little uncomfortable for you to wear, but they present a nice, clean image, a formal voice—but these aren't the clothes that you would wear every day. Perhaps you're more comfortable in a pair of blue jeans or sweatpants or shorts and a T-shirt. Maybe a polo shirt and khakis. This style seems more natural to you. You're more at ease with this form of dress because it's more "you." I like to think of my own voice as being something like the polo shirt and khakis—not too formal, but not slouchy, either.

Exercise: Dressing Up/Dressing Down

Take a sheet of paper and make two columns. Label the first one "descriptive words" and the other one "examples of a type of writing." After reading a description of clothing below, try to describe what you think the writing style would be in the first column; that is, what characteristics of the clothing can you transfer over into a description of voice? Then, in the next column, name a few types of writing that share the characteristics that you give to the clothing. For fun or a follow-up, as a class contribute some outfits of your own imagining and complete the exercise again.

  black suit, white shirt, red tie

  jeans, tennis shoes, T-shirt

  evening gown, pearls, white gloves

  sandals, shorts, polo shirt

  khakis, dress shirt, brown belt, no tie

  skirt, flats, white linen blouse

Your own voice is a great one—it's your essence. But, I'll level with you. There will be times when you will have to assume the formal voice of an academic paper whether you want to or not. And, in fact, there will be times when you'll choose to, because there is power involved in gaining the ability to choose how you appear to others (readers). There are other times when you'll be able to play around more freely, especially in creative writing, where pushing the boundaries of voice is valued. And, of course, there's always e-mail and journaling. But your voice has a place in each of these forms of writing. To become more fluent in adapting your voice (to the rhetorical situation), however, you need to know yourself.

And there's an added benefit to being yourself: You might actually begin to enjoy writing. I look at it from a rather conservative standpoint. Every payday I deposit $100 into my savings account from my paycheck. Sure, I'd rather spend it on something frivolous, but I'm disciplined enough to know what's good for me (and that's savings, i.e., writing). Every few months or so, I check my balance, and it gets bigger and bigger—and I'm happier and happier with myself. The more I save, the easier it is to save, and the larger my account gets. I'm proud that something I worked on so hard is developing so nicely. I like seeing the results, and it motivates me to keep working. And writing.

Be Yourself

Here's a story. I had a student, Doug (not his real name, of course), in one of my summer classes. He was a tremendously bright and intuitive guy. But whenever he wrote a paper, he tried to make it sound overly academic. I'm including a sample below.

> Although the interracial mix continues to improve by generation progression, elements of discrimination still exist between ethnicities in America. Many Americans view racism as an inability for whites and blacks to interact and the solution varies directly with the social impediment. . . . Throughout childhood and school we have been taught antiracial values, but without reinforcement, how will we interact when we are free?

What do you hear? And,

> In the theory of interracial interactions we are taught the diversity between races is the beneficial difference. . . . Stereotypes are a natural response in the situation of an unknown, but the willingness to allow the person to defend themselves against the accusations differentiates the usage of racial discrimination.

I hear this writer trying to ratchet up his level of discourse to talk to me on (what he assumed were) my terms. He misused words frequently. He tried to write overly complicated, lengthy sentences. He tried to imitate a style that wasn't uniquely his.

And that's the point: The voice wasn't his. Although certainly with time and practice a more formal voice is within his grasp.

So, how do *you* find *your* voice? I'll repeat myself: The first thing you need to do is write. I don't care what it is. Drafts for your instructor, letters home to friends, e-mails, instant messages, personal journals. Voice is like a muscle: The more you use it, the stronger it becomes. The stronger it becomes, the more visible it is.

Eventually, Doug and I had a long conversation about the voice he was using, and we determined that he was more worried about me thinking that he was stupid than anything else. He obviously wasn't—he was just wearing the wrong set of clothes.

Writing Behaviors to Develop Your Voice

Freewriting: Freewrite without stopping for ten minutes. If you are stuck and don't know what to write, simply write, "I'm stuck I'm stuck," until you get your train of thought back. Or, simply write whatever it is that you're thinking at the time. Do this every day for a week. Every day, try to write a little more than the previous day.

Compulsive e-mail: Everyone likes getting a letter. Write several e-mails a day to several different types of acquaintances (mom, dad, sister, brother, friend, grandmother, teacher).

Diary: Write an honest and personal diary—sort of a letter to yourself every night. Make yourself vulnerable, and then after a month you can burn it. Confess, whine, delight, and scream.

When to Use Your Own Voice

Like I said, there are times when you'll have to write a paper that seems bland and dry. That's life. Other times you'll be free to do as you please. I maintain, though, that in every situation you can incorporate elements of your own voice, traces, hints, a fingerprint or two. It's obvious how you can use your own voice in personal writing and in letters to friends—you write like you speak, as if (like we are here) having a conversation. But in areas like academic and public writing, you might not be certain what parts of your voice are appropriate to include.

I think that what you're reading here fulfills an academic need. I'm giving you an overview that I hope will help improve your writing skills. I could have used a ton of sources, written in precise, analytical terms, and in general been much more formal than I'm being. Instead, I've incorporated personal stories and examples of student work (which, when you think about it, is a source), and I've tried to talk in a straightforward manner. I hope my natural voice is coming through to you. Of course, some instructors frown upon using the first-person and personal examples in formal papers. In those cases, there's not much that you can do—except use this writing time to hone your skills, to add techniques to your toolkit, style to your closet, range to your voice. In any event, you have a lot more leeway in academic writing than you think, and the trend lately is for a more relaxed style in articles that deal with subjects in the humanities.

Last Thoughts

At first, I typed, "Don't worry about your writing." I had to delete it, though, because you *should* worry about your writing. What I meant to type was don't *fret* about your writing. Improve by doing, and *do* often. *Think* about the ways you write, the voices you use, your audience, your rhetorical situation, and the writing clothes that you want to wear. And remember: You have many outfits and many options. Your writing matters because you leave traces of yourself behind for your readers. Let them hear your voiceprint lingering in the background of your work. Chances are, you'll delight your audiences with who you are. Make them come back for more.

Sharing Ideas

- Draw some connections between Kate Ronald's observations in the following chapter about style and Jay Szczepanski's observations about voice. Can you use his essay to help you elaborate on what Kate is observing? Would these two teachers agree or disagree with each other? Would Kate offer similar or different advice to you than Jay does? If you like, write a short scenario where you're having lunch with these instructors and interrogating them about their observations, comparing their thinking with your own experiences in sharing your writing voice and writing style in classes across the university.

- Can you make an argument that learning how to adapt and adopt your writing voice will help you create writing that is more literary in nature and is valued as such? Look at the claims about student writing as literature in Wendy Bishop's essay in light of what Jay explains about voice and writing.

- Compose a critique directed toward some aspect of your own college experience and do so in two or more voices. Use Jay's advice about dressing this piece of persuasive writing in two sets of clothes. Dress it down, then up. Be yourself. Be someone else.

- Pose some difficult yet predictable college writing tasks and then give other writers your advice for composing those tasks in the most interesting voice possible. For instance, how do you develop your own best voice in the school genres of the in-class essay, the lab report, the oral presentation, (as) group discussion leader, the take-home exam, the research paper, and so on?

- Whose writing voices do you most admire? Make a list of your five favorite authors; find four excellent quotes from two of these individuals; and analyze and report on what makes each author's voice recognizable and distinct. Along the way, imitate these voices and present your findings in an essay that makes readers want to go read more work by these authors.

- With classmates, comment on the voices you find in the chapters in this collection. Which writers' voices do you warm to and why? Be specific.

10

Style: The Hidden Agenda in Composition Classes; or, One Reader's Confession

Kate Ronald

Kate Ronald is the Roger and Joyce L. Howe Professor in English at Miami University. She teaches writing and rhetoric courses at all levels, and she works with faculty across the curriculum on the teaching of writing. With Hephzibah Roskelly, she has written *Reason to Believe: Romanticism, Pragmatism, and the Teaching of Writing*, whose title comes from a Bruce Springsteen song. With Joy Ritchie, she has published *Available Means: An Anthology of Women's Rhetoric(s)*, whose title comes from Aristotle.

In some ways I see this essay as a confession. I have been teaching writing and theorizing about how it should be taught for almost fifteen years now. During those fifteen years, you, the students reading this essay, have been in school, taking English classes and writing compositions. I have been teaching those classes and reading those compositions; plus I've been teaching some of your teachers for the past ten years, and so I feel responsible to you even though I've never had you in one of my classes. Now I'm going to tell you something you might already know. Since you started school in the first grade, there's been a revolution in the way you've been "taught" to write. It used to be that teachers focused on and evaluated your writing according to two main things: its structure and its correctness. Those were the days of diagramming sentences and imitating types of organization. In the 1960s and '70s, however, many people who studied writing began to talk about teaching the "process" of writing rather than the "products" of writing. In other words, the focus shifted in the 1980s from organization and correctness to generating ideas, appealing to audiences, and developing a "voice" in writing.

Composition or "rhetoric" as it used to be called, is an ancient discipline going all the way back at least to Plato and Aristotle in the third century B.C.E. You are the most recent in a long, long line of students sitting in classes where teachers assign writing tasks and evaluate your ability. In ancient times, the art of writing was divided into five steps: invention (coming up with ideas), arrangement (organizing them), style (making them sound right), memory (remembering speeches), and delivery (oratorical ability). One way to think about the history of writing instruction is to look at the different emphases that different eras have put on these five steps. Today, with computers and photocopy machines, we don't worry much anymore about memory, for example, but it was terribly important in the time before the printing press. And we don't "deliver" what we write orally very much anymore, although the kind of font you choose from your word-processing program might be considered a matter of delivery. Of course all writers have to think about invention, arrangement, and style, no matter what age they work in. However, different eras have emphasized different parts of composition. Plato and Aristotle were upset by what they saw as an enchantment with style; they worried that writers could dazzle audiences without caring much about telling them the truth. And so they focused on invention, on figuring out issues by thinking and writing. By the sixteenth and seventeenth centuries, the focus had shifted back to style, going so far as giving students manuals that provided hundreds of ways to say "I enjoyed your letter very much." How a person sounded was more important than what a person had to say.

I see the shift from "product" to "process" while you've been in school as a reaction to that overemphasis on style. Once again, the focus has changed back to make *invention* the most important step in composition. Writing teachers who are up-to-date these days (including me) tell you (our students) not to worry, for example, about grammar or spelling or organization as you write your early drafts. We invite you to choose your own topics for writing and to get feedback from responsive small groups in your classes. We don't grade individual papers, but instead ask you to write multiple drafts and submit for final evaluation the ones you think best represent you as a writer. We don't lecture on punctuation or topic sentences. It's what you say, not how you say it, that counts. No doubt you all are familiar with this kind of teaching—I doubt you'd be reading this essay right now if you weren't in a class with a thoroughly "new rhetoric" teacher. Obviously this whole collection is focused on the *processes* of writing, the main theme of writing instruction since the 1980s.

But here comes my confession. Your teacher, and I, and all the others who were part of this latest revolution in rhetoric, haven't been exactly honest with you about the matter of style. We say we aren't overly interested in style, that your ideas and your growth as writers is uppermost in our minds, but we are still influenced by your writing style more than we admit, or perhaps know. In other words, despite all the research and writing I've done in the past ten years about composing, revising, responding, contexts for writing, personal voice, and all I know about the new rhetoric, I'm still rewarding and punishing my students for their writing styles. And here's the worst part of my confession: I'm not sure that I'm teaching them style. Of course any teacher quickly realizes that she can't teach everything in one semester, but I worry that I'm responding to something in my students' writing that I'm not telling them about—their style, the sound of their voices on paper. This essay is my attempt to atone for that omission in my own teaching. Despite that selfish motive, I also want to suggest to you ways in which you might become aware of your own writing styles and your teachers' agendas about style, as well as show you some strategies for studying and improving your own style in writing.

Let me stop to define what I mean and what I don't mean by "style." I don't mean spelling, grammar, punctuation, or usage, although if I'm going to be completely honest, I'd have to tell you that mistakes along those lines do get in my way when I'm reading. But those can be fixed, easily, by editing and copyreading. By style, I mean what my student, Margaret, said last semester after another student, Paul, had read a paper out loud for the whole class. She got this longing look on her face and cried, "I want to write the way Paul does!" You know students like Paul. He's clever, he surprises with his different perspectives on his topics, and he has a distinctive voice. I call this "writing where somebody's home," as opposed to writing that's technically correct but where there's "nobody home," no life, no voice. Let me give you some examples of these two kinds of voices.

Much Too Young to Be So Old

The neighborhood itself was old. Larger than most side streets, 31st Street had huge cracks that ran continuously from one end to the other of this gray track that led nowhere special. Of the large, lonely looking houses, there were only six left whose original structures hadn't been tampered with in order to make way for inexpensive apartments. Why would a real family continue to live in this place was a question we often asked and none of us could answer. Each stretch of the run-down rickety houses had an alley behind them. These alleys became homes, playgrounds, and learning areas for us children. We treasured these places. They were overgrown with weeds and filled with years of garbage, but we didn't seem to care. Then again, we didn't seem to care about much. (Amy)

The Dog

In 1980 I lived in a green split level house. It was a really ugly green but that is beside the point. The neighborhood was really rather pretty, with trees all over the place and not just little trees. They were huge. My friends and I played football in my backyard right after school every day. The neighbors had a white toy poodle that barked forever. You would walk by the fence and it would bark at you. I had no idea whatsoever that the dog was mean. (Corey)

Even though both these writers begin these essays by describing the settings of their stories, and both end with a suggestion of what's coming next, Amy's opening paragraph appeals to me much more than Corey's. I could point out "flaws" in both openings: I think Corey's suffers from lack of concrete detail, and he takes a pretty long time telling us only that the trees were "huge." Amy uses too much passive voice ("hadn't been tampered with"). However, I'm much more drawn into the world of 31st Street than I am to the neighborhood with huge trees. And I think that's because I know more about Amy from this opening—her words and her rhythm evoke a bittersweet expectation in me— whereas I'm not sure what Corey's up to. In other words, I get the distinct feeling that Amy really wants to tell her readers about her childhood. I don't see that kind of commitment in Corey. I know Corey's going to write a dog story, and usually those are my favorites, but somehow I don't very much want to read on.

But teachers have to read on, and on and on, through hundreds and hundreds of drafts a semester. So I can't just say to Corey, "This is boring." And, being a believer in the "new rhetoric," I'm interested in the process that leads to these two different styles. How does Amy come up with this voice? Was she born clever? And why does Corey make the decision to take himself out of his writing? I can think of many reasons why he would choose to be safe; in fact, he admitted to me later in that course that he had "copped out," choosing to write in what he called his "safe, public style" rather than take chances with what he thought was a more risky, personal style. That makes sense, if you consider the history of writing instruction up until the past fifteen to twenty years. Certainly it's been better to get it right, to avoid mistakes, than to get it good, to try for a voice. And it makes sense that Corey wouldn't want to expose his personal style—writing classrooms traditionally have not been places where students have felt safe. Writing and then showing that writing to someone else for evaluation and response is risky, a lot like asking, "Am I OK? Am I a person you want to listen to?"

And so, to play it safe in a risky environment, it's tempting to take on a voice that isn't yours, to try to sound like you know what you're talking about, to sound "collegiate," to be acceptable and accepted. There's also a sort of mystique about "college writing," both in composition courses and in other disciplines. To write in college, this thinking goes, means to be "objective," to take your own opinions, your own stake in the subject, completely out of your writing. That's why people write, "It is to be hoped that" rather than, "I hope" or, "There are many aspects involved" rather than, "This is complicated." And then there's also a real fear of writing badly, of being thought stupid, and so it's tempting simply to be bland and safe and not call too much attention to yourself.

And teachers have encouraged you, I think, to remain hidden behind your own prose. Remember when you got a "split grade" like this: "C/B"? One grade for content and another for style. That sends a clear message, I think, that what you say and how you say it can be separated and analyzed differently. That's crazy—we can't split form and content. But teachers tend to encourage you to do that when they ask you to read an essay by Virginia Woolf or E. B. White from an anthology and then tell you to "write like that." Or, we teachers have been so concerned with form that we've discouraged you from real communication with another person. One of my students just yesterday described her English classes this way: "I wanted to learn how to write and they were trying to teach me what my writing should look like." Preoccupation with correctness, with organization, and with format (margins, typing, neatness, and so on.) all get in the way of style and voice. So, too, do prearranged assignments, where each student in the class writes the same essay on the same subject ("Compare high school to college," "Discuss the narrator's attitude in this short story," "My most embarrassing moment"). Such assignments become exercises in competition, in one sense, because you've got somehow to set yourself apart from the rest of the essays your teacher will be reading. But they are also exercises in becoming invisible, for while you want to be noticed, you don't want to be too terribly different, to stick out like a sore thumb. And so you write safely, not revealing too much or taking many chances.

I used to teach that way, giving assignments, comparing one student with another and everyone with the "ideal" paper I imagined in my head (although I never tried writing with my students in those days), correcting mistakes and arriving at a grade for each paper. The new rhetoric classes I teach now have eliminated many of these traps for students, but I've also opened up new ones, I'm afraid. Now my students choose their own topics, writing whatever they want to write. And sometimes I'm simply not interested in their choices. In the old days, when I gave the assignment, naturally I was interested in the topic— it was, after all, *my* idea. Now I read about all sorts of things every week—my students' families, their cars, the joys and sorrows in their love lives, their athletic victories and defeats, their opinions on the latest upcoming election, their thoughts about the future, and so on. Frankly, I don't approach each of these topics in the same way. For example, a dog story almost always interests me, while a car story might not. Or, a liberal reading of the latest campus debate on women's issues will grab my attention much more quickly than a fundamentalist interpretation. That's simply the truth. But, as a teacher of "process," I try my best to get interested in whatever my students are writing. And, I'm usually delighted by how much my students can move me with their ideas. So what makes me interested? I'm convinced it has to do with their style. And here I'm defining style not simply as word choice or sentence structure, but as a kind of "presence" on the page, the feeling I get as a reader that, indeed, somebody's home in this paper, somebody wants to say something—to me, to herself, to the class, to the community.

Mine is not the only response students receive in this kind of classroom. Each day, students bring copies of their work-in-progress to their small groups. They read their papers out loud to each other, and we practice ways of responding to each writer that will keep him or her writing, for starts, and that will help the writer see what needs to be added, changed, or cut from the draft. This can get pretty tricky. It's been my experience that showing your writing to another student, to a peer, can be much more risky than showing it to a teacher. We've all had the experience of handing in something we knew was terrible to a teacher, and it's not so painful. People will give writing to teachers that they'd never show to someone whose opinion they valued. But sitting down in a small group with three or four classmates and saying, "I wrote this. What do you think?" is, again, like asking, "Do you like me? Am I an interesting person?" And so my classes practice ways of responding to one another's writing without being overly critical, without taking control of the writing out of the writer's hands, and without damaging egos. And they become quite sophisticated as the semester goes along. Still, one of the worst moments in a small group comes when someone reads a draft and the rest of the group responds like this: "It's OK. I don't see anything wrong with it. It seems pretty good." And then silence. In other words, the writer hasn't grabbed their attention, hasn't engaged the readers, hasn't communicated in any meaningful way. What's the difference between this scenario and one where the group comes back with responses like "Where did you get that idea? I really like the way you describe the old man. This reminds me of my grandfather. I think you're right to notice his hands"? I think the difference is in *style*, in the presence of a writer in a group who is honestly trying to communicate to his or her readers.

But I know I still haven't been exactly clear about what I mean by style. That's part of my dilemma, my reason for wanting to write this essay. All of us, teachers and students, recognize good style when we hear it, but I don't know what we do to foster it. And so for the rest of this essay I want to talk to you about how to work on your own writing styles, to recognize and develop your own individual voice in writing, and how to listen for your teachers' agendas in style. Because, despite our very natural desires to remain invisible in academic settings, you *want* to be noticed; you want to be the voice that your teacher becomes interested in. I think I'm telling you that your style ultimately makes the difference. And here I'm talking about not only your writing styles, but the reading styles of your audiences, the agendas operating in the contexts in which you write.

I'll start backward with agendas first. There are several main issues that I think influence English teachers when they are reading students' writing. First, we have a real bent for the literary element, the metaphor, the clever turn of phrase, the rhythm of prose that comes close to the rhythm of poetry. That's why I like sentences like these: "As the big night approached I could feel my stomach gradually easing its way up to my throat. I was as nervous as a young foal experiencing its first thunderstorm" (from an essay about barrel racing) and "Suddenly the University of Nebraska Cornhusker Marching Band takes the field for another exciting half-time performance, and the Sea of Red stands up *en masse* and goes to the concession stand" (from an essay about being in the band). I like the surprise in this last sentence, the unexpectedness of everyone leaving the performance, and I like the comparison to a young foal in the first one, especially since the essay is about horses. I tell my students to "take chances" in their writing. I think these two writers were trying to do just that. And I liked them for taking that chance.

But you don't want to take chances everywhere. Of course this kind of writing won't work in a biology lab report or a history exam, which brings me to another troublesome issue when we talk about style in college writing. You move among what composition researchers call "discourse communities" every day—from English to Biology to Sociology to Music to the dorm to family dinners to friends at bars—you don't talk or write the same way, or in the same voice to each of these groups. You adjust. And yet many professors still believe that you should be learning to write one certain kind of style in college, one that's objective, impersonal, formal, explicit, and organized around assertions, claims, and reasons that illustrate or defend those claims. You know this kind of writing. You produce it in response to questions like "Discuss the causes of the Civil War," or "Do you think that 'nature' or 'nurture' plays the most important role in a child's development?" Here's a student trying out this kind of "academic discourse" in an essay where he discusses what worries him:

> Another outlet for violence in our society is video games. They have renewed the popularity that they had earlier in the 1980s and have taken our country by storm. There is not one child in the country who doesn't know what a Nintendo is. So, instead of running around outside getting fresh air and exercise, most children are sitting in front of the television playing video games. This is affecting their minds and their bodies.

Why wouldn't Jeff just say "Video games are popular again" instead of saying that "they have renewed their popularity" or "Kids are getting fat and lazy" rather than "This is affecting their minds and bodies"? Besides using big words here, Jeff is also trying to sound absolutely knowledgeable: He states that every child in this country knows Nintendo, they are all playing it, when if he thought about that for a minute, he'd know it wasn't true. I don't like this kind of writing very much myself. Jeff is trying so hard to sound academic that "there's nobody home," no authentic voice left, no sense of a real human being trying to say something to somebody. I prefer discourse that "renders experience," as Peter Elbow (1991) puts it, rather than discourse that tries to explain it. He describes this kind of language (or style) as writing where a writer "conveys to others a sense of experience—or indeed, that mirrors back to themselves a sense of their own experience, from a little distance, once it's out there on paper" (137). Here's an example of that kind of "rendering" from Paul's essay about a first date:

> Her mother answers the door. My brain says all kinds of witty and charming things which my larynx translates in a sort of amphibious croak. (Ribbitt, Ribbitt. I can't remember what it was I actually attempted to say.) She materializes at the top of the stairs, cast in a celestial glow. A choir of chubby cherubim, voices lifted into a heavenly chorus, drape her devine body with a thin film of gossamer. (No, not really. She did look pretty lovely, though. I tried to tell her as much. Ribbitt. Ribbitt.)

Now, perhaps Paul goes too far here, trying a little too hard to be clever, but I like this better than the discussion of video games. (And not just because I like the topic of dating better—since I've gotten married, I don't date anymore and I confess I'm addicted to Mario Brothers 3.) Paul here is conveying the *feeling* of the moment, the sense of the experience, and he's complicating the memory by moving back and forth between the moment and his interpretation of it. In other words, he's letting me into the story, not explaining something to me. Paul is involved in what he's writing while Jeff is detached. And Paul's funny. Besides dog stories, I like humor in my students' writing.

Now, this brings me to another issue in the matter of style. I prefer the rendering style over the explanatory style, perhaps because I'm an English major and an English teacher, and therefore I like the allusion over the direct reference, description over analysis, narrative over exposition. But perhaps there's another reason I like the more personal style: I'm a woman. There's a whole body of recent research that suggests that men and women have different writing styles, among all sorts of other differences. Theorists such as Pamela Annas and Elizabeth Flynn suggest that women writers in academic situations often are forced to translate their experiences into the foreign language of objectivity, detachment, and authority that the male-dominated school system values. Women strive for connection, this thinking argues, while men value individual power. Feminist theory values writing that "brings together the personal and the political, the private and the public, into writing which is committed and powerful because it takes risks, because it speaks up clearly in their own voices and from their own experiences" (Annas 1985, 370; see also Flynn 1988). Here's an example of that kind of writing, an excerpt from an essay titled, "Grandma, You're Not So Young Anymore":

> My grandma was always so particular about everything. Everything had to be just so. The walls and curtains had to be spotless, the garden couldn't have a weed, the kolaches had to be baked, and the car had to be washed. . . . Each spring she was always the first to have her flowers and garden planted. She could remember the littlest details about our family history and ancestors. . . . There were always kolaches in the oven and cookies in the refrigerator. . . .
>
> I really didn't notice the aging so much at first. . . . When I would come home from college Mom would always say, "Grandma's really lonely now. Grandpa was

her company, and now he's gone. You should really go and visit her more often. She won't be around forever."

I had to admit I didn't visit her all that often. . . . I didn't notice how much slower she'd gotten until Thanksgiving Day. Grandma took us to Bonanza because she didn't want to cook that much. I noticed the slower, more crippled steps she took, the larger amount of wrinkles on her face, and most of all, her slowed mental abilities. She sometimes had trouble getting words out as if she couldn't remember what she wanted to say. She couldn't decide what foods she wanted to eat, and when she did eat, she hardly touched a thing. I didn't think my grandma would ever get old. Now I don't think she will last forever anymore.

Here, Deanna uses her own experience and observations to go on and talk about how the elderly are treated in our culture. She could have written a statistical report on nursing homes or a more formal argument about how Americans don't value their old people. But she chose instead to draw from her own life and therefore she draws me into her argument about the "frustration" of getting old. I like old people, and I can identify this woman's deterioration with my own mother's several years ago. But I still think it's more than my personal history that draws me to this essay. I suspect it's Deanna's willingness to explore her own experience on paper. Deanna definitely needs to work on editing this draft to improve her style (something more specific, for example, than "larger amounts of wrinkles" and "slowed mental abilities"). But she doesn't need to work to improve her style in the sense of her commitment to this topic, her presence on the page, or her desire to figure out and to explain her reaction to her grandmother's aging.

Each of these three issues might lead me to advise you that you should write metaphors for English teachers, formal explanations for male teachers in other disciplines, and personal narratives for your women professors. But you know that would be silly, simplistic advice about style. You have to maneuver every day through a complex set of expectations, some of which aren't made explicit, and the whole idea of teacher-as-audience is much more complex that simply psyching out a teacher's background or political agenda. "Style" in writing means different things to different people. I have to be honest and admit that my definition of style as presence on paper is simply my own definition. I hope this essay will lead you to your own thinking about what style means, in all contexts. But I am going to end by giving you some advice about your own style in writing anyway—the teacher in me can't resist. That advice is: Work on your style without thinking about school too much. Here are five suggestions to help you do this.

In School or Out, Write as if You're Actually Saying Something to Somebody. Even if you're not exactly sure who your audience is, try to imagine a real person who's interested in what you have to say. Probably the most important thing I can tell you about working on your style is: Think of your writing as actually saying something to somebody real. Too often in academics we can imagine no audience at all, or at the most an audience with evaluation on its mind, not real interest or response. When I'm able to get interested in my students' writing, no matter what the topic, it's because I hear someone talking to me. My colleague Rick Evans calls this kind of writing "talking on paper," and if you keep that metaphor in mind, I think you'll more often avoid the kind of "academese" or formal language that signals you're hiding or you've disappeared.

I can illustrate the difference in style I'm talking about through two journals that Angie gave me at the beginning and the end of a composition and literature course last year. All through the course, I asked students to write about how the novels we were reading connected to their own lives:

> January 24: Well, I'm confused. I haven't written a paper for an English class that wasn't a formal literary analysis since 8th grade. Now, all of a sudden, the kind of writing my teachers always said would be of no use in college *is,* and what they said *would* be, *isn't.* Go figure. Now, if Kate had asked me to churn out a paper on some passage or symbol in *Beloved*—even one of my own choosing—I could get out 5–8 (handwritten) pages easy. But this life stuff? Who wants to know about that anyway?

> May 1: This portfolio represents the work closest to my guts. It's *my* story, not *Beloved's* or Carlos Rueda's. I hasten to point out that this may not be my best work or even my favorite work, but it's the work that sings my song. My goal was to communicate a set of ideas, to spark a dialogue with *you,* as my reader, to inspire you to think about what I have written, not *how* I have written it. So here it is, bound in plastic, unified, in a manner, ready for reading. I hope you like what I have woven.

Notice how Angie's attitude toward me as her reader changed from January to May. At first she referred to "Kate" as if I wouldn't be reading what she had written, even though this was a journal handed in to me; later I become someone she wants to engage in a dialogue. (She had expected the kind of writing class I described at the beginning of this essay, but she found herself writing for a new rhetoric teacher.) Notice, too, how at first she talks about how she could write five to eight pages *even if she had to choose her own topic.* The implication is clear—that it's easier to write when someone else tells her what to do, what to write about. In other words, it's easier to perform rather than to communicate. Notice, finally, Angie's relationship to the literature we were reading in these two journals. At first she wants only to write about the symbols in Toni Morrison's novel *Beloved* (1987), focusing all her attention on the literary work and not on herself. At the end off the course, she subordinates the novels almost completely to her own stories. This is an engaged writer, one with a clear sense of her own style, her own presence.

Write Outside of School. Play with writing outside of school. You'll need to write much more than just what's assigned in your classes to develop a beautiful writing style. (Sorry, but it's true.) One of the truisms about good writers is that they are good readers; in other words, they read a lot. (And they were probably read to as kids, but we can't go into that right now.) So, here's an exercise in style that I recommend to my students. Find an author whose writing you admire. Copy out a particular, favorite passage. Then imitate that style, word for word, part-of-speech for part-of-speech. Here's an example from one of my students last semester. We were reading *Beloved*, and Sarah used its opening passage to talk about the first day of class. I'll show you Morrison's passage and then Sarah's:

> 124 was spiteful. Full of a baby's venom. The women in the house knew it and so did the children. For years each put up with the spite in his own way, but by 1873, Sethe and her daughter Denver were its only victims. The grandmother, Baby Suggs, was dead, and the sons, Howard and Buglar, had run away by the time they were thirteen years old—as soon as merely looking in a mirror shattered it (that was the signal for Buglar); as soon as two tiny hand prints appeared in the cake (that was it for Howard). Neither boy waited to see more. (3)

> Andrews 33 was quiet. Full of a new semester's uneasiness. The students in the room knew it and so did the teacher. For a few minutes, everyone took in the tension in their own way, but by 12:45 the roll call and Kate's lame jokes broke the ice a little bit. The course, a new program, was explained, and the syllabus, papers and papers, looked simple enough by the time Kate explained her marvelous approach—as soon as really deciding on a topic excited us (that was the reason for the authority list); as soon as four friendly voices read to each other (that was the reason for small groups). No students lingered to write more. (Sarah)

Sarah told me later that doing this imitation surprised her—she had never written with parentheses before, nor had she stopped sentences in the middle this way ("the syllabus, papers and papers"). She wasn't sure she liked this imitation, but it showed her she could write in different ways. And playing with different voices on paper will help you make choices about your own style in different situations.

Read Your Work-in-Progress Out Loud, Preferably to a Real Person. Looking back over this essay, I realize that so much of what I've said about style revolves around the sense of sound. Teachers have good ears, and so do you. Listen to your own voice as you read out loud. Do you sound like a person talking to someone? Or a student performing for a grade?

Practice Cutting All the Words You Can Out of Your Drafts and Starting from There. This is one of the hardest things for any writer to do, and yet I think it's one of the most effective ways to make your writing more interesting. Most of the time there are simply too many words getting in the way of your meaning, making too much noise for you to be heard. Look closely at your drafts and be hard on yourself. Let me give you a few quick examples:

> The first thing that really upsets me is the destruction of our environment due to ignorance, capitalism, and blindness in the world. The attitude that most people take is that by ignoring the problem it will go away. An example of this attitude is the turnout for elections in America.
>
> Revision: Ignorance, capitalism, and blindness destroy our environment. Most people look the other way. Many don't even vote.

Once Jim revised this opening sentence from an essay on what worries him, he realized that he hadn't said much yet and that he was moving way too quickly. He learned that he had several ideas he felt strongly about, ideas worth slowing down to develop. Here are two more examples:

> I also think that we need to provide more opportunities for the homeless to receive an education so they can compete in today's job market. Another reason for educating these people is because the increasing numbers of unemployed persons is a factor that is contributing to homelessness in our country. There are declining employment opportunities for unskilled labor in todays job market, and since many homeless are unskilled laborers, they are not able to acquire a decent job. Therefore they cannot afford to buy a home. I think it is critical that these people be educated if the homeless problem in our country is going to be resolved.
>
> Revision: We need to educate the homeless so they can compete in a market where jobs are becoming more scarce.

> There are so many things that a person can fill their mind with. I find that when talking with friends the majority of their thoughts are filled with worries. I don't really believe that it is all negative to worry unless it becomes an obsession. So many people are worried about so many different things. Some of which are personal while others are more societal. When I try to figure out what worries me most I find it to be on a more personal level.
>
> Revision: I'm sort of worried that I worry so much about myself.

Each of these last two writers realized that they hadn't said much of anything yet in their initial drafts. Going back to cut words, asking themselves questions about what they meant to say to a reader, allowed them to start over with a different, clearer perspective. I know this isn't easy, especially in school, where you've been trained to "write 1,000 words" and, by God, you'll write 1,000 words whether you have one or 1,000 words to say on the subject. Try to stop padding and counting words in the margins. Cut words. This is probably the most practical piece of advice I have.

Finally, Write About Your Own Writing Style. Keep a record of your reactions to what you write, a list of your favorite sentences, and a reaction to the reactions you get from readers. Most of all, forgive yourself for writing badly from time to time. One of my professors in graduate school told me that I was capable of writing "awkward word piles," and here I am with the nerve to be writing an essay to you about style. I've tried to practice what I preach, and now I'm suggesting that you throw out more than you keep and to notice and remember what works for you. Writing about your own writing is another piece of practical advice.

This is really my last word: Don't let *me* fool you here. Even though I understand what Angie meant in her last journal to me about my being more interested in what she has to say than *how* she said it, I'm still very in tune with the how, with her style; I'm happy that her focus has moved away from me as evaluator toward herself as a creator. But I'm still influenced by her style. Don't forget that. And I'm happy that the emphasis in composition has shifted from style back to invention. But I still reward and punish style in my reactions to students' writings. Yes, I try to be an interested reader, but my agendas also include listening for the sound of prose I like.

I suppose what I'm really confessing to you all in this essay is that I am not only a teacher, but I'm also a reader, with her own tastes, preferences, and phobias about what I like to read. And, as a reader, I look for style. There's a play that I love that I think can show you what I mean by style, by presence in writing. *The Real Thing*, by Tom Stoppard (1983) is about real love and real life, but it's also about real writing. At about the end of Act One, Henry, the playwright/hero, talks about good writing. He's picked up a cricket bat (could be a Louisville slugger, but this play is set in London) to make his point. (Read this out loud and listen to the sound):

> This thing here, which looks like a wooden club, is actually several pieces of particular wood cunningly put together in a certain way so that the whole thing is sprung, like a dance floor. It's for hitting cricket balls with. If you get it right, the cricket ball will travel two hundred yards in four seconds, and all you've done is give it a knock like knocking the top off a bottle of stout, and it makes a noise like a trout taking a fly. What we're trying to do is write cricket bats, so that when we throw up an idea and give it a little knock, it might . . . *travel*. (22)

This image has stayed with me for seven years, ever since I first saw and read Stoppard's play, and it's an idea that I think all writers and readers understand. "Ideas traveling"—surely that's what I want for myself as a writer and for my students. I love the image of the dance floor too—the idea of a piece of writing as an invitation to movement, a place to join with others, a site of communal passion and joy. But I don't think people in school always think of writing as something that travels, or as a dance floor, and I would like somehow to help you a little toward Henry's vision. Later in the same speech he picks up a badly written play that he's been asked to "fix" and describes it:

> Now, what we've got here is a lump of wood of roughly the same shape trying to be a cricket bat, and if you hit a ball with it, the ball will travel about ten feet and you will drop the bat and dance about shouting "Ouch!" with your hands stuck in your armpits. (23)

I've read writing, my own and my students' and professionals', that makes me want to do this different kind of dancing. Many of your textbooks read like "lumps of wood," yes? Henry tells us that no amount of simple editing will fix something that has no life or passion to begin with. But how to transform lumps of wood into cricket bats? It seems to me the key lies in this play's other theme—the "real thing," meaning real love and real passion. When I encourage you to develop your style in writing, I'm inviting you into the game, onto the dance floor, encouraging you to commit yourself to your ideas and to your readers. That's the essence of *style*, which, without knowledge and passion, amounts only to a performance that dazzles without touching its readers, and which, without practice, amounts to very little. In that sense, Plato and Aristotle were right to say that we shouldn't emphasize style over invention, ideas, and voice. And in another sense, my last piece of advice would apply to students in ancient Greece as well as modern America: Write about something you care about to someone you care about. Even if you are writing in school, try to have a presence—show them that somebody's home, working. Writers must know and love not only their subjects but their audiences as well, so that ideas will dance, so that ideas will travel.

Works Cited

Annas, Pamela (1985). "Style as Politics." *College English, 4*, 370.

Elbow, Peter (1991). "Reflections on Academic Discourse." *College English, 2*, 137.

Flynn, Elizabeth (1988). "Composing as Woman." *College Composition and Communication, 39*, 423–435.

Morrison, Toni (1987). *Beloved*. New York: Knopf.

Stoppard, Tom (1983). *The Real Thing*. London: Faber & Faber.

Sharing Ideas

- In different eras writers have been encouraged to pay more or less attention to style. In fact, style doesn't just manifest itself in our writing but in our living, also. We often talk about lifestyle and style of dress. Do you see any connections between your writing style (or the style you'd like to attain) and your lifestyle and style of dress?

- Kate Ronald talks about a shift from product to process but indicates such shifting can be problematic. She reminds you that "mistakes along those lines [spelling, grammar, punctuation, or usage] do get in my way when I'm reading" and then she suggests that writing teachers tend to listen for certain types of difficult-to-describe writing voices. What do you think of her discussion?

- Looking through some of your writing, find samples of pieces where you, the writer, are "not at home" and where you, the writer, are clearly "at home." Do Kate's discussions of style and voice explain differences in voice in your own writing?

- Have you ever taken a piece of writing to class to share and had it flop? Why do you think that happened? Did you ever take a piece to share that you felt lukewarm about and it was a hit? Again, what do you think was going on, what were readers responding to in that piece of writing?

- Kate tells you that English teachers tend to like certain types of writing—writing that renders, writing that uses allusion, narrative, and (particularly for women teachers perhaps) personal style. Do these attributes help you understand past teachers' responses to your writing? Explain by using examples of your own writing with the teacher's response if you still have them.

- Do you think it's silly to think that you might write "metaphors for English teachers, formal explanations for male teachers in other disciplines, and personal narratives for your women professors," or do you find yourself already making some of these shifts?

- How do you learn what type of writing a professor expects from you? How able or willing are you to deliver writing in that style? Are you comfortable or uncomfortable when meeting teachers' demands?

- Look at Kate's five writing suggestions, offered at the end of her essay. What in your own writing practices would you have to change to follow her advice?

Part III

Special Topics:
Craft and Skills Advice

The real secret to good writing, for most writers, is rewriting. It's true that a few gifted writers compose, understand, and edit all in one draft—but neither I nor my students seem to do our best writing that way. Even when writers are pleased with their first drafts, those drafts don't usually tell the whole story that could be told—the one revealed only in second- and third-draft writing. In other words, it's the act of writing itself that explains the whole story to the writer. There are no shortcuts to full understanding, even for good writers.

—Toby Fulwiler, writing teacher

Part of your life story as a writer will include stories of your previous writing classrooms. You too have an important history of writing, one you will want to explore even as you continue to write today's papers and share them with your peers and teacher. You might share your thoughts in a literacy autobiography, in journal entries, during classroom discussions, or in conferences with your teacher. When reading essays about writing and talking about your own writing past, I hope you'll notice how all of us start writing courses already informed by significant writing experiences. All of us, too, have the ability to grow, more fully, into our writing.

—Wendy Bishop, writing teacher

Racial difference is almost impossible to talk about honestly in a class—or in any public place for that matter. We often recognize stereotypes for what they are, but we're not sure how to address other differences productively as teachers and students. Many of us hurry to define ourselves as color-blind or, at least, just nicely color-aware. Others of us turn away. Some of us seethe. Very little true dialogue occurs when the topic is raised.

—Lizanne Minerva and Melanie A. Rawls, writing teachers

. . . speakers and writers are bound to make some errors. In fact, they could not learn anything new about the language unless they did make some errors. The errors are likely to be in some way logical or consistent because the learner is searching for patterns . . . error is an important sign of active learning, for the error shows how speakers and writers are making predictions and trying out solutions, and of taking risks with the language they are using.

—Eleanor Kutz, writing teacher

My past writing classes had not developed too much of me. I've either analyzed texts without really including personal views, or I've written stories that sounded pretty but had no depth. . . . Writing, revising, editing, workshopping, revising again—these all motivated me to rework my texts (or at least think about different ways to revise as I showered, walked to class, brushed my teeth, and ate lunch).

—Haley Belt, writing student

11

Virtually Inspired
Computer Strategies for Revision
Shelley Aley

Shelley Aley, an associate professor, directs the Writing Program at James Madison University. She teaches freshman composition, a graduate-level course in composition theory, and courses in writing and rhetoric. Her interest in rhetoric took her to Scotland to do archival research. She lives on a farm near Broadway, Virginia, with her five dogs, four quarter horses, and three longhorn steers (who help the horses keep the grass from taking over the farm).

I like to compose on the computer keyboard. If you're like me, then you know how difficult it is to draft a piece using pen and paper. But what happens when it comes time to revise? I used to revert to my old hands-on approach—going over a printed copy of my work by hand with a pen. But now I've found that anyone with access to a computer can easily employ strategies that can enhance revision. In fact, the virtual approach can actually inspire me to address revision with more awareness than I had poring over a printed copy of my writing. For example, like many of you, I became savvy about using the spell and grammar checkers provided by my word-processing software, but I didn't realize that I could also split the screen to see different parts of my paper at the same time. This is particularly helpful when I'm cutting and pasting material during the revision process or checking sources against my list of references at the end of a paper.

Computer software that is standard on most university computers can help you maintain a spirit of invention throughout your writing process, including during revision, not just at the beginning. Before going on, I want to say a few words about the spirit of invention and the word *invention* itself. Invention, as you may know, is the first of the five canons of rhetoric taught by the ancient Greeks and Romans for creating and giving speeches; the others are arrangement, style, memory, and delivery. To the Greeks and Romans, invention meant finding something useful to say; in Latin *invenire* means "to find." Invention is the art of discovery. Writing instructors and textbooks today tend to place invention at the beginning of the writing process, since you have to discover what you want to say before you can write it. But, like Amy Hodges, in her chapter "Invention Throughout the Writing Process," I believe that invention—finding what to say—runs from the beginning of the writing process to the end, perhaps even leading to a new beginning.

Actually, the writing "process" isn't a step-by-step procedure; it's more recursive, a word that means something that can repeat itself, sometimes indefinitely. When composing, the writer moves back and forth from one task to another. Everyone's writing process is different. Seldom would a writer think that he or she had to move rigidly in a linear path from prewriting (sometimes called invention), to drafting, to revision, to editing, to publishing. Writing just doesn't happen that way. Invention, just because it is listed as the first canon of rhetoric, does not have to be left behind in the writing process. While the computer is a great place to begin the inventive design of your paper, when you begin to review your work with revision in mind, don't stop thinking about invention just because you've developed the first draft. Instead of thinking that creativity stops when you look critically at your work, shift back and forth between these two purposes as you draft and revise your writing. Let the two stages (creation and revision) overlap; allow your process to be recursive.

Turn Off Your Monitor

While we write, we tend to struggle with two opposing sides of ourselves that compete for our attention. In TV cartoons and sitcoms, characters occasionally struggle with the forces of good and evil. You'll see a fellow with an angel perched on one shoulder and a devil perched on the other. That's just about how our two competing sides struggle to control us as we write. The angel seems concerned with creativity and the devil seems concerned with being critical and correct. When these two forces start tugging on us, writer's block can result.

When the angel of creativity is blocked by the devil of correctness, some writing teachers suggest simply turning off your computer's monitor and freewriting. The idea is that if you can't see what you're writing on-screen, you can't become distracted by the grammatical and mechanical concerns that the devil points out (those squiggly red and green lines that automatically appear when you've misspelled something or slipped into the passive voice). Some people call writing with the monitor off invisible writing; others call it writing blindfolded because it's like closing your eyes as you compose, which is a better idea than it sounds. This works when you're getting started on a writing project, but you can also do this exercise when you find yourself stuck somewhere in the middle or at the end of your paper. Our creative side flourishes in a space absent of critics.

AutoSummarize to Collect Your Thoughts

Before computers, my writing instructors would tell me to cut wordy phrasing and unnecessary passages, the way a cook boils the fat off the bones to create good soup stock. I'd pore over my work; sometimes I'd be successful, but I wouldn't always know what my main points were. There's no real shortcut to studying what you've written to know what to cut, but if you've been freewriting and want to boil some ideas down quickly, try the AutoSummarize feature available in Word and many other word-processing programs.

The AutoSummarize feature is designed to let you see in a nutshell what you've been trying to say. First, save your work, so you don't lose anything, but instead of using Save or Save As, try using the Version feature. With your draft open, click on File and then on Version. This feature allows you to create a description for each draft you save, so you can distinguish one version from another at a glance. When you save your work in a series of versions, you can watch your writing process progress right before your eyes. Sometimes you wish you could go back and retrieve passages that you previously cut; this way those passages will be saved in earlier versions, and you'll be able to go back and find what you need.

Once your work is saved, click on Tools and then on AutoSummarize. A dialogue box will appear that reads, "Word has examined the document and picked the sentences most relevant to the main theme." That, in itself, may sound scary, but don't worry. You saved your original, right? If not, go do that before you go on.

In the box that AutoSummarize brings up, you have the following options:

- Word will highlight the most relevant sentences within the original document. These highlights can be removed with the use of a radio button that will pop up on the screen.

- Word will create an executive summary or abstract and place it at the beginning of your original document.

- Word will generate a new document and place the summary there.

- Word will replace your original document with the summary. This is the most drastic option, so be careful if you don't want to lose anything.

You are also given the option of choosing how much of your original you want in the summary, from just a few sentences up to 75 percent of the original. What you choose to do with AutoSummarize is up to you. Experiment and see what each option produces. The results of the AutoSummarize feature don't always make sense, but many times they do. With the "collected" ideas I get from AutoSummarize, I can sometimes more easily move toward clarity and organization in my revision.

Use PowerPoint to Revise for Arrangement and Style

Another strategy I like to show my students is how they can use PowerPoint, a presentation software that many are familiar with or can learn easily, to revise for arrangement and style, two of the five classical canons of rhetoric mentioned earlier. Arrangement has to do with order, originally the order in which an orator mentioned things in his speech. The ancients used a type of organization, which we now call the classical argument, that divided a speech into a series of tasks: the *exordium, narratio, propositio, partitio, confirmatio, refutatio,* and *peroratio.* In the exordium, the orator would introduce the piece; in the narratio he would state the facts; in the propositio he would state his proposition or thesis; in the partitio he would create a division; in the confirmatio he would present his proofs for his argument; in the refutatio he would refute his opposition; and in the peroratio he would conclude. Sound pretty familiar? The classical argument set the stage for the five-paragraph theme (introduction; three-paragraph body; conclusion), among other forms of writing.

Style has to do with the *way* in which something is said—the fashion, the design, the cleverness, the art, the wit, the elegance of speech. In the past, so much focus was placed on style that rhetoric lost respect and speakers became accused of just mouthing fancy words that didn't really say much—empty rhetoric. Today, we still understand the significance of style, but we put it into perspective with matters of invention and arrangement, so that style itself does not take over. PowerPoint can help us balance these three important canons of rhetoric.

To use PowerPoint to help you revise your paper for arrangement and style, begin by outlining your paper; you might try using the AutoSummarize feature in Word to help you do this. Working from the outline of your entire paper, create your presentation using PowerPoint's drag-and-drop property to produce a separate slide for each of your main points. On each slide, bullet your subpoints under the main point. Many times, you'll find that you need separate slides for subpoints.

As you work, you may find that the way you arranged your paper when you originally wrote it is not the best way to present it. PowerPoint can help you see where you have confused your points or played them in the wrong order.

PowerPoint also allows users to employ themes and color schemes while creating a presentation that can communicate particular moods or impressions to the viewer. These elements can help students revise their writing to accommodate their style to the presentation. As you transform your paper into a PowerPoint presentation, pick an overall theme that goes well with your ideas. PowerPoint allows users to tie image and sound files to the presentation to add appeals relating to the rhetorical appeals the writer is trying to make. Pull out the Slide Master so that you can view it as you create your presentation. To do this, pull out on the left-hand screen border with your cursor. On the Slide Master, you can look at the entire presentation either as an outline or in slide format. Using the View button, you can see your presentation in Slide Sorter mode, a screen where you can drag and drop your slides into any order you choose. This allows you to try different arrangements, checking how ideas flow in a variety of sequences.

The association of ideas with images helps students connect abstract words to concrete elements, which can then be written into the paper in revision if they are not presently in the text. As you create your PowerPoint presentation, surf the Web to see if you can find images that relate to your main ideas and subpoints. Include graphics and visual elements to help an audience see what the paper is saying. You can also use some of the special display features in PowerPoint to determine how your slides will appear. These features include recording narration, creating a broadcast, and setting up animation and slide transitions. You can include sound, images, and movement on your paper's outline and make your words really come alive. Just remember not to make the presentation so fancy or distracting that it becomes the virtual equivalent of empty rhetoric.

It may sound like putting the cart before the horse to write and revise using PowerPoint, but the experience of creating the presentation generates such a sharp awareness of an audience that my students begin to think of arrangement and style rhetorically, as a way to influence that audience, maybe for the first time in their lives. This kind of attention to audience is not always explicit in writing assignments, as it is when using PowerPoint. Once you see what you would like to achieve with your presentation, you can return to revise your original written work so that it does what you want. Using PowerPoint should help you determine the best style and arrangement for your paper.

Draw Your Argument!

After students have written a draft of a paper, I have them use the Microsoft Paint program, available on our university lab computers, to "see" what they are trying to say. I got this idea after viewing a display of manuscripts written by British Romantic poets during the nineteenth century. It was amazing to see how a poet like Percy Bysshe Shelley would sketch as he wrote. William Blake, who wrote "Tyger! Tyger! burning bright," was actually better known as an illustrator than as a poet during his lifetime. Most of his famous manuscripts are beautifully hand-illustrated using a method that is still a mystery to us today. In that spirit, my students follow my instructions for using Microsoft Paint to draw their argument, as it were—to create images that represent what they are trying to say with their words.

One student a few semesters ago, who was writing about the Napster controversy, drew a big, ugly monster to symbolize the music corporations that priced musical recordings so high that young listeners were easily lured to join Napster, where they could download their favorite artists' music for free. The monster was crushing and devouring small musical artists as a backdrop of protesters (Napster users) tried to defeat it. It was a vivid image that helped the student find even more vivid language to express himself in his writing.

While not everyone is as inventive or as skilled with Paint software as this writer was, many students who draw their arguments find that they add elements to their drawings that are not explicit in their papers. The act of drawing helps students see what they are arguing and where they may need to revise.

Virtual Peer Review

An important part of revision is peer review, which I have my students do on-line using BlackBoard, a virtual community. Perhaps you've had experience in the past with peer review, but BlackBoard gives you a comfortable "place" to meet other students, without the time restrictions inherent in in-class peer review.

I set up the groups for my students in BlackBoard, configuring the e-mail and discussion-board area for each. In the discussion-board format, my students are able to share their work with each other by attaching it electronically to their discussion-board thread. Peers can then give feedback in a variety of ways: in e-mail messages, in posts to the discussion board, or as attachments to a discussion-board thread.

In the absence of BlackBoard or some other program like it, another way to get your work peer reviewed is by creating a blog (computer talk for Web log) or a wiki (a collaborative space for writers). These online places allow you to share your work with a community of writers and receive feedback. The wiki (named by concept creator Ward Cunningham) is unique in that it allows multiple users to freely create and edit a Web page using any Web browser. Several writers can use a wiki to coauthor and coedit a text on the Web. One of the most famous wikis today is *Wikipedia* (http://en.wikipedia.org/wiki/), a free-content encyclopedia that anyone can edit.

Web sites such as blogger.com, google.com/googleblog/, and blogwise.com allow you to set up a blog that can be personal or shared. To create a wiki, go to www.seedwiki.com or another wiki site of your choice. You can invite others to participate in your blog or join your collaborative wiki group, making your writing open to your teacher, classmates, and even outsiders, depending on your preference.

Besides being used to post drafts and elicit feedback, blogs and wikis are also great places to share ideas for writing and great sources. Wikis allow you to invite others to write collaboratively with you. Blogs give you that feeling of being published, which helps make you aware of your audience.

———— ◆ ————

It may sound a bit corny, but you can be "virtually" inspired as you write and revise your work in the on-line environment. It's a good idea to remember that writing is a technology—always has been. From early stone carvings and the invention of the pen and pencil to the typewriter and word-processing software, writing has always changed with the latest technologies, which influence what you are able to do as a writer. Within the virtual environment, writers have a pretty good sense of shared space and audience, which can make revision more real and necessary than most traditional types of classroom assignments can. So although your teacher might still ask you to pull out a sheet of paper and a pencil to write in class, the texts you produce on-line, which can be revised, updated, and read at any time, give you a true sense of what other writers do. Who can resist tweaking a piece of writing when it is reflected in such a public sphere? After all, what is the Last Updated feature for, if not for revision?

Sharing Ideas

- Do you like to compose on the computer keyboard, or are you a pen-and-paper kind of writer? Talk about your preferences and how they suit your writing style.

- What about revision—do you revise on the computer, or do you like to go over your writing with pen and paper first? Talk about your preferences and how they fit your writing style.

- Critics of PowerPoint feel it imposes a particular linear structure on users. After using PowerPoint as a revision tool, write about your experience in light of this complaint. Did the program restrict or liberate you, or did it do something else for your revision process? What features of PowerPoint did you use? Were they effective for revision?

- Have you ever tried writing a blog? If so, describe the experience.

- How comfortable are you with the idea of collaborating with another writer? How do you feel about giving people in the on-line environment the opportunity to edit your work? Go examine and participate in a wiki and then weigh in on what you saw and experienced. Would creating a wiki with a collaborative group be a beneficial experience in your opinion?

12

Does Spelling Count?

Rebecca Bowers Sipe

Rebecca Bowers Sipe is an Associate Professor of English Education at Eastern Michigan University, where she serves as a codirector of the Eastern Michigan Writing Project. Blessed with a husband, son, and daughter who all enjoy trips back to their home place in Alaska, she enjoys traveling, e-mailing, calling, and writing to keep in contact with good friends who are still there. She's a cook-aholic, too, particularly on stressful days when a piece of writing is due.

I remember my first year of college like it was yesterday. As a student who loved school, I was exhilarated by the atmosphere of the university. I loved the feel of putting words on paper, but I lived in dread of the day when I would have to write under timed conditions and without my dictionary close by. It would be at that moment, I was sure, that my professor would discover I was a fake, a pretend writer who wasn't particularly smart either. The problem? I struggled with spelling, especially when I was under pressure. Under moments of stress, my brain was as likely to go completely blank as not.

I had, of course, learned some tricks along the way. I knew that I could try to sound out words, breaking them into parts. I could also write the word several different ways and try to see which looked right. When all else failed, I could substitute a different word, which would mask the fact that I couldn't spell the word I wanted, even though it didn't sound as good or function as well as the word of choice. Still, plenty of times I concentrated so completely on my answers that I simply didn't notice the spelling errors in my text.

If this sounds familiar to you and if you, too, struggle with spelling, you are clearly not alone. Though estimates vary, it is likely that as many as 30 percent of all Americans struggle with spelling to some degree; many of them are excellent readers and writers. Because I struggled, and because I have worked with my own son and many others who struggle, I've focused my own research on trying to understand the causes of spelling difficulty and to see if there are strategies that can help high school and college students. What I've found has helped me think about spelling in some new ways.

Poor spellers are reluctant to admit their spelling difficulties to others because of the many assumptions that are made about spelling, one of which is that poor spellers aren't very smart. Two others are that poor spellers don't care about their writing and are lazy. What is true, however, is that some employers and teachers believe spelling is a social convention, one that indicates whether the writer cares enough about her work to take the time to spell words correctly. Often people assume that poor spellers are also struggling readers and writers. While it is true that some poor spellers avoid reading and writing, many read widely and enjoy writing in a variety of genres and for different purposes and audiences, both in school and for pleasure. These students understand that spelling is a small part of their overall writing and that with adequate tools and strategies, they will be able to address their spelling concerns. And yet, it's also true that among challenged spellers, some are more willing than others to put forth the effort it takes to activate strategies to help address their difficulties.

If you are like most students, your earliest spelling instruction focused first on paying attention to the way words sounded and later on learning lists of words, using practice exercises that were visually oriented. One of the things I found was that many challenged spellers have difficulty with short- or long-term visual memory, and, for this reason, they have more difficulty than others remembering the way a word looks in print. They have a greater need to learn about predictable patterns and rules that provide some sense of logic in the language. Unfortunately, this overdependence on visually oriented learning leads many challenged spellers to think most words have to be memorized separately, quite a daunting task if you consider that there are more than 750,000 words in the English language.

I also found that the spelling errors we make are not random. Generally, our errors reflect our level of spelling development; they offer clues about the patterns or rules that we haven't yet fully mastered or, perhaps, ways that we pronounce certain sound combinations that lead us to predictable but incorrect spellings. Knowing more about the types of errors we make, of course, leads to greater control over our spelling.

It's important to remember that spelling is a writing skill; it really counts only when we write. And even then, there are some times when spelling doesn't count. For example, I rarely worry about my spelling when I write in my diary or when I write notes in class, as long as I can read what I've written. It's when

I'm writing for a more public audience—for my classmates, a professor, or an employer—that spelling becomes more important. Spelling becomes important when we're writing to get our thoughts and our interests into the public conversation, when we're writing to influence the thinking and enjoyment of others. If you struggle with spelling, it will be helpful to have a repertoire of strategies to draw upon when spelling counts. These spelling strategies fall into several broad areas.

- *High-Use Words.* Learning to spell high-use words at a level of automaticity is important, so knowing about high-use words—both those that are in general use and those you use often—is essential.

- *A Sense of Logic.* Knowing about rules that apply to groups of words will be helpful in building a sense of logic in the language.

- *Your Own Writing Process.* The more you know about your own writing process, the easier it will be to identify and draw upon final editing strategies to be sure your writing represents the message and care you intend to send to a reader.

Dealing with High-Use Words

Despite the fact that our language contains a rich collection of words, we generally use a limited number in routine written communication; a mere one thousand words represent approximately 89 percent of all the words we use in our daily writing. This number includes very basic words that we could hardly do without, like *a, and, the, use, such, about, two, to,* and *too.* If we learn two thousand high-use words, we have mastered 95 percent of the words we generally use. These two thousand words include troublesome words like *whether, weather,* and *familiar.* Think how much time it would take if you had to look up all the words that we use frequently! By learning high-use words so well that we don't have to think about them, we are able to write faster, concentrating less on spelling and more on what we are trying to say.

You may find that your troublesome high-use words are different from those that others find vexing. These may include content-specific words or just favorites. One of the easiest ways to address high-use words is to actually begin to pay attention to the words you use all the time. Once you find yourself checking the spelling of a word over and over, either with a dictionary or a spell checker on the computer, make a conscious effort to remember the correct spelling. One way is to write the word in a personal dictionary, which could be a conveniently placed small spiral notebook or a special file on your hard drive. This will make the word easy to find the next time you need it. Another way is to try to notice something about the word to help you remember. For example, I often use the word *accommodate,* but I had to look it up every time for years until someone suggested that I only have to remember to *accommodate the twins.* That was it: two *c*'s and two *m*'s. Since learning that trick, I haven't looked up the word again. Sometimes you'll find words within words, like when you *correspond*, you *respond* to your friend. Recognizing the parts will make the spelling easier to remember. For example, once you know how to spell *essence*, then you have a clue to spelling other words, such as *essential*, *inessential*, *quintessential*, and *nonessential.* Not only does the base word give you a hint about spelling, but it helps you understand what related words mean.

Homonyms—words that sound the same but have different spellings and meanings—are particularly difficult high-use words because they are generally not picked up by spell checkers. For example, if you wrote *rite* for *write* or *right*, the spell checker would never notice. It also wouldn't notice words that look similar but have completely different meanings, like *through* and *though.* So, while the spell checker is certainly a good tool to use, it will not be a cure-all for spelling in the absence of basic proofreading skills! Think of the embarrassment that might arise if you inadvertently made a substitution like *pubic* for *public*, as did one of my students last year when she wrote, "Since coming to college I've found myself increasingly concerned about pubic affairs." Trusting a spell checker to pick up errors without proofreading can lead to trouble.

If there are homonyms (sound alike but have different meanings) or other words that cause particular problems for you, consider creating a mnemonic device—a strategy that helps you remember the word through some association or exaggeration. For example, "<u>a</u> <u>r</u>at <u>i</u>n <u>T</u>om's <u>h</u>ouse <u>m</u>ight <u>e</u>at <u>T</u>om's <u>i</u>ce <u>c</u>ream" provides a quick way to remember the spelling of "arithmetic." Mistakes with words such as *to, too, two* and *there, their, they're* tend to drive teachers crazy! If you find yourself frequently confusing these or other homonyms, consider taking a moment to reflect upon why you confuse the words and create a strategy to prevent confusion in the future. For example, we might remember the word *there* deals with place by paying attention to the *here* found in *there.* For *they're*, the apostrophe is a clue to the contraction that signals two words coming together—*they* and *are*—to create a new word.

Once you have created a strategy for remembering the varying definitions of homonyms, add these to your personal word list or personal dictionary. You might even use a binder ring to attach index cards with particular homonym clusters to your notebook. Though this process may seem time-consuming, just think of all the minutes you'll save in the future when you never have to look up the word again. Further, you'll have a higher level of confidence as you respond to the various writing-on-demand tasks that you confront at school and at work.

Developing a Sense of Logic in the Language

For those of us who struggle with spelling, one of the most useful things we can acquire is a sense of the logic that exists in the language. For example, there are rules that help with the spelling of large numbers of words that are very common and definitely worth knowing. You can find four of the most basic sets of rules in the appendix at the end of this chapter. These sets of rules govern

- using *i* before *e* except after *c*;
- creating plurals;
- adding prefixes; and
- adding suffixes.

Many words in the language are put together from building blocks: prefixes, suffixes, and roots. Knowing a little about these can give you tools to help unlock many different words. For example, if we know that the prefix *pre-* means "before," then we have a clue to begin defining and spelling dozens of words. For example, *preview, premier, preliminary*. Knowing common prefixes, suffixes, and roots not only helps with spelling but aids in understanding new vocabulary as well.

One of the reasons English spelling challenges many of us is because the language is composed of words from many different languages. For example, words like *pneumonia* and *pneumatic* are from Greek, and the initial *p* is silent. Words from French, such as *bureaucracy*, tend to have multiple vowels clustered together as well as other predictable word parts. Knowing something about where words originate from can be immensely helpful for understanding and remembering their spelling.

Knowing Your Own Process

As noted earlier, spelling is a writing skill that becomes important when pieces of writing have a public audience. Whether the piece is written as a school assignment, as a letter to the editor, or as a communication with an employer, the more the writer knows about her writing process, the better. I prefer to think about individual pieces of writing for a while before I begin to compose. I think while driving, cleaning the kitchen, and walking the dog. This think time gives me the opportunity to "talk" the piece of writing out in my head before committing the first word to paper. When I write, I'm addicted to a computer keyboard. For me, typing frees me from worrying about forming words and the laborious process of revising with pen and paper. And revision is a process that begins after the first paragraph: I constantly reread, move words or sentences around, and substitute or add information. After a page or two, I'm apt to print the piece off and then walk up and down the hallway, reading it aloud to hear how it sounds: Does it flow? Does it say what I meant to say? Reading aloud—and reading only what is on the page—helps me find words that are used incorrectly or may have been left out altogether. Then I revise again.

When I'm writing with a pen, I may underline or highlight a word whose spelling I'm unsure about, but I probably won't stop to check it until I'm sure that I'm happy with the piece and plan to take it to a final draft. I don't want to waste time looking up words I may not use. If I'm composing on a computer, my word-processing program will automatically place a little red line under some words; in any case, I'll do a careful proofreading once I'm ready to edit. If the piece is really important—that is, if the audience is one that could be particularly critical—I may ask a colleague to read it to see if he or she catches anything that I missed.

That's my process. The more you know about your own process for writing, the better you are able to hold concerns about spelling at bay until you get to the time and place where spelling matters. Good spellers have a host of strategies they draw upon. Some are internalized strategies that build from knowledge about rules, patterns, and associations. Others are externalized, such as the use of dictionaries, spell checkers, and editors. Good spellers may have these strategies so firmly ingrained that they use these tools automatically, while challenged spellers need to use the same strategies more consciously.

Developing a Plan

Sometimes spelling is a big deal. If you experience difficulty with spelling, there are a number of things you can do to make your challenges more manageable. All require taking control of your writing in deliberate ways.

- *Concentrate on learning high-use words that continue to challenge you.* Since high-frequency words are ever-present in your writing, taking the time to master them will enhance your writing fluency. Create a personal word list or dictionary or invent mnemonic devices, such as acrostics (*geography* = George Edward's old goat ran a pig home yesterday), chants, visuals, or cute reminders like the one I use for *accommodate.*

- *Learn rules that work most of the time.* These rules will help you when you encounter new words that represent a certain pattern. Maintaining lists of words that fit these rules, as well as ones that predictably don't fit, will provide a shortcut as you continue using them and learning their spelling.

- *Pay attention to the ways words are constructed.* Many words in English are made up of parts: prefixes, suffixes, and roots. Each of these has a meaning and, when placed in a new word, contributes to its definition as well as to its spelling. Becoming more perceptive about language and how prefixes, suffixes, and roots combine helps you think about the words that trouble you and find patterns to your errors.

- *Develop a clear sense of your writing process and allow sufficient time for revision and editing.* While all students benefit from multiple drafts, challenged spellers particularly do so. Thinking about your writing process and the strategies you use to compose, revise, and edit will give you tools to use when you come to new writing tasks. The more strategies you have for spelling and editing, the more secure you will be with your writing. To that end, have resources available including dictionaries, personal word lists, and spell checkers. Although it's not a substitute for proofreading, a spell checker is a good tool. And try to always read your paper aloud as a part of your editing process. You may spot a misspelled word as well as hear incorrect words or places where words are omitted.

- *Develop a circle of editors.* For really high-stakes writing, ask a trusted individual to review the piece with you. Although you're not obliged to take your editor's advice, it's good to remember that all published writers have the benefit of an editor at some level.

- *Discuss your writing and spelling concerns.* Most teachers truly want their students to develop competence and confidence in writing. Helping teachers understand your need for multiple drafts will likely benefit you and others. You may want to ask your teacher, a friend, or peer tutor from the writing center to look over a draft and highlight all the spelling mistakes he or she finds. Then, together you can discuss any patterns you can see in the errors. Do you tend to have problems with doubling consonants within words? With adding suffixes or prefixes? Building awareness of the types of errors you make and then building lists of words you use that exhibit those patterns will help you remember the correct spelling in the future.

Remember, if you struggle with spelling, you are not alone. Struggling with spelling has nothing to do with being unintelligent or incapable as a thinker or writer. Some of our best thinkers and writers have also been poor spellers. However, the reality is that even though the playing field is not level—some of us have difficulty with visual memory and associated problems with spelling—nonetheless, the expectations for correct spelling in formal writing in school and the world are the same for all of us. Poor spelling can affect the message we want to communicate. That means we who struggle with spelling have to take additional steps to master spelling and to be sure that our writing goes into the world reflecting the message we intend to send.

Appendix: Four Basic Rule Sets for Challenged Spellers

Set #1: Rules for *I* Before *E*

Write *i* before *e* except after *c* or when it sounds like *a,* as in *neighbor* and *weigh.* Examples include *fiery* and *friend.*

When the *ie/ei* digraph is not pronounced *ee,* it is usually spelled *ei,* as in *reign.*

If you develop a personal word list that includes words you use often, this would be a good place to begin collecting examples of words that fit the general rule (*i* before *e* except after *c*) as well as words that are exceptions to it. For example,

Words That Fit the *I* Before *E* Rule	**Exceptions to the *I* Before *E* Rule**
1. receive	1. neighbor
2. friend	2. weigh
3. fiery	

Set #2: Rules for Plurals

When forming the plural of most words, just add -*s,* as in *books* and *coats.*

When forming the plural of a word that ends with a *y* that is preceded by a vowel, add -*s,* as in *monkeys* and *turkeys.*

When forming the plural of a word that ends with an *o* that is preceded by a vowel, add -*s,* as in *patios* and *ratios.*

When forming the plural of a word that ends with an *o* that is preceded by a consonant, add -*es,* as in *tomatoes* and *porticoes.*

Set #3: Rules for Prefixes

Generally when a prefix is added to a word, do not drop a letter from either the base word or the prefix. For example, *dis* + *approve* = *disapprove.* Exceptions include *ad-, com-,* and *in-,* which can be absorbed by the base word so that the last letter in the prefix changes to match the beginning consonant of the base word, as in *illegal* instead of *inlegal.*

Set #4: Rules for Suffixes

When a one-syllable word (*run*) ends in a consonant preceded by one vowel, double the final consonant before adding a suffix that begins with a vowel, as in *running.*

In a two-or-more-syllable word ending with a consonant-vowel-consonant, double the final letter before adding a suffix beginning with a vowel if the final syllable is stressed, as in *commit/committed.* If the final syllable is not stressed, do not double the final letter, as in *cancel/canceled* and *blanket/blanketed.*

If a word ends with a silent *e,* drop the *e* before adding a suffix that begins with a vowel, as in *ice/icing* and *take/taking.*

When *y* is the last letter in a word and the *y* is preceded by a consonant, change the *y* to *i,* before adding any suffix except those beginning with *i,* as in *happy/happiness, happy/happily.*

When adding the suffix -*ly* or -*ness,* do not change the spelling of the base word unless it ends in *y,* as in *careful/carefully, fond/fondness, gay/gaily.*

If a root is not a complete word, add *-ible,* as in *visible, edible, illegible.*

If a root is a complete word, add *-able* as in *suitable, dependable, workable.*

If a root is a complete word that ends in a silent *e,* drop the *e* and add *-able,* as in *advisable, likable, valuable.*

Exceptions to the *-ible/-able* rule occur when the final sound is the hard *g* or *c.* Then the suffix used is *-able,* as in *apply/applicable.*

If the root ends in *ct,* add *-ion,* as in *select/selection.*

If the root ends in *ss,* add *-ion,* as in *discuss/discussion.*

If the root ends in *te,* drop the *e* and add *-ion,* as in *educate/education.*

If the root ends in *it,* change the *t* to *ss* and add *-ion* as in *permit/permission.*

If the root ends in *de* preceded by a vowel, drop the *e,* change the *d* to *s,* and add *-ion,* as in *explode/explosion.*

Sharing Ideas

• Do you consider yourself a challenged speller? Try to recall early experiences you had with learning to spell.

• Discuss the misconceptions about challenged spellers being lazy, unmotivated, and not very smart.

• Think about strategies you use to spell a word correctly if you don't automatically know the spelling. How many strategies can you immediately draw upon? Note them and then think about others that you could develop to gain more confidence in your spelling.

• Did you take a moment to reflect on your own spelling background? What types of strategies and supports were most helpful to you? How can you use them now, as a college student, to be more successful with your spelling and writing?

• Do you misspell words more easily when you type or when you write by hand?

• How do you feel about keeping the spell checker (and grammar checker) turned on when you write with word-processing software? Do you ever ignore those red and green lines? Why?

• As a child, do you recall being in spelling bees or having weekly spelling tests? How did you feel about these activities?

• What are some of the troublesome words that you are proudest of conquering? How did you do it?

13

Developing Sentence Sense

Anne Ruggles Gere

Anne Ruggles Gere is Professor of English and Professor of Education at the University of Michigan, where she serves as codirector of the Joint Ph.D. in English and Education. Her family includes her husband, a six-year-old named Denali, and a sweet-natured golden retriever whose IQ is about equal to his weight. She enjoys skiing, listening to the radio, and picking flowers someone else has planted.

Recently I visited an elementary school, and my tour guide showed me the books that kindergartners and first graders were writing. They wrote a string of words (using invented spellings) and then went to the computer lab and (with help) typed the words conventionally. Then they returned to their classroom, where they cut the words out and pasted them onto a larger page, adding an illustration. They bound several of these pages together to make their books. As I watched the children cutting and pasting their sequences of words, I wondered if they knew they were writing sentences. These youngsters, like most of us, fell naturally into using words to create sentences, even if they didn't know what a sentence was.

This ability to produce words in sentences, almost automatically, is one of the things that gets us started as writers, even in kindergarten. It sustains us as we begin to add one sentence to another and another, creating longer stretches of prose, so that by the third grade or so we can write whole stories. If you've been lucky, you've had teachers who have encouraged you to write as much as you've been able, so that you've moved comfortably from writing a few sentences to writing whole essays. Some less fortunate students may have been told that they had to learn how to write sentences before they could write paragraphs and paragraphs before essays. I say "less fortunate" because everything I know about writing tells me that it isn't like learning math. You don't need to learn it in discrete steps, the way you master addition and subtraction before multiplication and so on. Writing doesn't need to be broken down into component parts because we all come to writing classrooms with lots of experience with reading, hearing, and, probably, writing sentences.

That said, I do want to suggest that even experienced writers can benefit from developing sentence sense. I'm convinced that one of the ways writers can improve is by becoming more aware of how they put sentences together. It's easy to fall into patterns or habits of sentence construction without being aware of it. Conscious attention to new ways of shaping sentences can make a big difference in the overall quality of your writing. More important, we can all improve as writers by expanding our repertoires for forming sentences.

Composing sentences, like much else in writing, is about making choices. Having an expanded repertoire of sentence-making strategies means that you have choices to make. When you can choose from among a variety of sentence structures, selecting on the basis of what you want to achieve with a given piece of writing, you can create an interesting and complex essay. The classic study of rhetoric, what Aristotle thought of as finding all the available means of persuasion, suggests two guiding principles to help you think about those choices and the effects you want to have: audience and purpose.

The first guiding principle centers on the audience; good writers always consider their audience. Since most students write for a teacher and/or evaluator audience, the qualities that your audience will be looking for can be found in rubrics, commonly used scoring guides that identify features of good writing. Most rubrics for writing include familiar features such as ideas, organization, style/voice, word choice, conventions/mechanics, fluency/structure, and presentation/verbal facility. All of these depend, in varying degrees, upon the choices you make at the sentence level. If your instructor hasn't discussed criteria for grades with your class, you might ask if the class can discuss what makes "good writing."

Of the features of good writing, word choice is probably the most obvious because individual words are combined to create sentences. It's easy to see how word choice shapes sentences, which, in turn, contribute to the overall quality of writing. Selecting an apt word to express an idea will always be impressive to a reader, and strong verbs are particularly helpful. In fact, word choice contributes to qualities that readers associate with verbal facility and/or good presentation of ideas because appropriate language gives writing an authoritative quality. Readers tend to trust and respond positively to writers who use words well.

Attention to conventions and mechanics at the sentence level also contributes to the quality of presentation and verbal facility because smoothness in syntax and lack of obvious errors makes reading easier. On the other hand, correctness alone in sentence structure does not equate particularly well with good writing. A string of perfectly correct sentences can be flat, and most readers, including your instructor, look for evidence of style or voice in addition to correctness. The overall effect of a piece of writing depends upon a combination of word choice, effective syntax, and connections between sentences. Each of these features is shaped by a writer's choices within individual sentences. Choosing the right words, constructing syntax to convey meaning effectively, and cueing the reader about the connections between sentences—each of these choices contributes to the effect a piece of writing has on its audience.

The other guiding principle concentrates on the purpose of the writing. Even when you are writing in response to an assignment, you can still make choices about your reasons for writing. Suppose, for example, that you have been asked to write an essay explaining why you chose to take a particular class. Your purpose in writing might be to explain how the class fits into your larger career plans, or to promote the good qualities of the class, or to warn other students away from the class. In each instance, sentence-based decisions, guided by the consideration of *why* you are writing and what you want the language *to do*, will contribute to the achievement of your purpose.

One way to start developing sentence sense is to analyze some of your own writing to find out what types of sentences you use most frequently. The four most common sentence types are the simple sentence (a noun and a verb); the compound, which has two joined simple sentences; the complex, which has a simple sentence modified by a dependent clause; and the compound-complex, which combines the compound (two independent clauses) and the complex (adding a dependent clause). The chart in Figure 13–1 explains the features of the four common sentence types. You can learn a good deal about your own writing by looking at several pieces of your writing and marking and counting the types of sentences you use in each.

One student, Jeremy, analyzed his sentence patterns in an essay he had revised several times, and then he created a chart of sentence types to learn about his sentence variety. Here is Jeremy's essay, "Adversity," and what he found:

> Adversity has played a major role in my life. [S] I was born with collapsed lungs, chronic asthma, jaundice, and amniotic band syndrome which claimed four of the digits on my left hand. [CX] My mother realized that many obstacles had to be overcome before I, her new baby, could thrive. [S] I persevered through two weeks of surgery but was finally allowed to go home. [CX]
>
> Overcoming adversity has become an inspiration in my life. [S] I have discovered that the missing digits on my left hand are not a limitation but a motivation. [S] I have played both baseball and soccer at the high school level, have reached a typing speed of eighty words per minute, and have strung my guitar backwards so that I can play music. [S] In spite of these triumphs the greatest adversity was yet to come. [S]

The morning of December 12, 2000 brought an immeasurable amount of pain and suffering into my life. [S] My mother served as my hope and my inspiration; she was a tutor, a mentor, a role model, and a friend. [CD] Our bond was torn apart, however, when a house fire claimed her life and broke my heart. [CX]

Jeremy's sentence variety chart:

S-CX-S-CX

S-S-S-S

S-CD-CX

Figure 13–1
Four Major Sentence Types

Sentence	Features	Example	Comment
Simple (S)	One independent clause (can have multiple subjects and/or multiple predicates)	Traders and buyers hurry to the center of town and usually arrive at the same time.	multiple subjects (traders and buyers); multiple predicates (hurry and arrive)
Compound (CD)	Two or more independent clauses but no dependent clause. Independent clauses may be joined by a comma and a coordinating conjunction or by a semicolon with or without a conjunctive adverb.	The guide dog stopped suddenly, so he did not fall into the hole. Rain poured for ten days; therefore, the festival had to be canceled.	S, and S S; however, S
Complex (CX)	One independent clause and one or more dependent clauses (dc)	She read the newspaper because she wanted to learn more about the candidates for mayor.	S / dc
Compound-complex (CD-CX)	Two or more coordinated independent clauses and at least one dependent clause	He majored in biology, but he became so fascinated by language that he changed to English.	S, but S that dc

Using sentence-type analysis, Jeremy realized that even though the length of his sentences varied, he relied heavily on one type—the simple sentence. An analysis of his own sentences helped Jeremy realize that his writing would benefit if he used a greater variety of sentence types. You might try doing a similar analysis of your sentence patterns, identifying the forms you use most commonly. Once you've done that, you can look for common patterns within the sentence types you use most often.

When Jeremy looked carefully at the simple sentences in his "Adversity" essay, he could see that most of them began with the same noun-verb pattern (*Adversity has played; My mother realized; I was born; I persevered*). He noticed that he used the same pattern again and again. When Jeremy read his essay aloud, he could hear the repetitive sound of this noun-verb pattern at the beginning of each sentence. He realized that he needed to use additional sentence types and to vary the sentence patterns in his writing.

If you think you need to introduce more variety into your sentence types, you may want to try some sentence-combining exercises to remind yourself of how many different ways sentences can be put together. You might try the three exercises in Figure 13–2. There is no answer key for this exercise since there are multiple possible versions. If you do the exercise in class, compare your version with those written by other students. You'll probably notice that each different combination of sentences yields a slightly different effect. Talk with your classmates about which combination you prefer and why.

Understanding and learning to use the various possible effects of sentences is the essence of developing sentence sense. Writing good sentences is not just a matter of learning how to construct more complex syntactic structures; it is also a matter of learning to connect rhetorical purposes with sentence structure. It's important to consider where you want to direct the audience's attention and then create the syntax to accomplish that goal. Consider, for example, the following two sentences: *Lacrosse is my sister's sport. It is strenuous and challenging.* This linear form, putting one subject-verb-complement sentence after another, is typical for many inexperienced writers, and this form makes it difficult for the writer to direct the audience's attention to the connection between the features of lacrosse and the game itself. Here is an alternative combination: *Lacrosse, strenuous and challenging, is my sister's sport.*

This combined sentence is clearly more effective than the two sentences from which it was formed because it uses a more sophisticated syntactic structure. At the same time, this particular combination has a rhetorical effect as well as a syntactic one. The arrangement of the words suggests the meaning the author wants the reader to take away after reading it. Putting the adjectives *strenuous* and *challenging* centrally in the sentence next to *lacrosse* focuses the reader's attention on the nature of lacrosse and makes it easier to move on to the next sentence, like this: *It attracts some of the strongest athletes in our school.*

Figure 13–2
Sentence Combining

How many different ways can you combine the following sets of eight sentences into one sentence?

Set One

1. There was a car accident.

2. Over twenty cars were involved.

3. There was fog on the highway.

4. The cars ran into one another.

5. The cars couldn't move.

6. Rescue vehicles had a hard time getting there.

7. Sirens blared and lights flashed.

8. The accident injured a dozen people.

Set Two

1. The wedding was over.

2. The guests were tired.

3. The guests were happy.

4. The bride and groom were ready to leave.

5. The guests got into their cars.

6. Their cars filled the parking lot.

7. They laughed and talked.

8. Suddenly the parking lot was empty.

Set Three

1. My desk is cluttered.

2. It is covered with papers.

3. It is covered with books.

4. My assignment is somewhere on the desk.

5. I can't find my assignment.

6. My teacher will be angry if I turn my assignment in late.

7. My teacher will lower my grade on the assignment.

8. I wish I could find my assignment.

These two sentences together direct the audience to qualities of the sport, and they work well if the author aims to inform the reader about the nature of lacrosse. However, if the writer wants to focus the audience in a slightly different way, another alternative may work better. For example, consider this combination: *Attracting some of the strongest athletes in our school, lacrosse is my sister's sport.* Here the audience is directed to think more about lacrosse as one among several school sports. The author does not want the reader to focus on lacrosse in itself but to consider its role within a larger program of athletics.

Cumulative sentences (not to be confused with compound and complex sentences) offer another way to broaden your sentence-making repertoire. Basically, cumulative sentences take a simple sentence (one independent clause) and amplify it with a series of modifiers. For example, more information could be added to this simple sentence: *The skaters are filling the rink.* Detail can be provided by modifiers that transform a statement into a scene of action: *The skaters are filling the rink, the girls gliding and spinning, the boys swooping and daring, their arms flapping like wings.* Many students worry that these modifiers will lead to run-on sentences because the modifiers feel like sentences hooked to the first sentence with a comma. However, these modifiers usually lack a verb (or part of a verb), so they would be incomplete sentences on their own. For example, *their arms flapping like wings* would have to be *Their arms* are *flapping like wings* to be a complete sentence (and this would then be a run-on if used without the proper coordinating conjunction).

Knowing how to write cumulative sentences can be very useful when you want to provide more detail in your writing and develop more sentence variety. Returning to the "Adversity" piece, we can see how revision to add a few cumulative sentences can introduce syntactic variety. Take, for example, the final sentence of the first paragraph, *I persevered through two weeks of surgery but was finally allowed to go home.* This sentence could be revised with modifiers: *I persevered through two weeks of surgery, pricked senseless by long needles, caught in a tangle of tubes, blinded by a light that shone night and day over my incubator, before finally being allowed to go home.*

Another sentence that might be revised into a cumulative one is the first in paragraph three: *The morning of December 12, 2000 brought an immeasurable amount of pain and suffering into my life.* One possible revision would read like this: *Freakish and stealthy, with exquisite precision, the morning of December 12, 2000, brought an immeasurable amount of pain and suffering into my life, upending my days, haunting my nights.* You might find it useful to practice creating cumulative sentences by trying the exercise in Figure 13–3.

Another way to develop sentence sense is to become more aware of some of the sentence patterns that classical rhetoricians have traditionally taught their students over the years. Figure 13–4 lists each pattern type (with its classical name) along with the features of the pattern and an example.

Figure 13–3
Cumulative Sentence Exercise

With each of the ten practice sentences, try to add at least three free modifiers to the main clause, varying the position of the modifiers. For example, *Four women in red walked to the podium* could become (a) *Four women in red, joint winners of the Nobel Prize for Chemistry, walked to the podium, arms linked in fellowship,* (b) *Four women in red walked to the podium, joint winners of the Nobel Prize for Chemistry, arms linked in fellowship,* or (c) *Arms linked in fellowship, four women in red, joint winners of the Nobel Prize for Chemistry, walked to the podium.*

Try to include as much sensory detail as possible. Compare your cumulative sentences with those written by another student, considering the details you added and the varying effects you achieved.

1. Four women in red walked to the podium.
2. Then I heard the siren blare.
3. She raised her hand.
4. The feather bed beckoned me.
5. Five sparrows huddled near the birdbath.
6. The speaker paused.
7. Joan could play the piano for hours.
8. The old man's eye remained fixed on me.
9. Ocean swells moved rhythmically toward us.
10. The little girl stood at the top of the stairs.

Knowing about rhetorical sentence patterns like these can help you develop sentence sense in at least two ways. One of the most common maxims is that good writers read widely. While it's true that extensive reading contributes to the quality of writing, the connection between the two can be strengthened if you can *recognize* sentence patterns when you see them. Becoming hyperaware of various patterns of repetition can help you notice how writers use these patterns. And, of course, one way to make the best use of patterns you find is to record them in a notebook where you can refer to them when you are writing.

In addition to recognizing rhetorical sentence patterns, you can develop your sentence sense by playing with them. You might, for example, take each of the example sentences from Figure 13–4 and restate it in other words. Consider the difference between sentences like *When the going gets tough, the tough get going* and *When things get difficult, people of character rise to the occasion.* You might also try imitating the structure of these sentence patterns with topics you are writing about.

Figure 13–4
Rhetorical Sentence Patterns

Type	Features	Example
Multiple repetitions (anaphora)	Repetition of same word(s) at the beginning of successive clauses	Our class has worked on school spirit for four years— four years of pep rallies and bonfires, four years of cookie sales and tag days, four years of cheering ourselves hoarse.
Phrase reversal (chiasmus)	The second half of a sentence reverses the order of the first	When the going gets tough, the tough get going.
Interrupted repetition (diacope)	Repetition of word or phrase with one or more words in between	Give me bread, oh my jailer, give me bread.
End repetition (epiphora)	Repetition of word or phrase at the end of several clauses	When I was a child, I spoke as a child, I understood as a child, I thought as a child.
Apparent omission (occupatio)	Emphasizing a point by seeming to pass over it	I will not mention her extravagance, her luxurious wardrobe, her credit card debts, her loyalty to fashion designers—austerity is her new mode.
Part/whole substitution (synecdoche)	Substitution of part for the whole	All hands on deck.
Triple parallels (tricolon)	Pattern of three parallel phrases	I came, I saw, I conquered.
Verb repetition (zeugma)	One verb governs several objects, each in a different way	Here, thou great Anna, whom three realms obey, dost sometimes counsel take—and sometimes tea.

Developing sentence sense, then, can be an ongoing part of your work as a writer. Moving from having an awareness of the sentence types and patterns you use most automatically to broadening your syntactic repertoire by considering sentence combining, using cumulative sentences, or trying rhetorical sentence patterns can lead you to write more varied and syntactically interesting sentences. But the real work of developing sentence sense lies in connecting your choices about sentences with rhetorical considerations. Of course it is good to be able to write sentences of varying length and type simply because it makes your prose more interesting and pleasant to read. The payoff comes, however, when you can use syntax to foster the larger purposes of your writing. Ultimately, developing sentence sense will help you connect more effectively with your audiences and convey your purposes more clearly.

Sharing Ideas

- Anne Ruggles Gere calls students lucky who have had teachers who encouraged them to write as much as they were able, moving comfortably from writing a few sentences to writing whole essays. The less fortunate students were told that they had to learn how to write sentences before they could write paragraphs and paragraphs before essays. See if you can recall how you were taught. Do you consider yourself lucky or unlucky?

- If word choice is one of the more obvious features of good writing, try to reflect on how much time you spend considering word choice when you draft your sentences.

- Some people think that correctness is the most important feature of sentences. How do you see the role of correctness in your own sentence construction?

- Did you analyze some of your own writing to find out what types of sentences you use most frequently? If so, comment on what you learned by looking at your use of simple sentences, compound sentences, complex sentences, and compound-complex sentences.

- Discuss your feelings about and experiences with writing cumulative sentences to provide more detail in your writing and develop more sentence variety. Do you find writing cumulative sentences exciting, or do you worry about making comma-splice errors and writing run-on sentences?

- Look back over several pieces of writing that you have recently completed. If you find any series of simple sentences, think about several different ways that you could combine the sentences to make them more interesting.

- Take the sentence *Winning isn't everything; it's the only thing* and try to develop your sentence sense by playing with it, restating it in other words, and revising it for these different audiences: kindergartners, peace activists, and members of a women's club.

14

Understanding Writing Assignments
Tips and Techniques

Dan Melzer

Dan Melzer is a graduate student at Florida State University who recently received his Ph.D. in Rhetoric and Composition. He's especially interested in writing across the curriculum. As a writing center tutor, he's worked with hundreds of students who have needed help understanding their class assignments, and that experience has provided the inspiration for this essay.

I'm sitting at a table in the Writing Center when my 2:00 appointment stumbles in, confusion evident in his bleary eyes. "I've been up all night trying to write this history paper," he says, "but I just don't understand what the professor wants us to do!" I tell him to take a deep breath, stay calm, and have a seat. I ask him if the professor has given him a handout explaining the process he should follow while composing, and I assure him that he's not the first college student who's ever arrived confused about what to do next. He's taken the time to come to the Writing Center for help, and that's a good start.

When your teacher presents you with a writing assignment, whether it's a first-year writing class or a class in a different subject area, she will usually hand out a written description, detailing what she's asking you to accomplish. Of course, not all teachers do this, a situation I'll discuss later in this chapter. For now, though, I want to discuss seven tips for understanding any kind of college writing assignment and provide an insider's view by discussing one of my own assignments in first-year writing, a review paper.

Review Essay

In the review essay, you're going to choose a campus event to review. It can be any kind of event—a lecture, a musical performance, a museum show, a fiction reading, and so on. We're going to include these reviews in our class anthology, so *your audience is your peers, not your teacher.* To get a sense of what a review might look like, we'll read some examples from the campus newspaper. Most reviews provide an audience with a brief *summary* of the events, as well as an *evaluation* by the reviewer. As you begin to brainstorm, you might ask yourself: What were the main aspects of the event that readers will want to know about? What did you like best about the event, and why? What did you like least about the event, and why? What descriptive details can help give the readers a sense of the event?

Your review essay should be between three and five pages long. *Your review essay will go through a number of drafts.* You'll bring a rough draft to a peer response workshop next Friday, and then you'll sign up for a one-on-one conference with me to get feedback on a revised version. The final draft will be included in your portfolio, so you will have until the end of the semester to revise the essay.

I will evaluate the review based on the *progress* you made in your revisions, the appeal of the review to a *peer audience*, and the development of your *summary* and *evaluation* of the event. Please take another look at the grading rubric I handed out the first week of class to review my general evaluation criteria.

Assume you're in my first-year writing class and I just gave you this assignment. Take a moment to think about some strategies you would use to better understand this assignment. What do you think are the most important aspects to focus on? What questions would you have for me about the assignment? Although every assignment and every teacher is different, the following tips will be useful in any writing situation.

Tip #1: Look for Key Verbs in the Assignment

Most assignments have key verbs, such as *argue, define, summarize,* and *evaluate,* that can help you understand what kind of thinking and writing skills the instructor wants you to demonstrate. Notice that in my review assignment I keep mentioning two key verbs—*summarize* and *evaluate*—again and again. I even highlight them twice. The reason these key verbs are so important to me is that I'm hoping they show classroom authors just what kind of approach they should take in a review essay.

Since these key verbs have different meanings in different classes and different subjects, teachers will often describe what they mean by these key verbs in the assignment sheet. Notice that I give writers a list of questions that will help them better understand what I mean by *summarize* and *evaluate*. Summarizing an event means getting across to the reader the "main aspects" of the event, and in this kind of summary I want writers to be descriptive in order to give the readers a sense of the event. Evaluating means talking about what you liked and didn't like about an event and why—making judgments and then backing them up with arguments and examples.

Of course, my definitions of *summary* and *evaluation* may be different from the definitions used by instructors in other subjects. These differences aren't just random. Each subject has its own conventions and methods. For example, here's one paragraph explaining the key verb *evaluate* from an assignment sheet in a sociology course. The instructor wants students to write a critical evaluation of an article in a sociology journal:

> What were one or two problems with this research? How could the author have done a better job of investigating the questions he or she posed? Did the author interpret his/her findings correctly, or did he or she overstate or understate their importance?

This instructor's definition of *evaluate* for his assignment is much different from my definition of *evaluate* in my review assignment. This kind of evaluation focuses on problems with research and whether findings were interpreted correctly by the author. My definition of *evaluate* in the review assignment focuses much more on the students' tastes and personal opinions. Reading an assignment sheet carefully and closely will help you make these kinds of subject area distinctions.

Sometimes teachers don't really describe what they mean when they say *argue* or *summarize* or *evaluate*, and this can get confusing when you're trying to understand their assignments. Let's pretend that a psychology professor has given you this assignment:

> Your paper will be a literature review of a topic in cognitive psychology. A literature review is a well-organized overview and evaluation of the relevant research or findings related to your topic. I place emphasis on the words "overview" and "evaluation." You will be interpreting the available information and research findings and then drawing conclusions.

Just like my review assignment, *evaluate* is a key word for this literature review. But it's hard to tell what the professor means by *evaluate*. Students are supposed to "interpret the available information," but what exactly does the teacher mean by *interpret*? If I were given this assignment, before I started trying to write, I would ask the professor to discuss *evaluate* and *interpret* in more detail. Most teachers appreciate it when students have questions about an assignment after they've looked over the assignment sheet, so don't be shy. You might also ask the professor if she can tell you where to find some examples of the kind of literature review she's asking for, since the literature review is a common type of writing you might find in a psychology journal. I talk more about assignment types and model assignments with Tip #2.

Tip #2: Figure Out What Genre—
What "Type"—of Essay You've Been Assigned

Many of the writing assignments you get in college will fit into genres. "Genres" are essay types that have certain forms and purposes, for example, lab reports, business letters, editorials, and scientific reports. Not all writing assignments fit into these genres, but many do. The review essay, for example, is based on a very common genre. Classroom authors have probably read movie reviews in the local newspaper or music reviews in magazines like *Rolling Stone*, so they can use this knowledge of the form and purpose of a review when they write their own. I also mention in class that we're going to look at example reviews in the campus newspaper. Of course, I don't want writers to just copy the exact form of someone else's review, but I do want them to think of other reviews they've read in the past to give them a better sense of different possibilities for shaping their own reviews—to give them options for making their reviews more effective.

If your teacher gives you examples of the kind of essay she's assigned, or if she gives you the names of journals or magazines to look at for examples, my advice is to take advantage of this. If your assignment fits into a genre, whether it's a lab report or an interview, it helps to look at models. This will also be true of the writing you do in your career after college. If your boss asks you to write a business plan or a brochure, learning from examples can help you be a more effective writer.

Here's an example of another genre, the chemistry class abstract:

> An abstract of the experiment is to appear on the first page of each lab report. An abstract of an experiment is a short paragraph (3–4 sentences) stating what was done (not what was set out to be done) in a given experiment. It is not a description of the experimental procedure. No data is given in the abstract. The correct form and wording of an abstract, which is found at the beginning of every research article published in chemistry, may be seen in any chemistry journal in the library.

An abstract for a history or psychology article might be much different from this chemistry abstract. This chemistry abstract should only be three to four sentences long, but I've written abstracts for English journals that were a page long. If I were given this assignment, even if I'd written an abstract before in another class, I would take the time to go to the library and look up a few examples from chemistry journals.

Thinking about the type of essay you've been assigned—the genre—can also help you think about things like purpose (Why are you writing?), audience (Who are you writing to?), and tone (How do you want to sound in your writing? Authoritative, personal, formal, humorous?). For example, a scientific paper written for a journal will have a formal tone and structure. A newspaper editorial will usually make an argument to persuade a specific audience. A personal journal entry will probably be less formal than an electronic bulletin board journal that the entire class reads. When your teacher gives you a writing assignment, think about what genre it is and how that might affect these elements. The better understanding you have of things like genre, purpose, audience, and tone, the better you will be able to persuade and influence your readers. [For more information about writing in different tones for differernt audiences, read Jay Szczepanski's chapter.]

Tip 3#: Figure Out Who the Audience for the Writing Assignment Is

In my review essay assignment sheet, I make it clear to my students that they're writing to a peer audience, not to me. Notice that I highlight the target audience a number of times. I do this because I know that most of the writing my students have done in high school, and a lot of the writing they will be assigned in their other college classes, had one audience: the teacher. But in this assignment, I want classroom authors to write to each other, not to me, which is one reason we put all of the essays in a class anthology for everyone to read. Of course, in the end, I'm the one who has to put a final grade on these essays. But notice that I tell students I will evaluate them on how well their writing appeals to their peers and not to me. I do this because I want them to see a writing assignment not as a boring task to please a teacher, but as something that generates an interesting idea that a writer can communicate to a real audience.

It's not uncommon for college teachers to assign a hypothetical audience—to ask for role playing. Teachers know that having students write in a situation they might encounter in the real world can lead to much better work. Here's an example from a bioethics course of an assignment that presents a hypothetical audience:

> You are on the board of medical ethics of a major hospital. Your board is still struggling with the best way to advise parents of newborns with an intersexual appearance. Specifically, you must decide if parents have the right to choose surgery and hormonal treatment for their newborns in cases where it is not required for medical reasons.

If you were given this assignment, you would need to keep in mind that your audience is *parents*, and that you're playing the role of an *expert*, a hospital board member. If you were writing this assignment professionally, for a hospital board of medical ethics, you'd also want to keep your audience in mind.

Tip #4: Pay Close Attention to How the Teacher Will Evaluate the Assignment

Notice that the review assignment sheet includes a paragraph devoted to how I will evaluate the essay. I highlight the fact that writers will be graded on the progress they made as they drafted and revised their essays, and this is no surprise considering that I require that students undertake peer response workshops and one-on-one workshops with me. In the evaluation paragraph of the assignment sheet, I also highlight the two key verbs writers need to keep in mind as they structure their essay: *summarize* and *evaluate*. Since my grading rubric discusses general things I value in any essay students write, I also remind them to look over the rubric again.

What if the teacher hasn't provided you with a grading rubric or doesn't mention how the assignment will be evaluated? I want writers to understand how to succeed when I give them an assignment, and if I haven't successfully explained how I evaluate an essay, then I hope they ask me questions as we discuss the assignment sheet. Don't be afraid to ask your teachers for more information about what they expect from an assignment and how they will evaluate your writing. Of course, you'll want to be tactful. Don't ask: "What do I need to do to get an A?" Instead, ask the teacher to expand on what she wants you to accomplish in the assignment and what she will value when she grades the assignment.

Keep in mind that every teacher grades differently, based on particular class goals and on the criteria of his discipline. I value originality, creativity, and lots of revision. Other teachers might focus more on how well you can use outside sources to support an argument, while others might be more concerned with grammar. For example, here's a passage from the evaluation section of an assignment in a sociology class:

> Present things in an organized way. I expect your work to be free of spelling errors and grammatical mistakes. Also, your essays should constitute a completed whole. Your paragraphs should be interrelated and work toward the completion of a single, but complex, idea or thesis.

I may grade on revision and originality, but this instructor is more focused on an organized essay structure and error-free spelling and grammar. Unlike a quantitative subject like math, writing is qualitative and subjective, and different teachers will value different things and read your work in different ways. That's why it's important to read each assignment sheet carefully and then ask questions.

Tip #5: Think About the Assignment in Terms of the Class as a Whole

I mention in my assignment sheet that the review essay is part of the class anthology, which is a *magazine* of all the writing the class does. The audience for this anthology is freshmen in college, and all of the pieces we write for it have something to do with college life. I don't grade my students' essays until the anthology is complete at the end of the semester, and students know that I use end-of-term grading because I want them to do a lot of revising. Knowing these details about the class as a whole can help my students understand this particular assignment and put it in the context of the goals of the class.

Here are some questions you can ask yourself about the context of the class whenever you receive an individual assignment:

- How is this assignment similar to/different from previous assignments? Does it ask me to build on skills I practiced in a previous assignment? Does it ask me to do something new?

- How does the assignment relate to the work I've done in class or for homework?

- How does the assignment relate to the subject area of the class? For example, writing in the sciences is usually logical and formal, but a journal in an English class will usually be more conversational in tone and more exploratory.

- How has the teacher evaluated assignments in the past? Does this assignment call for any new ways of writing and thinking the teacher might be evaluating me on?

All of these questions are also something you could ask your teacher, discuss with fellow classmates, or review with a tutor at your college's writing center.

Tip #6: Don't Be Afraid to Ask the Teacher Questions

I'm a teacher who appreciates thoughtful questions about an assignment. It shows me that students are trying to understand the assignment. And, as hard as I try, when I'm writing an assignment sheet, it's difficult to imagine all of the information writers will need to understand the assignment. So don't be shy. Even if you're in a big lecture class that doesn't allow for a lot of discussion, take the time to visit the professor during her office hours. If she has given the class her e-mail address, then that's another option for communicating about questions you have concerning an assignment. It's helpful to understand an assignment before you start writing, and if questions come up after you start writing, it's crucial to talk to your instructor before you turn in the paper.

When you first come to college, it can seem as if teachers will see you as a pest if you stop by during their office hours and ask questions. But for most of us, just the opposite is true. Most teachers really appreciate students who take the time to visit during office hours and ask thoughtful questions about their assignments. After all, even though it doesn't always feel like it to you, the teacher has created the assignment to help you learn something, not to try to torture or trick you.

Tip #7: If the Teacher Lets You Choose the Topic, Pick Something That's Original and That You're Genuinely Interested In

I can say without a doubt that I'm the world's foremost expert on the death penalty and legalizing marijuana. Why am I such an expert? Because I let my students choose their own topics for research papers, and many of them choose these or other well-known issues. So one reason to pick an original and interesting topic is that most teachers have become a little numb to debates that they've already read about over and over again. Of course, it isn't just teachers who are sick of these issues. Arguments about the death penalty and legalizing marijuana have gotten so much attention from the media that almost everyone is familiar with the opposing sides in the debate. And that makes it harder to find something interesting to say about these kinds of topics.

But here's an even more important reason to pick an original topic: You'll be more excited about writing the paper. Students who pick topics that fascinate them, topics that they really want to know more about, almost always write better essays than students who rely on the same old topics. I've had very few students who were genuinely excited about researching euthanasia or abortion. But I've had plenty of students who chose interesting, original topics and wound up actually enjoying their research and writing. For example, one student who liked rap music compared the attitudes of female and male rappers and included lyrics and images from CD covers; another student who was an environmental science major investigated a controversy over the pollution of a river in her hometown, and her research paper turned into an editorial she mailed to her hometown newspaper.

It's not easy coming up with original topics, I know. But here are some ideas to help you brainstorm if your teacher lets you choose a topic to write about:

- Jot down a list of things that you're an authority on, hobbies you have, and things you want to know more about. Use this list to brainstorm topics that might interest you. You can start broadly and then narrow down (for example: Movies > Tarantino > *Pulp Fiction* > Gender roles in *Pulp Fiction*).

- Look over class notes and other class materials. What were some of the issues you discussed in class that interested you the most? Which chapters in your class text were the most interesting to read or raised the most questions for you?

- Think of the personal relevance the course has for you. Why did you take it to begin with? What connections does the course have to your personal goals, interests, and experiences?

- Glance through books, journals, magazines, or websites in the general area of the class or assignment and find out which issues are being debated or which topics might need further exploration.

- Bounce ideas off your classmates, your teacher, or a tutor at your school's writing center. Sometimes just brainstorming with another person can lead to new topics you never considered.

The seven tips I've discussed can be helpful if the teacher provides an assignment sheet, but what if the teacher doesn't give you any written description of the assignment? Some teachers explain their assignments verbally and expect students to take careful notes, but it can be difficult to fully understand an assignment without some written description from the teacher. If your teacher doesn't give you an assignment sheet, my advice is to take detailed notes about her verbal description of the assignment and ask questions about anything you're not sure of. Again, don't be shy about visiting the teacher during her office hours and asking her to elaborate on what she's looking for in the assignment.

Another place to get help with understanding a writing assignment is your school's writing center. Writing center staff are experienced with helping students who are struggling to understand an assignment or find a topic. They can help you understand key verbs, figure out the audience for the writing, and interpret the teacher's evaluation criteria, much like I've done in this chapter. With all this in mind, good luck with your next writing assignment!

Sharing Ideas

- Think back to writing assignments you were given in high school or in other college classes. Do you have any tips for understanding those assignments that you could add to Dan Melzer's list?

- Make a list of the kinds of key verbs Dan mentions in Tip #1 that you've come across in high school or college writing assignments. How are these key verbs different in different subject areas (for example, how is arguing different in science than in English?).

- What genres have you encountered in your high school or college writing assignments? How did the genre affect the audience and purpose of the assignment? What kinds of genres might you encounter in your career after college?

- In Tip #7, Dan has a list of techniques for coming up with a topic. Think back to times that you've had to come up with your own topic for a writing assignment. Are there any techniques you used that aren't on Dan's list?

- Think of a list of possible questions to ask your teacher about an assignment.
- How does Dan's chapter complement other chapters in this book that deal with finding and developing your own topic, voice, writing style? How does a writer negotiate between the desire to make a topic or assignment personally significant and the need at the same time to meet the requirements of a course or a teacher or a discipline?

15

Tips for College Writing Success

Nathan Timm

A junior at Florida State University when he composed this essay, Nathan Timm was studying writing and was an active member of the university track team.

Every college student has to write. Some love it, others dread it. Welcome to college. Deal with it. If students want to be able to succeed in college, they must learn to write well in almost every subject. Writing has become just as much a part of college as late-night pizza delivery. Still, students always seem to be complaining about writing papers, even English majors, including avid writers who are trying to write successfully outside of class. Writers can get so entangled in their assignments that they think of each assignment as torture instead of a challenge. Any method found to alleviate this frustration can be a sanity-saver. To help, I came up with eight helpful hints for writing success-fully in and out of class in college.

1. Set Measurable Goals

If I didn't set goals for my writing, I would lose my hair by age twenty-one. Put your goals in writing. Keep them simple. Write them in your journal. Tape them to your mirror above your sink. I have Post-it Notes all across my room. I set goals to get my writing done ahead of time because then I can spend the remaining extra time concentrating on feedback, comments, and revision.

Setting goals will allow you to make time for your writing. I set a goal for this year to spend an hour writing a day with at least twenty minutes on my personal writing. When I meet this goal my writing improves, but when I don't it suffers.

2. Allow Time

College students vary in their ability to manage time. Some students attempt to balance school, work, and sports all in one day. On the other hand, I've seen college students seem to spend their entire Saturday afternoon sitting on the porch drinking the day away. Writing takes time. It's not like some subjects where you can never open a book and hope to pass. English classes consume time because essays can't be written with the help of Cliffs Notes. I spend over half my homework time doing writing assignments. I have to make time. I set up appointments to write.

3. Have Fun with It

Whether you're an English major or not, you still are required to write. It might be journals, papers, e-mails, or even letters. Writing isn't fun for everyone, but if you hope to be successful having fun needs to become a major component of your writing. Maybe it's the end result, which puts a gleaming smile on your face or produces a sigh of relief. Or you find joy in the process which you go through in order to get to the product of your writing. I heard a quote once that I try to follow, especially with my writing endeavors. "I never worked a day in my life. It was all fun."

When I'm reading a paper on the bus to the trials, my teammates from the cross country team say:

"Nathan. You're writing another paper. That's gotta suck."

"No, not really," I usually respond.

I would rather be writing than studying for other classes. I don't find much enjoyment in reading the same text over and over to get a decent grade on a midterm. I enjoy English classes. In order to get writing done, students need to make the paper fun. Write more in different areas. Make it a challenge. Don't ever think of writing as a bore. I think everyone wants to improve their writing in some shape or form, but often they don't have the discipline.

In his book, *Writing Without Teachers*, Peter Elbow discusses the idea of forming a writing group. Sharing with others is one way to make writing more fun because I'll be the first to admit that writing for school all the time can get draining.

4. In Your Free Time—Write

I can't tell you how many papers I've written or found ideas to if I write while watching television. I'll just be relaxing in front of the television while eating dinner. Then something on the television will trigger an idea for a paper. Then

I pick up a pen and my journal and start writing. Every part of life can dictate your writing life. That's why I make a conscious effort to write for myself sometimes. Whether it's a motivating quote I came upon or just a piece of advice for that day, I write it down. I sometimes just write a story, chronologically going through my day.

If you're living a boring life, your writing will probably reveal that. Equally, too much partying can cause your writing to suffer. You're probably going to have a hard time feeling up to writing when you're out later, but then again if you're a late-night person, maybe writing late at night would be your specialty. Make it a point to sit down and write before and after you go out— maybe you'll find out something new about your writing abilities. Maybe you will find new motivation to write before you go out. Find your best writing window. Capitalize on your strengths. You could feel so relaxed after you get home that you'll write freely. This will help you reach your writing potential, and also prove relaxing. Plus, you'll learn that you can do two things you enjoy doing at exactly the same time, useful for a time-pressed college student.

5. Write with Music

You'll never know if this will work for you if you don't try it. You'll be amazed at the writing you'll get by having music in the background. You'll find it easy to write along to the beat of the music. The different moods in the music will change the pace and break up the mood in your writing. You'll be more likely to write with a varied sense of style going to the beat of the music. The longer, slower songs will help you think more deeply and relax while constructing your piece.

Faster paced music will help you to type faster and get into a stronger rhythm while you write. Some writers feel they must write in silence, but I disagree; you have the best of both worlds while writing with music. I prefer to let my Aimster play list go and dictate the song selection because if I were selecting I would get distracted from the writing task. The focus still needs to be on writing and letting music become a helper, but not a distraction.

6. A Procrastination Solution

A trick I started using my freshman year in college helped me eliminate the majority of my procrastinating habits. If you're a procrastinator, give yourself an hour to complete your assignment, but do it a week in advance. Most procrastinators would never think of trying this mind-boggling idea, but under the proper conditions it can work successfully. Imagine your assignment is due in an hour and work furiously with adrenaline pumping. You can be excited about the writing and overloaded with motivation because the time is so short. You'll discover what you can do when you have only moments to spare, and then find yourself a week ahead. An extra week to edit and get feedback from friends or the teachers means you won't be stressed about writing.

This is the best secret of my writing process. Work ahead and you'll be amazed how well you can write, using each minute and experiencing a new-found joy of writing under the time constraints, but with less actual pressure. Leaving you time to edit. I think the biggest struggle of college writers is editing; it's either they don't have enough time or they just feel their writing doesn't need to be edited. Using procrastination creatively allows you to find time to (learn how) to edit.

7. Try Working with a Partner

So many students are good writers, but you'll never really know unless you ask them. Others can help you with your paper, but you have to ask. Let them read it. Edit it. Let them break down their reading of your paper and tell you what they got out of it and what they still want from the paper. You'll be amazed at how two people interpret the same section of an essay when they read it together at the same time. So find a friend in your class and work together. Go out for coffee. Go watch a movie together after you've completed your work. This way, writing will become social instead of being such an individual activity.

8. Take Breaks

I know we've all seen tired and exhausted students literally falling asleep in front of the computer. They drink five cans of Mountain Dew to surge them through the last two pages of a paper. They have so much caffeine in their system that they can't even sit still. When this happens, I say: "I need a break. I'll be back in a second." I call this proactive relaxing. I work first then I take breaks. After a certain amount of time, the mind is going to wander and lose focus on the goal ahead.

After a long semester of writing papers for class and your own personal work, plan a week-long break from writing. Time to relax. Maybe even try to read more. No writing allowed. Then after that week get back to writing. You'll be more motivated than before. You finished a tough semester and deserved a break, but now it's time to see the results of the hard work.

After your week-long break challenge yourself to complete something new, maybe a poem, an essay, or a short story. Make it a goal to show it to someone.

Most of these ideas may seem odd and unfamiliar and I doubt all of them will help you personally with your writing. But, if even one idea helps you become a more effective writer then I feel that I've succeeded in sharing my processes with you. I battle the same things that every college student does with writing, but some of my own ideas and suggestions from writers I read have helped me get through the rough times of writing. I think if you give some of these techniques a try you might become quite surprised at the new look you'll find in your writing. Then, writing will be the first assignment you'll finish, instead of the last.

Sharing Ideas

- Read Nathan's Timm's essay in light of Susan Wyche's essay in Part I. Do these writers agree on the habits of college writers? What other writing habits have you observed among your friends?

- Consider Nathan's advice in light of the notion that college resituates and shapes students in relationship to their methods of study and in relationship to their family members. Do you feel Nathan's tips are influenced by the sorts of changes he knows college students are experiencing in their new lifestyles? Explain and explore.

- If you write with music, discuss what music, what it means to your composing process, and why. Take one of your papers and annotate the margins, telling how listening to music while composing affected that draft. Make your "best composing" playlist. Do you invent to the same music you revise to? Why or why not? If you're one of those who needs silence, not music (or TV!) for writing, argue against music (or TV) as a writing aid.

- Tell some tales of working with a writing partner. What helped you be productive? What kept you from doing your best work together? Consider on-line collaboration (if you've done some)—how has that worked for you so far? What skills do you have to learn to help others write? How does Nathan's advice connect to Donald McAndrew's observations in a later chapter about college writing classrooms?

- Plan an optimal writing calendar for your next paper. Look at the syllabus, consider the assignment (using Dan Melzer's previous chapter to help you do this), and write out a time line that would let you do your very best work. Now, troubleshoot: add complications to that schedule (what might draw you away from your work and how can you avoid interruptions and distractions?). Even if such detailed planning is unlike your normal practices, try to follow this schedule and see if it makes a difference in the quality of your final writing product for this paper, the unit, or the term.

- Read Amanda McCorquodale's process narrative (Part I). To what extent does she seem already to be following Nathan's advice? To what extent do you follow it yourself?

- Add three more writing tips to Nathan's essay based on your own writing habits.

Part IV

Writers and Other Writers

I simply write about my chosen topic for as long as I feel inspired, and go off on as many tangents as I need to get my thoughts down. Structure, formation, word choice, sentence balance, sentence placement, and overall readability are all things that I pretend do not exist. It took a long time to teach my internal editor to shut her mouth during this process, and it's something I have to keep in mind every time I write. My critical brain and creative brain do not play well together, so I try to train them to keep away from each other. The critical brain can be so demanding too.

—Rebecca Bybel, writing major

When I was eighteen, my writing was an extremely personal activity. I didn't just throw words on pages, I invested myself into the work. Everything I wrote was full of personal insights, personal style, and voice. A good writer, I was regularly praised and awarded for my high school writing efforts. I was totally unprepared for the shocking comments that my college professors would place on my writing. Part of the problem came from a natural maturing process: The valued and original insights of a high school senior were suddenly the trite and common repetitions of a college student. And part of the problem came from style. The original, personal, whimsical voice of a young writer was not enough to assure my spot in the academic community.

—Kevin Davis, writing center director

The story you pick draws on your knowledge of culture, people, and verbal arts. When you retell it in your workshop, you need to add background that will help your peers appreciate it as you do. Along with the narrative you should provide information about where it comes from, how the characters in it relate to each other, when it's been told, who usually tells it and who usually listens, what events accompanied previous tellings that might increase its significance. You should also include insights you have about the way people use the story to express themselves and about the influence the narrative has had on you.

—Ormond Loomis, writing teacher

I need deadlines. This class provided me with more than an adequate number of them (I have a gift for understatement). I write my best from about 10 until 2 in the morning (I edit the following afternoon). I think this is a result of habit, but it is nonetheless true. Without deadlines, I have trouble forcing myself to work at those hours. I am concerned that after this class I will do less work since I am deprived of those deadlines.

—Jason Fink, writing student

Textbooks and teachers are sincerely trying to help students become better writers. But you are the person in control of deciding what works best for you. Some people don't want to accept that responsibility because it takes some effort and experimentation to find out how they write most effectively. They'd rather have someone tell them exactly what to do—it's a "no brain" activity since they then merely have to do what they are told. Other people shy away from the close consideration involved in making choices because they are so unsure of their skills. They'd rather trust "the experts." But you are the expert on the subject of yourself.

—Muriel Harris, writing teacher

16

Changing as a Writer

Audrey Brown

Audrey Brown was a student at the University of Vermont when she wrote this essay.

I don't like to write.
I never did.
It always takes me a long time to get done.

—age 9

Eleven years later and I still feel this way. So what am I doing? I don't like my writing. I'm mad right now. I'm irritable. I just bit my sister's head off because she came in my room with an essay she wanted me to proofread. I always liked math. Maybe I should have been a math major. Math is good because it's straightforward and always either right or wrong. There's no emotional involvement with math. Writing, any kind of writing, drains me.

When writing, I have always felt that I am struggling with myself. The only reason I have continued to write is that once in a while I like what comes out. But I really don't want to write this paper that is supposed to trace the development of my voice. I've been sitting here for hours. Struggling. My brain is so jammed with all the possible ways to write this that I'm having trouble producing anything at all. Well, I have to write

157

something, and analytical writing is a safe way to go, so. . . . I wrote my first descriptive piece when I was eight.

> September 14, 1976
> I like flowers. They smell nice. They are pretty.

I didn't take advantage of my youth and inexperience to write something off the wall here like "flowers are ugly" or something fantastic and imaginary like "the flowers are dancing." Although at the time, I'm sure I didn't even realize I had that option. I described flowers the way I saw them and the way I still see them. They *are* pretty and they *are* nice. Basic words for a basic subject.

Much of my writing actually reminds me a little of math. Don't take any chances, because if you take chances, you get the answer wrong. Just like math. Subject + verb + object = a sentence. $2 + 2 + 2 = 6$. Sometimes this strategy works well, as in the flower piece. Other times, this mathematical prose makes me sound very emotionless.

When I was nine my family had a dog named Tan. He was a great dog, and we all loved him a lot and were really upset when he disappeared during hunting season one year. But this is how I relayed the event in a school journal:

> February 18, 1977
> Last year my mother found a dog with no collar. We called some of our friends. The dog didn't belong to any of them. We had it on the radio but we couldn't find the owner. We kept him for a little while. One day in winter he didn't come home. We didn't see him the next day we didn't see him either. We never saw him again.

I never even mention being sad in this, but this lack of expressed emotion is typical of a lot of my writing.

Even when I was excited about something, I didn't express it well on paper. Having school canceled because of bad weather was always a highlight of the school year. That fact is completely obscured by the following bit of writing.

> January 1977
> Yesterday morning about six-o-clock my father came in to see me before he went to work. He told me school was canceled. He said my mom was going to work but he wasn't. When I got up my friend called and I went to her house for a little while. We went outside for a little while and the snow was past my knees.

Believe it or not, I was very excited about that day, although there is not much evidence of that in my words. There's a sense of distance here between me and the reader. In all of my early writing I was very conscious of writing for some sort of audience. I can't quite identify who that audience was, but I know it never varied much, regardless of whether I was writing an analytical paper or a school journal or even a personal diary entry.

This mystery audience never knew me too well. I felt the need to identify the people I wrote about, to justify my beliefs or emotions, and to tie up any loose ends in my life's events. I think sometimes, mostly in the diary entries, the audience was myself. Not me as I was then, but as I would be in the future. I assumed, when writing, that in the future I wouldn't remember much of my past so I was careful to clearly explain everything. In the above passage, I was sure to say "my mom" and "my friend" instead of just "mom" and "Celina." I am careful not to confuse my audience by using a name without any explanation. This adds a touch of formality, of distance, to my writing.

In my final year of high school, I took a course in expository writing. I had intentionally put off taking this class, which I usually called the "dreaded Expo," until my senior year because I was terrified to take a class that was all about writing.

It turned out that the dreaded Expo wasn't really too bad. I actually liked the class, and I learned that writing is not *always* dreadful. I wrote some really good papers in that class and some really bad ones, too. But my absolute worst piece was the essay I wrote for my University of Vermont application.

One of our assignments for Expo was to write a practice essay for a college application. Since I had already sent in my UVM application, I just handed in a copy of the essay I had written. My teacher, not knowing I had actually sent in this essay, ripped it apart in front of the class, as an example of what *not* to write for a college essay. I was in tears the minute I left the classroom, convinced I would never get into college. Here's why:

> My main reason for wanting to attend this college is to expand my education and therefore develop a satisfying career.
>
> At this time, I have many interests, but no single outstanding interest. I would like to attend this college because of its wide range of areas that interest me both academically and socially. I hope that by attending this college I will be able to use its wide range of curriculum to develop a single strong interest. . . .

The subject of the essay was "why you want to go to this college and why you should be accepted." My teacher wrote four comments on my paper. "This is awfully *vague*," "vague," "such as?" and "repetitive and vague."

I think the reason I wrote such a "vague" essay was that I was uncomfortable writing about myself. There is a sense of discomfort in much of my writing. Even in my diary (I call it "the book" because I hate the word diary) where I write my most personal things, my words often sound stiff and contrived. My writing there is always controlled. Whenever I was mad or excited I would always express it in the size of my letters or with exclamation marks. In my life too, I tend to control my emotions, to hold a lot of my feelings inside: especially negative feelings. I don't express sadness very openly, and if I'm angry, the object of my anger rarely knows it, and I just hold it in until the feeling blows away.

Here is what I wrote in the book at age 11 about the traumatic death of a kitten. Don't laugh. People always laugh when they hear about this, but it's not funny, it's very sad.

> August 9, 1979
> Last night Wellington got killed. He was in the dryer when mom turned it on. At least he died fast and we can keep Mish.

When first considering what I would write about in this paper, I thought I might be able to get some good information from the book. I sat down and read the thing from cover to cover, entries from 1978 until 1989, although the entries in the last several years are few and far between. After all that reading, I felt I owed an entry. So this is what I wrote:

> November, 1989
> I have to write a paper on my personal voice—an analysis of it. So I just read this whole book hoping to get some good material but the whole thing is mostly the ravings of a lunatic.

And it is too. I really thought that the book would be the best place to see my true voice. But I'm having a hard time with that because in most of the book I am a stranger. Now I want to say that what I wrote was not my true voice, but how could it not be? I have mentally divided the book up into three categories: the obligation entries (including the death of the cat entry), the hate entries, and the high school entries. The obligation entries evolved somehow into hate entries like this one:

> February 23, 1979
> Today was terrible. I went to the Wheelers. I hate Dawn and Dawn hates me. There were these dumb girls there named Heather + Holly. Now my parents won't let us see "Hulk" on TV. My mom gets to see "Roots." Why can't we see "Hulk"? My braces don't hurt any more.

This series of unfortunate entries are probably the most emotional things I ever wrote. Even here though, it still sounds as if I am writing for someone other than myself. I say "*my* mom" rather than just "mom," and I'm careful in my attempt to define "Hulk" and "Roots" as television shows with the use of quotation marks. Pretty academic considering the writing was completely personal.

The high school entries are unmentionable, and if I wasn't such a pack rat, I'd throw them out. I refuse to quote any of these entries, but this is what I wrote about them in May of 1989:

> I wonder if it's normal for almost this entire book to revolve around the male sex? . . . Why not write about my friends or my family or school or my apartment or the sunset or my car or exercising or any other thing that is important to me. Writing might just not be for me—seems like pictures are better. . . .

My voice starts to change slightly during my senior year in high school. I become a little more present in my writing and start to relax a little. The following passage was written in a journal for an American Writers class:

Nov. 5, 1985
I really admire Thoreau for what he did about his taxes. . . . I respect and agree with Thoreau that he shouldn't pay his taxes when he doesn't agree with what they are for. I also know that if I was in the same situation, I wouldn't be able to do what he did. I would pay my taxes so that I wouldn't have to have the difficulties that not paying the tax would present. I'm not proud of that but I know that's what I would do.

The best paper that I wrote my senior year was called "Oceanside." It was the first piece of writing that I actually remember feeling good about. The description was of a house on the Outer Banks of North Carolina that my family stayed in for two weeks one summer.

The white and gold tiles on the kitchen floor are cool to the feet. The cupboard shelves are full of plates, glasses, mugs, bowls, and cooking utensils. The dishes from breakfast are stacked in the sink while the supper dishes still sit, sparkling clean and untouched in the dishwasher. Sand, collecting in the corners of the room, is hardly noticed and the broom and dustpan are left stationary in the corner. A note to all late sleepers says "Gone to the beach. It's beautiful out!" The radio plays soft music from "Beach 95, F." A few smile-faced magnets gaze cheerfully from the refrigerator door.

It's interesting that I do not physically exist in this paper even though the place I described was very special to me. I said that the tiles were cool to "the" feet, but they were really cool to *my* feet. It's as if this robotic eye is viewing the surroundings and putting the data down on paper. A note has been written but who is the author? Who is the reader? I suppose the reader must be the same person who is listening to the radio and I suppose that person is me, but the magnets in this are more alive than I am.

Just last spring I wrote another memory description of a favorite place: Montmartre, in Paris. This is how I began my paper:

I smile uncomfortably, shake my head and try to blend into the crowd, but I am stopped by a persistent hand on my elbow. I had made the mistake of looking a little too interested in this particular artist's charcoal portraits. "Come, sit. Let me draw you," he insists in a heavy French accent. I ask how much. Three hundred francs. I do some quick mental arithmetic; 300 francs equals 30 pounds, which equals about 40 to 45 dollars. I shake my head, more emphatically this time, and start to back away. "Okay, 200 francs. Just for you, 200 francs." But I really want to look around first, at the other artists. "No good," he says, "now 200 francs, if you leave, you have to pay 300. I am good. If you don't like it, you don't pay . . . huh? Where are you from? America! Ah, rich American, come . . . come on," he beckons. I look to my friend for help, but she just smiles and shrugs.

I am tempted. Perhaps because I would like my portrait done, but it's more likely that I'm flattered because he is the first Parisian who had treated me with anything better than annoyed indifference.

This was scary for me to put myself so fully into that paper, but since then I've done it more and more. I'm realizing that it's OK to be expressive and emotional in writing. And in person too. If I could write poems I would. Lots of times when something really strikes me, I want to write a poem or draw something to convey how I feel. But if I ever start doing that, some more rational part of me springs out, and I tear up the paper.

Last weekend I did something weird. On Saturday morning I went with Nancy to Swanton to see a fortune-teller. The fortune-teller is an elderly Abenake Indian woman. She is very poor and living in a run-down house behind a block of warehouses, with nothing but trailers for neighboring houses. We each paid $15 for her to read us through a regular deck of cards. Don't conjure up an image of her as a gypsy-type with a crystal ball in front of her; she's very normal looking, and we sat at her kitchen table with the breakfast leftovers still on it.

Nancy went first and got a pretty accurate reading. Then I went. Now, I don't necessarily believe in everything she said to me, but I don't not believe it either. You see, she's not really a fortune-teller, but more of a present-teller. Either way, it was pretty amazing. This woman told me things about my life that there is no way she could have known because she didn't even know my name when I went in to see her. She started my reading by talking about—of all things—men. She described my relationship with my old boyfriend to a tee and told me that he was BAD for me (which I had already discovered), and I should send him to "you know where" (which I have already done), but reinforcement is always good.

She described my brother as a devil but a good devil (which he is) and saw a lot of darkness around my sister (which there is). She asked me why I stopped playing the flute (which I did) and told me I should start again (something I have considered). She told me that whatever is bothering my mother is not my fault (it's not) and that I shouldn't be worried because everything will be OK.

What made me angry was coming home from Swanton and being very excited about what had happened and telling another roommate some of the things the woman said and having him say, scornfully—well of course she just made an easy guess—or something to that effect. Why can't people believe in things that are a little stranger than normal? Why does everything have to be so rational all the time? Life is interesting because of things that are magical and strange and unusual and really beautiful or really ugly, and it upsets me when people say That's stupid or That's weird and turn up their noses.

I think in this country, and in a lot of other places, people are often raised thinking it is bad to be emotional. If you feel something or write something or say something that veers away from the traditional, then you are making a big commitment to being "radical" like that and setting yourself up for criticism. The reason I struggle with my writing is because what I write is usually not exactly what I feel. Instead, it is what I feel is a proper presentation of what I feel. It's the same thing as smiling when someone asks you how you are and just saying Good, thanks, when you are actually feeling lousy or even when you are feeling really great.

I have done a lot of growing up in the past few years, and my writing has grown with me. I have become a more outgoing and expressive person. I am happier and more comfortable with myself, and my writing shows this. In fact, just the other day, I wrote a poem. And I didn't tear it up.

Sharing Ideas

- Audrey Brown talks about different attitudes she has toward numbers and words. Sometimes I hear individuals talking about themselves as number people or word people. Is that distinction meaningful to or necessary for you? What do you mean when you make it?

- Have you ever found yourself in Audrey's situation, keeping your emotions out of your paper? Why did you do that? Were you worried, as she was, about your audience? Did you use any of the same techniques—passive voice, avoidance of first person, the robotic, reporting eye? Did you use any other techniques?

- Audrey talks about her struggles to achieve a personally satisfying writer's voice; still, I think her essay certainly sounds like someone talking to someone else. Can you describe her voice? How does it strike you? Whom do you think she imagined as the audience for her piece? Why?

- In Audrey's essay, what do you think about her visit to the fortune-teller and her thoughts about emotion and writing?

- I noticed that Audrey mentions the importance journal writing had for her as she traveled to other countries and experienced different cultures. Have you had similar experiences? Have you kept a journal? With what results?

17

The Friendly Neighborhood Writing Center—Your Personal Trainer for Writing

Katherine Holahan and Elizabeth Boquet

Katherine Holahan is a recent graduate of Fairfield University. She became involved in the Writing Center her freshman year, long before she declared her English major. Since graduating she has moved back to her home state of Massachusetts, where she is attempting to organize her future.

Elizabeth Boquet is a Professor of English and Director of the Writing Center at Fairfield University in Fairfield, Connecticut. Born and raised in Louisiana, she is still adjusting to New England winters. Her favorite things are boat rides, backyard cookouts, and long summer days.

Both writers wish to thank their helpful readers (Sally Stratakis-Allen, Kathleen Doherty, and Tara Cushman) and Geena DeFrancesco, their favorite tutee.

Welcome to the writing center! You're probably already aware that writing is a process, that successful writers use a variety of writing strategies, and that all writers need readers to help gauge the impact of their words on an audience, but you may wonder what exactly a writing center is. A writing center is a place where writers write, where readers read, and where writers and readers talk together about things like process, strategies, and audience. A writing center is all this and more. It is also a place where words rule, a place where magnetic poetry scrolls across the filing cabinets and inspirational quotes line the walls, a place where students rethink their papers as they serenely drag a rake through a mini Zen garden, and a place where tutors and students take a break from an intense writing session by blowing off a little steam with a rousing game of crocodile dentist. In other words, it's not your college classroom; it's someplace else.

What Is a Writing Center, Anyway?

Writing centers are designed to respond to the needs of students, so writing centers are different from one campus to the next. But all writing centers, no matter how different they are, share some common features:

All writing centers have writing tutors. These writing tutors have both training and experience in working with students at all stages of their writing. Some writing centers are staffed by undergraduate peer tutors—students like you—who have taken part in workshops or classes designed to sharpen their writing and response skills. Other writing centers are staffed by graduate students who have completed their undergraduate degrees and are now pursuing a highly specialized field of study. Still other writing centers are staffed by faculty members who tutor in the writing center in addition to teaching their regular classes. Many writing centers will have a mix of undergraduate, graduate student, and faculty tutors. You also might be surprised (and happy) to learn that not all tutors are English majors. Many writing centers consider diversity of academic disciplines an essential element of what they offer. So don't be surprised if a history major sits down to tutor you on your nursing care plan or if a Spanish major works through Heidegger with you for that big philosophy paper. While some writing centers try to match tutors to disciplines or classes, others (like ours) think random hook-ups are part of the fun. We encourage students to find tutors whose coaching styles best match their own learning styles, rather than worry about disciplinary expertise. (We'll have more to say later on selecting your tutor.) Tutors might meet with you in different ways. Most places offer what's called face-to-face tutoring, where you sit down next to a tutor and focus on your writing. In addition to face-to-face tutoring, however, many schools offer on-line tutoring, some even in real-time chats. So you're likely to find everything from hour-long sessions to instant messaging on grammar questions available to you through your college writing center.

The writing tutors will work with you at any stage in your writing. Do you have an assignment but don't know where to start? Walk into the writing center with nothing written, tell the tutor you'd like to work on generating some ideas, and watch the tutor's eyes light up. Or are you the type of writer who generates lots of words quickly but then has trouble organizing them? The tutors in the writing center can help you think about how to shape your ideas. Does your teacher keep talking about "coherence," but you can't figure out whether your text "flows"? The tutors can talk with you about the internal movement of your writing. Do you (admit it) love to hear your words read out loud? Do you get excited knowing that the ideas that were rolling around in your head are now out in the world? The tutors get excited about that stuff too. We promise.

Talk is a key feature of any writing center session. For a meeting that's about writing, you might be surprised by how much talking goes on in a writing center session. Most of that talking will probably be done by you, as the tutor prompts you with questions, guides you through your thinking and writing, and shares observations and reflections with you—about writing in general, about the specific writing task that you're working on, even about negotiating the demands of college life.

Why Should *You* Go to the Writing Center?

You've probably figured out some of the basics of college, like why you should go to class or why you should go to the bookstore and the library, but you might be wondering why you should go to a writing center. We thought we'd let some of our regular writing center users tell us why they chose to come to the writing center for the first time and why they keep coming back for more. We've grouped their responses into some common categories and summarized them below.

Adjusting to College Life

If you haven't already noticed, college is all about adjustment. The biggest and most obvious change (which may be the one you're going through right now) is the move from high school to college. Everyone warned you that expectations in college would be different, but no one could tell you exactly how. Now you're trying to figure it out for yourself. One of our writers described it as the Fear Factor. You're buried under the piles of books you lugged back from the bookstore, and you're feeling the weight of your initial writing assignments. For the first time, maybe, you have to come up with your own ideas for your papers. You also have lots of other smaller, less obvious adjustments throughout your college years: Negotiating different expectations in writing requirements from one class to the next; experiencing what it's like to write in your major for the first time; figuring out how to manage a research writing task when you think of yourself as more of a creative writer (or vice versa). Our writing center users appreciate the tutors' abilities to work on the things that students think are important. Also, as Geena, one of our regulars, said, "Coming into the writing center for the first time was intimidating. I assumed the tutors would be like teachers, but they're not; they are students just like us. Many of them had the same teachers I have and they knew what the teachers were expecting. The tutors always guide me to creating a paper that I am proud of. And they are happy to help someone in a position that they were once in themselves."

Adjusting to American Life

As we mentioned earlier, college is a time of huge transitions. Few students have bigger transitions to make than international students studying in a foreign country. Whether you speak English as a first language or as a foreign language, if you are studying in a place other than your country of origin, writing centers are terrific resources for all sorts of information that might help you in your courses and in your adjustment to a new country. Writing center tutors frequently work with students from other countries, and both tutors and students learn from those experiences. For example, one of our favorite sessions recently was with a student who came in with an assignment for a history course. To write the paper, the student needed to consider the class readings in light of the upcoming Columbus Day holiday. While the student had a good grasp of the assigned readings, she didn't know what Columbus Day was, so she really couldn't engage in the kind of analysis necessary to complete the paper. She and the tutor talked and researched Columbus Day together; both of them got a history lesson that day!

Offering a Friendly Focus

We're tutors, but we're students, too. We've been through it all—the room-mates from hell, the crunch weeks when it seems your professors have assigned papers and tests just to stress you out, and the food in the cafeteria that makes you hungry for home. Tutors realize that all these factors affect your personal writing process and that sometimes it's hard to disconnect yourself from the flurry and flutter long enough to construct a coherent sentence. They know that's when it helps to have another perspective. The writing center can be a world unto itself, a secret vacuum floating within the tumult—a center with one aim: to create coherent prose (or poetry) from the chaos that is the student brain. This is where the give-and-take of a session comes into play. In a writing center session, students have the opportunity to explain not only their assignments but what (if anything) has been holding them back. We can focus, organize, and reorganize ideas, thoughts, or writings with ease, because it always helps to have someone offer another perspective. Tutors are like Vanna White: We can showcase your thoughts, holding them up for you so you can fill in the blanks. Perhaps we can provide a few categories to help stimulate the creative juices. We won't give the answers (because Vanna never tells), just encouraging smiles. You and your tutor will get to know, challenge, and (hopefully) trust one another. Believe it or not, it is ridiculously rewarding—for both the tutor and the student—when we make a breakthrough. That's because writing center sessions are a two-way street; when students put forth the effort, tutors like nothing more than to help them out. This is one college relationship guaranteed not to cause stress. We'll never "need to have a talk" or keep you from "branching out and meeting other people" during your four years in college. The more the merrier, we say!

Working with Professors

We know, we know—your professor has an *office*, and worst of all, she wants you to go there. During her office hours. With your paper. To talk about your ideas. Have no fear: your friendly writing center tutors are here to help. The whole meeting-with-the-professor thing is new to you, but the tutors in the writing center can help you to get a handle on it. Sometimes we offer a sort of dress rehearsal (though baseball caps and flip-flops are dressy enough for us)—to help you think through your questions, your frustrations, your likes and dislikes—before you meet with your professor. Other times we help you to get some distance from your own work—after receiving a particularly disappointing grade, for example—so you can separate your substantive questions about a professor's comments from simple complaints about your grade. Still other times, we might meet with you after you've received a grade and comments to help you act upon your professor's suggested strategies for revision or try to figure out what it is the professor wants you to do.

Helping Writers for Whom English Is a Foreign Language

Whether you are an international student for whom English is a foreign language or you grew up in this country but speak a language other than English at home, your college or university writing center has resources that can help you make all the transitions we've already discussed and respond to some of your concerns about doing college-level academic work in English. Writing center tutors aren't just people who are interested in the English language; we are people who are interested in languages in general. We think it's amazing that you can study biology in your second (or third) language while we struggle with it in our first. Maybe you're a student who loves to write in your native language, but you find it frustrating that you can't manage the same degree of fluency with the English language. Maybe you feel pretty confident with your English speaking skills, but you find the formality of written English confusing. You wonder what a thesis-driven essay is, but lots of native English speakers have the same kind of questions. If pesky idiomatic expressions drive you crazy, come to the writing center. And don't forget, since writing centers involve a lot of talk between tutors and students, you'll also get a bonus: lots of conversational practice as you're focusing on your writing.

Writing for Personal Enrichment

Life in writing centers revolves around words—words on paper, words in our brains, and words on the tips of our tongues. The beauty of writing is that it doesn't have to be confined to the academic world; not all writing has to be done for papers or tests. Believe it or not, over the course of your college career, you will find reasons to write outside of class, times when you will be motivated by more than an assignment that needs to be turned in to your professor. Really. It's true. And your friendly neighborhood writing center can help you with that writing as well. Some of that writing may be pretty task oriented: application essays, personal statements, résumés, and internship reports. Some of it may be just for fun: If you enjoy writing poetry, see whether your writing center sponsors poetry slams. Budding fiction writer? Find out whether your writing center sponsors writers' groups or publishes collections of student work. And if you're truly interested, check into what you need to do to become a tutor in the writing center at your school. It's such a great place to be—why not get paid for it?

How Should You Prepare for a Session?

Making an appointment at the writing center shouldn't be a stressful situation, but it does require a little forethought. To the preparation question, we answer: Think, bring, and don't worry!

Think back over your course and figure out how your particular assignment fits into the greater scheme of the class. Is your professor trying to make you analyze something in particular? How has your class been structured thus far? What kind of things have you talked about in class that might have some relevance to this assignment? These are some of the things that your tutor will ask you about. The two of you will be trying to figure out the answers together, but it's always good to start thinking ahead of time.

Jot down some notes if it helps you feel more prepared. If your head starts to spin, take a deep breath—we're here to help! Think about some of the ways you like to work. Do these methods seem to be working for you, or would you like to try something new? If you always write your first draft on paper, would you like to try working on the computer? If you like to talk out your ideas, would you like to try writing everything down? Feel free to let your tutor know either way. Having comparable or disparate writing methods can teach you both something new. In the writing center, we love it when writing and learning happily coexist.

Bring anything that makes you comfortable (no pets, please). Bring the syllabus for your class, the specific assignment sheet, and any relevant books or previous assignments. Of course, if you have a draft (rough or otherwise), bring that along, too. Favorite pens, notebooks, and laptops can make the writing experience that much more comfortable, so always feel free to bring these.

Don't worry! The most important thing to remember about the writing center is that we're here to help. If you have no idea where to start or are so bogged down by your ideas that you think you will never write again, don't give up. Nobody is a perfect writer. Everyone needs some help in the planning and/or implementing stages—take advantage of a helping hand.

When It's Over . . .

Tutors will offer you a variety of strategies during writing center sessions that should help you extend and revise your work once your session is over. Your tutor might have taken notes while you brainstormed aloud; the two of you might have mapped out ideas on a sheet of construction paper; maybe you engaged in brief writing during your tutoring session; or you might have written a descriptive outline that will help make your paper more organized and coherent. If you were tutored on-line, then you will have a transcript of the entire session to refer to as you revise. Most tutors will also spend some time at the end of the session (face-to-face or on-line) briefly summarizing the session and helping you plan your next steps.

Many of the students we work with also say that the environment in the writing center has taught them to change their approach to writing. Writing centers are places where writers try out ideas. Some of those ideas work; some don't. That's the process. Writing centers are places where even small successes are celebrated because sometimes those improvements are the lasting ones. Developing skills in writing, like developing skills in any other area, takes time and interest. Time and interest are two of the many things writing tutors can offer you.

Finally, speaking of interest, we would encourage you to be an active participant in your writing center sessions. You are in charge! (How often do you get to say that in school?) You get to decide when to visit the writing center, which tutors you like to work with, and what you want to work on. But your active involvement doesn't stop there. The more engaged you are in the work of the session, the more willing you are to fully participate with your tutor, the more likely it is that you will leave the session prepared to make even more progress on your own. One of our students described her writing center tutor as a "personal trainer for her writing." Think about what you might want out of your personal trainer: Someone with habits very much like yours, so that she will understand your roadblocks? Or someone whose habits are very different from your own, so that he can offer you ideas you wouldn't have thought of? Someone with whom you might meet only occasionally, just to check in? Or someone you'll see weekly, to help keep you on track? These are your decisions to make.

Now You're on Your Own

No two writing centers are exactly alike, so we encourage you to find out what you can about the writing center at your own school. Maybe you got a brochure or a bookmark (here at Fairfield, we give out magnets) with your orientation materials. Maybe your college or university writing center has a website that you can check out for more information. (We've listed a few sample websites, including our own, at the end of this chapter so you can compare for yourself.) Your best option might be to find out where the writing center on your campus is located and to go there directly. Check the place out. Talk to some of the tutors. Try out a session, now that you have an idea of what's involved. We bet you'll find the writing center a laid-back, welcoming place.

Appendix

Below you'll find some of our go-to websites. These sites offer everything from tutor profiles and writing center mission statements to grammar hints and documentation information. From these sites, you can link to others, so you'll be totally writing center networked. Enjoy!

http://owl.english.purdue.edu/handouts/index2.html

The Purdue University writing center webpage includes practical grammar and punctuation handouts for both native and nonnative English speakers. These exercises can help boost your confidence about specific grammatical features of your writing.

http://writingcenter.usu.edu/

Utah State University's writing center website contains information helpful for students who have never been to a writing center session before. It incorporates background information on what to expect when coming to a writing center, including a mission statement, tutor humor, and resources for ESL students.

www.muhlenberg.edu/students/writing/basics.html

This Muhlenberg College website has important foundational information about different writing approaches. It gives guidance about essay organization and explanations about different essay styles, including personal essays, interpretive essays, and critiques.

www.evergreen.edu/writingcenter/

Evergreen State College's website includes links to the writing center's mission statement, opportunities to meet its staff members, and its Top Ten Writing Center Myths. Students can access writing and grammar handouts and MLA and APA citation formats and can participate in word games like scrabblelicious.

www.xu.edu/writing_center/index.html

Xavier University's writing center website contains grammar tips and documentation information for students. It also includes a webpage that answers the question, "Why Go to the Writing Center?"

www.fairfield.edu/writingcenter

No explanation necessary—you've heard enough from us already.

Sharing Ideas

- Locate the writing center at your college or university. Make a reconnaissance visit to discover as much as you can before you visit with a writing assignment. For example, are the tutors students? Graduate students? Special staff? Can you walk in without an appointment? Do tutors fix grammar, spelling, and usage errors? How long do tutors spend with each writer (thirty minutes? As long as needed?)? What is the environment like?

- Once you've become a writing center regular, describe your favorite tutor. What are the qualities you appreciate in your tutor?

- Visit some of the writing centers that are available to you on the Internet (see the URL addresses in this chapter's appendix). How does an on-line writing center compare with the one on your campus?

- Besides your professor, who regularly reads and gives you feedback on your writing? How would you characterize the response you get from that person or those people?

- Make a list of all of the writing you know you will do this semester. Be sure to include non-class related items like résumés, cover letters, newspaper articles, fiction, and poetry. Which of these pieces could most benefit from a writing center tutor's assistance? What kind of response would be most helpful to you?

- Did your high school have a writing center available to students? If so, did you ever use it? How did it compare with your college or university writing center?

- Would you ever consider becoming a tutor in the writing center at your college or university? If so, what is appealing to you about that job? If not, why not?

18

The Cupped Hand and the Open Palm

Hephzibah Roskelly

Hephzibah Roskelly teaches a variety of writing courses at University of North Carolina–Greensboro, from freshman composition to graduate theory. She writes about composition and reading theory and has published a book with Eleanor Kutz on the theory and practice of teaching English, *An Unquiet Pedagogy*. She received her Ph.D. from the University of Louisville in 1985 and remains an avid basketball fan.

When I was in first grade, I was a bluebird. Funny that I remember that after so many years. Or maybe not so funny. I suspect you remember your label too. I remember being proud of being in the group I was in. Somehow everybody in Mrs. Cox's class knew it was pretty awful to be a yellowbird, common to be a redbird, and therefore best to be a bluebird. One student of mine remembers her experience in first grade this way: "My first-grade teacher waited for us to make a mistake in our group and then she'd pounce. She always stood behind our desks. That's because I wasn't in the fast reading group. I was in the bears." She laughs. "To this day I think bears are stupid." For Susan, like for many of us, the first-grade reading group is our first real experience with group work, and for many of us, like for Susan, it's not remembered fondly. Especially if you happened to be a yellowbird or a bear.

By third or fourth grade, though, your early memory may have dimmed a little as group work began to get less attention. You and your fellow students were "tracked" by this point, grouped into classes according to the results of standardized achievement tests, so the need for "ability level" groups like the blue/red/yellowbirds within the classroom became less pressing. And by the time you entered middle school or seventh grade, probably there wasn't much group work at all. In its place was "seat work," which meant some sort of writing. If you were like most students, you wrote alone. Nobody ever saw your writing except your teacher and, very rarely, other students, if they happened to look at the bulletin board where the teacher occasionally posted the "A" papers. If you were writing answers to questions or coming up with ideas in class, you were often reminded to "cover your work" so that your friend in the desk across from you wouldn't be tempted to copy. So you used a sheet of paper to cover your writing, or you hid your marks behind a wall you made with your hand, cupping it to keep what you wrote private. Covering your work became so natural that you might have even cupped your hand anytime you wrote *anything* in school—the beginning of a short story, a letter to the editor of your school paper or to your girlfriend—the kind of writing where "copying" would never occur. But you continued to cup your hand because by this time you had gotten the message. Writing is solitary, individual, something others can take away from you if you don't keep it from them, and something others don't see except when it's "clean."

These elementary school lessons about groups and about writing are deeply imbedded, so much so that you may react with suspicion or even hostility now when your writing class—a freshman composition course or some other—encourages group work. Your past experience with group work in reading hasn't led you to feel that it will do much more than put you in some category you'd rather not be in, and past experience with writing suggests that sharing your work with someone else is foolish or illegal. Your college, after all, probably has an honor code that says something about giving and receiving help. Why should a composition teacher force the connection between writing and the small group, asking you to come up with ideas together, make plans together, read and revise together, and, strangest of all, write together?

I try to answer that question here. One of the reasons that group work fails in the classroom is that neither our past experiences in the reading group nor those with the writing lesson have given us much of a rationale for working in groups. When a person doesn't know why she's doing something, doing it seems relatively useless. Working in small groups, even though it's an idea touted by theorists and teachers in composition, is limited in actual practice for just this reason: Students and sometimes their teachers don't know why they're doing what they're doing when they meet in the small group. Just as important, students and their teachers aren't aware of why they're often so disposed against working in groups. I describe what underlies these attitudes so that you can begin to understand why group work fails sometimes and why it's so potentially useful for your development as a writer.

Why Group Work Fails

I asked a group of students who will be student teaching in high school English classrooms this semester to use their own past experiences and their developing ideas about teaching to speculate about what makes groups fail in the classroom. Their list may mesh with your own feelings about the small group in the classroom.

Too Many Chefs; No Chefs; Untrustworthy Chefs

Students mentioned the possibility of the "one member who dominates," who "thinks he knows it all," who "can't let the group decide." Or the possibility of having several members who all wanted to lead. What some described as a domineering personality in the group, others saw as responsible. "Somebody always ends up doing the most work. And that's usually me," says Beth, one of my first-year students at the beginning of the semester. "When I was in high school there were always a few who didn't want to do the work and goofed off, and they left the rest of us poor slobs to do it." The fear that the work won't be shared but shuffled off to one wimpy or guilty person is echoed in comments about who's prepared, who volunteers, who shows up. A student teacher reports on her experience with being given too much responsibility for her group's operation: "My classmates saw me as one of the smart kids and so in groups I was always expected to emerge as a leader and to get things done. There were many times when I felt I was carrying the load."

An even bigger fear about responsibility and personality centers on trust. "I don't know the other people in my group. Why would I want to talk to them about how I feel about anything?" asks a student teacher. And one freshman writer writing in her journal before her group met for the first time writes about her fears that the group won't be responsible to her: "What if they think my ideas are terrible? What if they think I'm stupid?"

Chaos Rules

At first, the fear of spinning out of control in the group may seem primarily to be a teacher complaint rather than a student one. And it's true that the fear that there will be too much talk or that the talk will quickly get "off task" does prevent teachers from using group work at all, or they use it only sparingly and with rigid guidelines to control it. But students fear loss of control as well. When students are conditioned to the quiet classroom where only one person has the right to talk (the teacher) and the rest have the right to remain silent (the students)—and this is the typical classroom—students aren't comfortable with a lot of noise and movement either. "It gets too disorganized," one student lamented. "I'm an organized person. And I don't like hearing what the other groups are saying."

If You Want Something Done Well—

One student teacher remembers her 101 class doing revision of essays in small groups:

> We had writing groups to comment on each other's papers. This was fine except that no one would make any comments about my papers. I guess because my grammar is sound they couldn't find anything to say because they didn't know what else to look for.
>   A typical group dialogue went something like this:
>
>> *First person*: I don't see anything wrong with your paper.
>> *Second person*: Me neither.
>> *Third person*: Yeah, it's a good paper. You'll get an A.
>> *Me*: Well, what did you like about it?
>> *First person*: Everything. The whole paper is fine.
>> *Second person*: I liked your topic. How did you think of such a good topic?
>> *Third person*: Yeah. You'll get an A.
>
> Not only did this fail to give me any useful feedback, but it also put me in an awkward position when the time came for me to comment on others' papers. They were so full of admiration and praise for mine, how could I say anything negative about theirs? So a vicious cycle where no one benefited was created.

Related to this feeling of the group not helping because no one knows what to do within the group is the feeling that the work they do is not very important. "It's a waste of time. I think teachers have us get in groups when they don't have anything left to say and don't want to let the class go. We just read the paper in my last class. Or maybe talked for five minutes and then read the paper." Another writer says, "I kept changing what my group said or changing what I said to match them. It would have taken a lot less time and been better just to do it myself."

Why—and How—a Group Works

These students tell the story of why group work fails in the classroom. The stories reveal deep and often unconscious beliefs about how the writing class is supposed to proceed, about how writers are supposed to work. The beliefs come from those old experiences with reading groups and with writing. But they also come from what we've all imagined about how people learn in school. School, we've determined, is competitive, not cooperative, and therefore it's the individual not the group effort that counts. And counting is what school is all about. Who has the most points, the most stars, the most As? Who's the bluebird? The fact is we assume that effort can only be measured by a grade and that a grade can't fairly be given to a group. So attempts to work as a group seem futile and unnecessary given what we've assumed school is all about—keeping not sharing, winning not collaborating, cupping the hand, not opening the palm.

If it were true that people learn to think and write primarily alone—in solitary confinement so to speak—it might also be true that group work is wasted effort, or unhelpful or too chaotic or too hard. But the truth is that people don't learn—in fact, can't learn much at all—in isolation. They learn *by engaging in the world.* They come to terms with what's around them, understand it, through sound and movement, through talk. A child who never hears talk, as tragic cases show, never talks or talks only very little. Talking presumes at least one listener or commenter. Group work, then, because it encourages engagement—talk and reflection and response—mirrors the way people learn things inside and outside the classroom, the ways in which they make sense out of the world.

So conversation, communication with others, is vital to our understanding of others and ourselves. And people can't communicate unless they listen— work toward a shared notion about how to proceed. Do you know the movie *Airplane*? It's actually one long joke about how communication gets muddled when that shared notion doesn't exist.

> "These people need to be taken to a hospital," the doctor says.
>
> Walking up, stewardess Julie looks at them. "What is it?" she asks.
>
> The doctor is impatient. "It's a big white building with sick people in it. But that's not important right now." Or:
>
> "Surely you can't mean it," Julie says.
>
> "I mean it," the doctor says. "And stop calling me Shirley."

Julie and the doctor don't communicate because they haven't decided on a shared basis for their talk. They mistake words and ideas and don't care enough (because then it wouldn't be funny) to get it right before they go on. In the class-room group, when shared work and talk do take place, real communication can occur. People learn to listen to one another and use one another's talk to test and explore their own talk more fully. This notion of learning and understanding as essentially shared rather than possessed by one individual can be tested using a little game I came up with called Trivial Literacy (after E. D. Hirsch's best-selling book *Cultural Literacy: What Every American Needs to Know*, 1987):

1. Choose part of Hirsch's list (or any list of words). A part of one list might read something like *hambone, harridan, Holden Caulfield, Huguenot.*

2. Mark every word you don't know or can't guess about.

3. In your group, see how many marks you can eliminate by getting information from others.

4. In class, see how many marks remain when the group pools all information.

5. Are there any words left? Guess about them. Ask somebody outside class.

You know what will happen before you do the test. You find out more and more by talking. You hear the contexts people have for knowing things like *Harlem Globetrotters*, and you bring up the context you have for knowing *Huguenot*. In other words, you'll illustrate how your knowledge gets stronger, better developed, more insightful, and more complete the more you combine your knowledge with others'. This combining always works better if it's informal, conversational, unpressured, in some way equal. That's why Trivial Literacy usually teaches so much. Because it's a game— it's fun, and the stakes aren't high. Group work needs to be nurtured because it works, often playfully, to encourage the development of individual thought.

All writers need to hear their own voices, but I think they can only hear them clearly when they find them in the chorus of lots of other voices. Otherwise, for many writers the writing is hollow, without a sense of commitment or *investment* that characterizes the voices of confident, effective writers. Kenneth Bruffee (1984), who's a composition teacher and writer, makes this connection between the social and the individual explicit. "Thought is an artifact created by social interaction," he says. "We can think because we can talk, and we think in ways we have learned to talk" (640). We're stronger and better developed individual thinkers and writers because we interact with people in groups.

Partially because so much of writing is done in silence and solitude, college writers often fear the investment required in writing. They don't trust their voices; the only thing they do trust is the certain knowledge that they will be graded on what that voice is able to produce. They want control, and so they ask, "How long does this have to be?" or "Can we use first person?" And they want to minimize risk, so they count words and number of footnotes, use simple sentences and forms they've read, and write with passive verbs that take them out of the writing. "It can be seen that Jane Austen was expressing feminist concerns," they might say, as a way of avoiding a declaration that *they've* been the ones to see it. They avoid the personal commitment that writing requires because it seems too dangerous to risk. It's as though you walked into a dark auditorium to speak to a group, knowing they were out there waiting but not knowing how many there were, how big the room was, or if you had a microphone. You'd probably clear your throat a few times, and test the sound, but if you could see nothing but your speech, and you knew you were being judged each time you opened your mouth, you might likely be stunned into silence.

Your small group functions as a visible audience, a literal sounding board for your voice, and, as Bruffee (1984) and others suggest, a source of your growing knowledge of the world. As such, the group alleviates the sense of powerlessness in writing (and thinking) that so many student writers feel and thus reduces the fear of commitment and investment by helping you to hear your voice clearly.

The Group at Work: First-Year Writers Writing Together

The group lessens writers' deep and real fear of taking responsibility for what's on the page in lots of ways—by supporting and strengthening individual writers' attempts, providing other perspectives on ideas, and sharing responsibility. All of these benefits for the writer occur when groups do all kinds of activities together—read, comment, discuss, plan, interpret—but they're most visible and dramatic when groups write together. That's why I'm using this example of the work of the group from my freshman writing course.

Students had been in their 101 class and in groups for five or six weeks when I gave the assignment. They were already comfortable talking about writing and ideas. But this task asked them to go a step further, to write together a short (two- or three-page) collective response to Dorothy Parker's funny and bitter short story "You Were Perfectly Fine." The story is primarily a dialogue between a male and a female character discussing the events at a party the night before. The man's guilt about getting drunk leads him to pretend he remembers a "promise" he's made to the woman, who pretends too in order to hold him to it. After reading the story and doing some quick in-class writing, groups met to begin to decide how they felt about the hungover, guilty man, the seemingly sympathetic woman, and the reasons for the dishonesty in the dialogue. As groups talked, they jotted down notes, often asking one another to repeat or clarify, often interrupting one another with revisions. Some groups talked mostly about the distinctions between social life in the twenties, when the story was written, and the present. Others concentrated on whether it was the man or the woman who was more to blame for the hypocrisy. In the next week and a half, groups argued about men and women and Dorothy Parker, and they worked out ways to allow for varying perspectives and to combine them. Everybody had to negotiate what to say and how to say it, who would write the final copy, where they would revise. All the talk and writing helped them find new ways to make points and gave them finally the new voices they needed to write together.

Here's the first paragraph of one of the papers:

Dorothy Parker's negative view of relationships between men and women is obvious in "You Were Perfectly Fine." We analyzed the story as readers and listeners. Reading it, we felt that the woman was basically honest and the man without credibility. Then listening to it our ideas changed. We got more of a sense of the female being manipulative, romantic and lovesick, but dishonest and deceitful. Peter, the man, seems sensitive and witty, although he ends up being weak and panic-stricken. They seem like real people. Between reading and listening, we've learned that both these characters are dishonest and the relationship probably doesn't stand a chance.

This group ends their piece with a modern tale of deceit that connects romance in Parker's time and in their own, using one of the group member's own experience with deceit in relationships: "It's hard for men and women to be honest with each other whether they live in the Roaring Twenties or right now. Nobody wants to hurt somebody or get hurt themselves."

Notice that the voice in this excerpt is strong. It's controlled; that is, students talk both about the story and the relationships within it, but they feel free enough to be personal too, using the personal pronoun "we" and including a real-life example. There's a clear sense of commitment, interest, and investment in the task.

Collaboration in the group removed or alleviated some of the most debilitating fears about writing for the freshman writers in my class, and this ability of the group to nurture confidence proves how useful the group can be in strengthening the writing process in individual writers. I bet that these fears about writing hit close to your own.

Fear of Starting

Many writers find a blank page of paper so intimidating that they delay beginning as long as possible, searching for the perfect sentence opening, the right title, the best word. But because in the group there were four or five sets of ideas about a particular sentence or a way to open or a character, no writer stared at her paper waiting for inspiration. Inspiration, in fact, came from the talk that went on in the group. "Wait a minute," a group writer would say. "Is this what you said?" And she'd read it back. Another member would say, "It sounds better like this." "And why don't we add something about his past?" another would add. Writing happened so fast that nobody had time to dread not being able to find the idea or the word they wanted to begin.

Fear of Stopping

One first-year writer told me once that her writing was like a faucet with no water pressure—"it won't turn on hard—it just dribbles till it stops." Lots of writers fear that once they get the one good thought said, or the two points down, they'll be left with nothing but dead air time, and that they'll have to fill it with what one of my students calls "marshmallow fluff." But none of the groups had difficulty maintaining writing after they began. The group kept ideas flowing, and changing, and if one person was losing momentum, another would be gathering it. Ken Kesey, the author of *One Flew over the Cuckoo's Nest* (1962) and a teacher, comments on this effect as he describes a collaborative project—an entire novel—that his creative writing class worked on in one group: "Some days you just don't have any new sparkling stuff. But when you got thirteen people, somebody always has something neat and it's as though somebody on your team is on and you're off" (Knox-Quinn 1990, 315).

Fear of Flying

When you have a personal stake in your writing, a belief in your voice and in what you're saying, and a trust in your reader to hear you out, your writing soars. "Everyone can, under certain conditions, speak with clarity and power," composition teacher Peter Elbow says. "These conditions usually involve a topic of personal importance and an urgent occasion." The group helped make the topic personally important since each writer had to justify decisions and ideas to the others, and the occasion was urgent since talk, writing, and real communication were necessary to make decisions in a limited time.

The Group and Changing the World

So what does this long example from my first-year class prove? First, the group validates rather than hurts or lessens the individual voice. The group reinforces the effort involved in writing, talking, by the energy and specificity with which they both support and challenge the writer's thinking. Ken Kesey watched larger perspectives get developed on character and plot in the novel his class wrote: "When we would sit down around the table . . . and start writing our little section, boy you could hear the brain cells popping. They knew they had to write and had to fit in with the other stuff. You couldn't be too much yourself" (Knox-Quinn 1990, 310). But knowing that gives writers a clearer sense of self when they write individually. Not being "too much yourself" is a way of finding what your writing self really is.

"People think it's about competing with each other," Kesey says, speaking of writers and writing. "But the real things that you compete with are gravity and inertia—stagnation" (Knox-Quinn 1990, 315). Writing is not some sort of contest between you and everybody else in the class, with the one who has the best grade—the fewest red marks—winning at the end of it, and that's why the cupped hand is a poor metaphor for what happens when you produce writing in a classroom. The struggle, the contest, is internal, between your desire to talk on paper and your fear or distrust of it. The group helps us compete with the real opponent of creative, critical thought—inertia, the fear of making a move.

As Kesey's work with his creative writers and my work with my first-year writers suggest, the group gives writers the strategies for winning that contest. I remember a few years ago, a freshman writer was writing an essay whose topic turned out to be something about the advantages of watching TV. She was bored with it, but chose it quickly as she was casting about for anything to do. The essay began, "There are many disadvantages to sitting in front of a TV. But there are some positive things about TV." Well, you get the idea. It was uncommitted, with no sense of the personal investment I've been describing, and a feeling in the writing of inertia. The writer wasn't just writing about couch potatoes; she was writing couch potato prose. When she read aloud her opening to her group the next day, she became aware that the group was growing glassy-eyed. She finally gave up. "It's bad, huh?" They laughed. Then she started talking. All of a sudden the couch potato had stood up. She was exploring an idea she was creating for and with her group.

Look back at the idealistic subheading that began this last section. Changing the world seems a pretty grandiose goal for group work, doesn't it? "Freshmen Arrive But Not to Change the World" read the headline in an article this fall in the *Greensboro News and Record* that described how first-year students in colleges across the country didn't believe they would make real changes in the world outside themselves. I think the article was wrong. I think people want to change the worlds they live in, but they feel increasingly powerless to do it. And here's the last and best reason for the group. Because they force writers and thinkers to consciousness, groups foster action and change.

Deciding on what's significant about what you're reading, what you're writing, what you're listening to, what you're writing in a group, is the beginning of an understanding that you make knowledge in the classroom. You don't just find it in a book, and you don't just apply it from a lecture. You *create* it. That's a potentially powerful piece of information. Once you realize that you make knowledge, you see that you can act to change the knowledge that's there. As students of writing, your work in the group can help you become aware that the knowledge of the subject matter you work with, of voice, of forms, and styles, can be determined by you and those around you. The more your group meets and talks about reading, writing, and ideas, the more your group collaborates, the more *authoring* you do. What seat work and the bluebirds taught you to see as private and unique the group can help you recognize as also shared and social. And that realization really can help you make a difference in the world around you and within you.

Works Cited

Bruffee, Kenneth (1984). "Collaborative Learning and the Conversation of Mankind." *College English, 46,* 635–652.

Hirsh, E. D. (1987). *Cultural Literacy: What Every American Needs to Know*. Boston: Houghton Mifflin.

Kesey, Ken (1962). *One Flew over the Cuckoo's Nest*. New York: New American Library.

Knox-Quinn, Carolyn (1990). "Collaboration in the Writing Classroom: An Interview with Ken Kesey." *College Composition and Communication, 41,* 309–317.

Parker, Dorothy (1942). "You Were Perfectly Fine." *Collected Stories of Dorothy Parker*. New York: Modern Library.

Sharing Ideas

- As a writing student, I've experienced positive and negative writing groups; Hephzibah Roskelly's essay helps me understand why this is so. And, she explains that group work actually doesn't take place all that often. Is that true to your life in school?

- Imagine that you're in a writing group and it's spinning out of control: One member is talking too much, or one member is never prepared, or two members are ignoring you and stranding you with that fourth person who never talks. Still, you believe in groups because last week even your struggling group gave you a great idea for revising your paper. How might you cope with each of these scenarios (and any other nonworking scenarios you can dream up)?

- For you, what is at stake in your classroom groups?

- Hephzibah claims that groups help writers by giving them voice. Is that true for you and to what degree?

- Can groups be useful even if not every member agrees? In fact, how effective are groups when every member does agree?

- Say that it's Christmas break. You're going home and telling your parents or a good friend about your writing class and writing groups because they've never experienced this method for learning to write.

- Share some tips for sorting out the different advice you receive from peers when sharing ideas or writing in a group.

- If you were able to form a writing group composed of your favorite authors, who would the members be, and how might they get along?

- Before this class, did you align yourself with the cupped hand or the open palm model? Tell some stories.

19

Responding—Really Responding—to Other Students' Writing

Richard Straub

Richard Straub taught courses in writing, rhetoric, and literature at Florida State University. A specialist on reading, evaluating, and responding to student writing, he was from Dunmore, Pennsylvania.

Okay. You've got a student paper you have to read and make comments on for Thursday. It's not something you're looking forward to. But that's alright, you think. There isn't really all that much to it. Just keep it simple. Read it quickly and mark whatever you see. Say something about the introduction. Something about details and examples. Ideas you can say you like. Mark any typos and spelling errors. Make your comments brief. Abbreviate where possible: *awk*, *good intro*, *give ex*, *frag*. Try to imitate the teacher. Mark what he'd mark and sound like he'd sound. But be cool about it. Don't praise anything really, but no need to get harsh or cutthroat either. Get in and get out. You're okay, I'm okay. Everybody's happy. What's the problem?

This is, no doubt, a way of getting through the assignment. Satisfy the teacher and no surprises for the writer. It might just do the trick. But say you want to do a *good* job. Say you're willing to put in the time and effort—though time is tight and you know it's not going to be easy—and help the writer look back on the paper and revise it. And maybe in the process learn something more yourself about writing. What do you look for? How do you sound? How

much do you take up? What exactly are you trying to accomplish? Here are
some ideas.

How Should You Look at Yourself as a Responder?

Consider yourself a friendly reader. A test pilot. A roommate who's been asked
to look over the paper and tell the writer what you think. Except you don't just
take on the role of The Nice Roommate or The Ever-Faithful Friend and tell
her what she wants to hear. *This all looks good. I wouldn't change a thing.
There are a couple places that I think he might not like, but I can see what
you're doing there. I'd go with it. Good stuff.* You're supportive. You give her
the benefit of the doubt and look to see the good in her writing. But friends
don't let friends think their writing is the best thing since *The Great Gatsby*
and they don't lead them to think that all is fine and well when it's not. Look
to help this friend, this roommate writer—okay, this person in your class—to
get a better piece of writing. Point to problems and areas for improvement but
do it in a constructive way. See what you can do to push her to do even more
than she's done and stretch herself as a writer.

What Are Your Goals?

First, don't set out to seek and destroy all errors and problems in the writing.
You're not an editor. You're not a teacher. You're not a cruise missile. And
don't rewrite any parts of the paper. You're not the writer; you're a reader. One
of many. The paper is not yours; it's the writer's. She writes. You read. She is
in charge of what she does to her writing. That doesn't mean you can't make
suggestions. It doesn't mean you can't offer a few sample rewrites here and
there, as models. But make it clear they're samples, models. Not rewrites. Not
edits. Not corrections. Be reluctant at first even to say what you would do if
the paper were yours. It's not yours. Again: Writers write, readers read and
show what they're understanding and maybe make suggestions. What to do
instead: Look at your task as a simple one. You're there to play back to the
writer how you read the paper: what you got from it; what you found interesting; where you were confused; where you wanted more. With this done, you
can go on to point out problems, ask questions, offer advice, and wonder out
loud with the writer about her ideas. Look to help her improve the writing or
encourage her to work on some things as a writer.

How Do You Get Started?

Before you up and start reading the paper, take a minute (alright, thirty seconds) to make a mental checklist about the circumstances of the writing, the
context. You're not going to just read a text. You're going to read a text within
a certain context, a set of circumstances that accompany the writing and that

you bring to your reading. It's one kind of writing or another, designed for one audience and purpose or another. It's a rough draft or a final draft. The writer is trying to be serious or casual, straight or ironic. Ideally, you'll read the paper with an eye to the circumstances that it was written in and the situation it is looking to create. That means looking at the writing in terms of the assignment, the writer's particular interests and aims, the work you've been doing in class, and the stage of drafting.

- *The assignment*: What kind of writing does the assignment call (or allow) for? Is the paper supposed to be a personal essay? A report? An analysis? An argument? Consider how well the paper before you meets the demands of the kind of writing the writer is taking up.

- *The writer's interests and aims*: What does the writer want to accomplish? If she's writing a personal narrative, say, is she trying to simply recount a past experience? Is she trying to recount a past experience and at the same time amuse her readers? Is she trying to show a pleasant experience on the surface, yet suggest underneath that everything was not as pleasant as it seems? Hone in on the writer's particular aims in the writing.

- *The work of the class*: Try to tie your comments to the concepts and strategies you've been studying in class. If you've been doing a lot of work on using detail, be sure to point to places in the writing where the writer uses detail effectively or where she might provide richer detail. If you've been working on developing arguments through examples and sample cases, indicate where the writer might use such methods to strengthen her arguments. If you've been considering various ways to sharpen the style of your sentences, offer places where the writer can clarify her sentence structure or arrange a sentence for maximum impact. The best comments will ring familiar even as they lead the writer to try to do something she hasn't quite done before, or done in quite the same way. They'll be comforting and understandable even as they create some need to do more, a need to figure out some better way.

- *The stage of drafting*: Is it an early draft? A full but incomplete draft? A nearly final draft? Pay attention to the stage of drafting. Don't try to deal with everything all at once if it's a first, rough draft. Concentrate on the large picture: the paper's focus; the content; the writer's voice. Don't worry about errors and punctuation problems yet. There'll be time for them later. If it's closer to a full draft, go ahead and talk, in addition to the overall content, about arrangement, pacing, and sentence style. Wait till the final draft to give much attention to fine-tuning sentences and dealing in detail with proofreading. Remember: You're not an editor. Leave these sentence revisions and corrections for the writer. It's her paper. And she's going to learn best by detecting problems and making her own changes.

What to Address in Your Comments?

Try to focus your comments on a couple of areas of writing. Glance through the paper quickly first. Get an idea whether you'll deal mostly with the overall content and purpose of the writing, its shape and flow, or (if these are more or less in order) with local matters of paragraph structure, sentence style, and correctness. Don't try to cover everything that comes up or even all instances of a given problem. Address issues that are most important to address in this paper, at this time.

Where to Put Your Comments?

Some teachers like to have students write comments in the margins right next to the passage. Some like to have students write out their comments in an end note or in a separate letter to the writer. I like to recommend using both marginal comments and a note or letter at the end. The best of both worlds. Marginal comments allow you to give a quick moment-by-moment reading of the paper. They make it easy to give immediate and specific feedback. You still have to make sure you specify what you're talking about and what you have to say, but they save you some work telling the writer what you're addressing and allow you to focus your end note on things that are most important. Comments at the end allow you to provide some perspective on your response. This doesn't mean that you have to size up the paper and give it a thumbs up or a thumbs down. You can use the end comment to emphasize the key points of your response, explain and elaborate on issues you want to deal with more fully, and mention additional points that you don't want to address in detail. One thing to avoid: plastering comments all over the writing; in between and over the lines of the other person's writing—up, down, and across the page. Write in your space, and let the writer keep hers.

How to Sound?

Not like a teacher. Not like a judge. Not like an editor or critic or shotgun. (Wouldn't you want someone who was giving you comments not to sound like a teacher's red pen, a judge's ruling, an editor's impatience, a critic's wrath, a shotgun's blast?) Sound like you normally sound when you're speaking with a friend or acquaintance. Talk to the writer. You're not just marking up a text; you're responding to the writer. You're a reader, a helper, a colleague. Try to sound like someone who's a reader, who's helpful, and who's collegial. Supportive. And remember: Even when you're tough and demanding you can still be supportive.

How Much to Comment?

Don't be stingy. Write most of your comments out in full statements. Instead of writing two or three words, write seven or eight. Instead of making only one brief comment and moving on, say what you have to say and then go back over the statement and explain what you mean or why you said it or note other alternatives. Let the writer know again and again how you are understanding her paper, what you take her to be saying. And elaborate on your key comments. Explain your interpretations, problems, questions, and advice.

Is It Okay to Be Short and Sweet?

No. At least not most of the time. Get specific. Don't rely on general statements alone. How much have generic comments helped you as a writer? "Add detail." "Needs better structure." "Unclear." Try to let the writer know what exactly the problem is. Refer specifically to the writer's words and make them a part of your comments. "Add some detail on what it was like working at the beach." "I think we'll need to know more about your high school crowd before we can understand the way you've changed." "This sentence is not clear. Were you disappointed or were they disappointed?" This way the writer will see what you're talking about, and she'll have a better idea what to work on.

Do You Praise or Criticize or What?

Be always of two (or three) minds about your response to the paper. You like the paper, but it could use some more interesting detail. You found this statement interesting, but these ideas in the second paragraph are not so hot. It's an alright paper, but it could be outstanding if the writer said what was really bothering her. Always be ready to praise. But always look to point to places that are not working well or that are not yet working as well as they might. Always be ready to expect more from the writer.

How to Present Your Comments?

Don't steer away from being critical. Feel free—in fact, feel obliged—to tell the writer what you like and don't like, what is and is not working, and where you think it can be made to work better. But use some other strategies, too. Try to engage the writer in considering her choices and thinking about possible ways to improve the paper. Make it a goal to write two or three comments that look to summarize or paraphrase what the writer is saying. Instead of *telling* the reader what to do, *suggest* what she might do. Identify the questions that are raised for you as you reader:

- Play back your way of understanding the writing:
  This seems to be the real focus of the paper, the issue you seem
      most interested in.
  So you're saying that you really weren't interested in her
      romantically?

- Temper your criticisms:
  This sentence is a bit hard to follow.
  I'm not sure this paragraph is necessary.

- Offer advice:
  It might help to add an example here.
  Maybe save this sentence for the end of the paper.

- Ask questions, especially real questions:
  What else were you feeling at the time?
  What kind of friend? Would it help to say?
  Do you need this opening sentence?
  In what ways were you "a daddy's little girl"?

- Explain and follow up on your initial comments:
  You might present this episode first. This way we can see what you
      mean when you say that he was always too busy.
  How did you react? Did you cry or yell? Did you walk away?
  This makes her sound cold and calculating. Is that what you want?

- Offer some praise, and then explain to the writer why the writing works:
  Good opening paragraph. You've got my attention.
  Good detail. It tells me a lot about the place.
  I like the descriptions you provide—for instance, about your
      grandmother cooking, at the bottom of page 1; about her house,
      in the middle of page 2; and about how she said her rosary at
      night: "quick but almost pleading, like crying without tears."

How Much Criticism? How Much Praise?

Challenge yourself to write as many praise comments as criticisms. When you praise, praise well. Think about it. Sincerity and specificity are everything when it comes to a compliment.

How Much Should You Be Influenced by What You Know About the Writer?

Consider the person behind the writer when you make your comments. If she's not done so well in class lately, maybe you can give her a pick-me-up in your comments. If she's shy and seems reluctant to go into the kind of personal detail the paper seems to need, encourage her. Make some suggestions or tell her what you would do. If she's confident and going on arrogant, see what you can do to challenge her with the ideas she presents in the paper. Look for other views she may not have thought about, and find ways to lead her to consider them. Always be ready to look at the text in terms of the writer behind the text.

Good comments, this listing shows, require a lot from a reader. But you don't have to make a checklist out of these suggestions and go through each one methodically as you read. It's amazing how they all start coming together when you look at your response as a way of talking with the writer seriously about the writing, recording how you experience the words on the page, and giving the writer something to think about for revision. The more you see examples of thoughtful commentary and the more you try to do it yourself, the more you'll get a feel for how it's done.

Here's a set of student comments on a student paper. They were done in the last third of a course that focused on the personal essay and concentrated on helping students develop the content and thought of their writing. The class had been working on finding ways to develop and extend the key statements of their essays (by using short, representative details, full-blown examples, dialogue, and multiple perspectives) and getting more careful about selecting and shaping parts of their writing. The assignment called on students to write an essay or an autobiographical story where they looked to capture how they see (or have seen) something about one or both of their parents—some habits, attitudes, or traits their parents have taken on. They were encouraged to give shape to their ideas and experiences in ways that went beyond their previous understandings and try things they hadn't tried in their writing. More a personal narrative than an essay, Todd's paper looks to capture one distinct difference in the way his mother and father disciplined their children. It is a rough draft that will be taken through one or possibly two more revisions. Readers were asked to offer whatever feedback they could that might help the writer with the next stage of writing (Figure 19–1).

This is a full and thoughtful set of comments. The responder, Jeremy, creates himself not as a teacher or critic but first of all as a reader, one who is intent on saying how he takes the writing and what he'd like to hear more about:

Good point. Makes it more unlikely that you should be the one to get caught.

Great passage. Really lets the reader know what you were thinking.

Was there a reason you were first or did it just happen that way?

Would he punish you anyway or could you just get away with things?

He makes twenty-two comments on the paper—seventeen statements in the margins and five more in the end note. The comments are written out in full statements, and they are detailed and specific. They make his response into a lively exchange with the writer, one person talking with another about what he's said. Well over half of the comments are follow-up comments that explain, illustrate, or qualify other responses.

The comments focus on the content and development of the writing, in line with the assignment, the stage of drafting, and the work of the course. They also

Figure 19–1

Jeremy

```
Todd
ENG 1
Rick Straub
Assignment 8b
```

                              "Uh, oh"

    When I called home from the police station I was praying   *I like this par-*
that my father would answer the phone. He would listen to what I *graph. It probably*
had to say and would react comely, logical, and in a manner that *lets the reader*
would keep my mother from screaming her head off. If my Mother *relate to you and*
was to answer the phone I would have to explain myself quickly in *also pictures*
order to keep her from having a heart attack.   *a "picture."*
                                                                 for reading

    When I was eleven years old I hung out with a group of boys
that were almost three years older than me. The five of us did
all the things that young energetic kids did playing ball, riding
bikes, and getting in to trouble. [Because they were older they
worried less about getting in trouble and the consequences of
there actions than I did.] *Good point, maks it more likely that you*
                           should be the one to get caught

what other   My friends and I would always come home from school, drop
things did you our backpacks off and head out in the neighborhood to find
do to get   something to do./ Our favorite thing to do was to find
into trouble?   construction cites and steal wood to make tree forts in the woods
this or is it   or skateboard ramps. So one day, coming home from school, we
irrevelant?   noticed a couple new houses being built near our neighborhood.
                  It was a prime cite for wood, nails, and anything else we could
                  get our hands on. We discussed our plan on the bus and decided
                  that we would all meet there after dropping our stuff off at
                  home. [I remember being a little at hesitant first because it was
of best writing close to my house but beyond the boundaries my parents had set
great passage   for me.] Of course I went because I didn't want to be the odd man
really lets the out and have to put up with all the name calling.] I dropped my
reader know   bag off and I headed to the construction cite.
what you were
thinking.]
                  I meet my friends there and we began to search the different
                  houses for wood and what not. We all picked up a couple of
                  things and were about to leave when one of my friends noticed a
                  what looked to be a big tool shed off behind one of the houses.
                  It looked promising so we decided that we should check it out.
                  Two of the boys in the group said that they had all the wood they
                  could carry and said they were going home.   The rest of us
                  headed down to the shed to take a look.

                  Once there we noticed that the shed had been broken in to
                  previously. The lock on it had been busted on the hinges were
was there   bent./ I opened the door to the shed and stepped inside to take a
a reason you   look around while my friends waited outside. It was dark inside
were first   but I could tell the place had been ransacked, there was nothing
or did it just to take so I decided to leave. I heard my to friends say some
happen that   thing so turned back around to site of them running away. I
way   thought that they were playing a joke on me so I casually walked

continues

view the writing rhetorically, in terms of how the text has certain effects on
readers. Although there are over two dozen wording or sentence-level errors in
the paper, he decides, wisely, to stick with the larger matters of writing. Yet even
as he offers a pretty full set of comments he doesn't ever take control over the
text. His comments are placed unobtrusively on the page, and he doesn't try to
close things down or decide things for the writer. He offers praise, encouragement, and direction. What's more, he pushes the writer to do more than he has

out only to see a cop car parked near one of the houses under
construction. As soon as I saw that cop car I took off but was
stopped when a big hand pulled at that back of my shirt. I
watched my friends run until they were out of cite and then I
turned around.

The cop had me sit in the squad car while he asked me
questions. He asked me if I knew those kids that ran off and I
said "Nnnnnooooooooo". He asked me if I had broken in to that
shed and I said "Nnnnnoooooo". The cop wrote down what I was
saying all the while shaking his head. Then he told me that I
wasn't being arrested but I would have to go down to the station
to call parents and have them pick me up. Upon hearing that I
nearly soiled my undershorts. "My God, I'm dead. My mom is going
to kill me".

what else happened at the police station? How long were you there? At the station the officer showed me the whole station,
jail cells and everything. An obvious tactic to try and scare
me, which worked. That plus the thought of my mom answering the
phone and me trying to explain what happened nearly made me sick.

"Wwwwhhhaatttt! You're where?" She would say.

"The police station mom," uh oh, hear it comes.

"Ooooohhhh my God, my son is criminal," so loud I would have
to pull the phone away from my ear.

maybe you could say more as to why you think your mom is like this. She had this uncanny ability to blow things out of
proportion right from the start. She would assume the worse and
then go from there. This was a classic example of why I could
never go to her if I had any bad news. She would start
screaming, get upset, and then go bitch at my father. My father
is a pretty laid back but when ever my mother started yelling at
him about me, he would get angry and come chew me out worse than
if I had just gone to him in the first place.

If my father were to answer the phone he would respond with
out raising his voice. He would examine the situation in a
logical manner and make a decision form there.

"Uhhmmm(long pause). You're at the police station."

"Yeah dad, I didn't get arrested they just had me come down
here so I had to tell you."

"Uhm, so you didn't get arrested(long pause). Well(long
pause), I'll come pick you up and will talk about then".

Did your Dad get into trouble as a kid? So he knows what it's like? Explain why he reacts as he does. I feel like I can relate to my father much better then I can
to my mother. He has a cool and collective voice that can take
command of any situation. I always feel like he understands me,
like he knows what I'm thinking all the time. This comes in real
handy when I get in trouble. *would he punish you anyway or could you just get away with things?*

I like the way you use dialogue in this section to illustrate how each of your parents would react and then explain to the reader what each of them are like. It works well.

continues

already done, to extend the boundaries of his examination. In keeping with the
assignment and the larger goals of the course, he calls on Todd in several comments to explore the motivations and personalities behind his parents' different
ways of disciplining:

Maybe you could say more as to why you think your mom is like this.

Did your dad get into trouble as a kid so he knows what it's like? Explain
why he reacts as he does.

continued   *Figure 19-1*

```
     I called home.  Sweet beading on my lip.

     "Hello", my mom said.  Oh geez, I'm dead.

     "Mom can I talk to dad?"

     "Why, what's wrong?"

     "Oh, nothing, I just need talk to him," yes, this is going
to work!

     "Hold on," she said.

     "Hello," my father said.

     "Dad, I'm at the police station,"  I told him the whole
story of what happened.  He reacted exactly as I expect he would.

     "Uhhmmm(long pause). You're at the police station..........
```

> I really like the ending, it tells the reader
> what is going to happen without having to explain
> it step, by step. Good paper, I like the use
> of dialogue. Perhaps more on your understanding
> of why your parents react as they do.

He is careful, though, not to get presumptuous and make decisions for the writer. Instead, he offers options and points to possibilities:

> Perhaps more on your understanding of why your parents react as they do.
>
> What other things did you do to get into trouble? Or is it irrelevant?

From start to finish he takes on the task of reading and responding and leaves the work of writing and revising to Todd.

Jeremy's response is not in a class by itself. A set of comments to end all commentary on Todd's paper. He might have done well, for instance, to recognize how much this paper works because of the way Todd arranges the story. He could have done more to point to what's not working in the writing or what could be made to work better. He might have asked Todd for more details about his state of mind when he got caught by the policeman and while he was being held at the police station. He might have urged him more to make certain changes. He might even have said, if only in a brief warning, something about the number of errors across the writing. But this is moot and just. Different readers are always going to pick up on different things and respond in different ways, and no one reading or response is going to address everything that might well be addressed, in the way it might best be addressed. All responses are incomplete and provisional—one reader's way of reading and reacting to the text in front of him. And any number of other responses, presented in any number of different ways, might be as useful or maybe even more useful to Todd as he takes up his work with the writing.

All this notwithstanding, Jeremy's comments are solid. They are full. They are thoughtful. And they are respectful. They take the writing and the writer seriously and address the issues that are raised responsibly. His comments do what commentary on student writing should optimally do. They turn the writer back into his writing and lead him to reflect on his choices and aims, to consider and reconsider his intentions as a writer and the effects the words on the page will have on readers. They help him see what he can work on in revision and what he might deal with in his ongoing work as a writer.

Sharing Ideas

- What are your experiences with responding to other students' writing? Have you done so in other classes? How did that work out? Were you able to discuss your responses? In small groups or large groups? Which situation did you like best?

- Do you have any papers where others have responded to your writing? Collect one or more and see how the responses stack up against Richard Straub's guidelines. Having read his essay, what would you say your respondent did well and needs to learn to do better?

- In the same way, after everyone in your small group responds to a first paper, go over those papers/responses together in a group and look at what was done and what could be done to improve the quality of responses. In addition, you might try to characterize each of you as a responder: What are your habits? What character/persona do you take on? Would you like to be responded to by the responder you find you are through this group analysis?

- Richard shows you a responder—Jeremy—and the comments he wrote on Todd's paper. If you were Todd, how would you feel about Jeremy's responses? Do you agree with Richard's analysis of Jeremy's comments? What three or four additional things would you tell Todd about his paper?

- What are your insights into responding? What has worked for you? What do you wish people would do or not do when they respond to your writing? What would make you most inclined to listen to responses and use them to change your work?

Part V

Larger Issues in Writing

The essay seems to have originated with Montaigne, a kind of adult French Bart Simpson, who seemed to hate the schools, school masters, and school-writing of that time, but who wrote for his own purposes, in his own way. Montaigne wrote very untraditional little sets of explorations, of tentative wonderings, about himself and his world that he called essays. Writers would do well to recover Montaigne's sense of essaying. Writing is a dialogue with one's world, open, unfinished, not always pretty, but often ongoing.

—James Zebroski, writing teacher

As I read, I find clues that help me to write my paper. I measure my ideas against the ideas of people who are considered experts. Their ideas force me to rethink my own. I conduct a dialogue between the author and me that sometimes causes me to change my mind and sometimes merely reconfirms my original ideas. But a book or article seldom leaves my thinking unchanged, and it always helps me put new words on the page.

—Marcia Dickson, writing teacher

A warning about Web research: Be selective about the source of information. Remember that anyone—anyone—can construct a site and put information on the Web. No one is really verifying that anything anyone puts out there is correct or true. Always ask yourself whether the information you get from a Web site is reliable and why you think it is reliable.

—Patricia Hendricks, writing teacher

Students often resist writing and writing teachers, and such resistance can be either healthy or unhealthy. As part of the classroom dynamic, resistance can play a role in promoting learning and critical thinking or it can be a way to refuse to learn or to become critically engaged. For example, with hours of drill on *lie/lay* and *sit/set*, tests on the eight comma rules, fill-in-the-blank questions about the ways to develop a paragraph, five points off for every misspelled word, students are probably right to resist such mindless "drill and kill" exercises often associated with being taught to write. Of course, usage, punctuation, paragraph development, and spelling are important in writing well, but we think that students realize that heavy emphasis on these issues by teachers often deflects attention from what students are thinking and saying. Unfortunately, schooling sometimes teaches students that the teacher is the enemy and that school work is irrelevant and alien to their concerns.

—Beth Daniell and Art Young, writing teachers

20

Writing Up Primary Research Observations

"Can We Use I?"

Danette DiMarco

Danette DiMarco is an Associate Professor of English at Slippery Rock University of Pennsylvania, where she teaches undergraduate and graduate students. In order to fine-tune her pedagogy and to stay in touch with the challenges that her students face when writing, she has been known to complete many of the assignments that she has designed. When not teaching and writing, two of her passions, she is happiest spending time with her family.

Several years ago I began asking my students to do something that is becoming more and more popular in first-year writing courses: include primary research like observing and interviewing in addition to gathering information from traditional sources such as the library and on-line and database sources. Many of your teachers believe that introducing this sort of research early in your college career will help you better recognize the depth and possibilities for research that is more clearly connected with daily life. But as I introduced this type of primary research writing, I began to notice a common pitfall that happened when students went to write up the results of their research: they wrote quite differently when discussing information derived from observations and interviews than they did about information gathered from other sources. The difficulty can be summarized in the age-old question of whether it's OK to use *I* in these primary research papers. For me, the question is a fair one, but it's really more a question of learning how to see past writing about ourselves doing research and instead writing about the discoveries we've made conducting that research. Paradoxically though, to get to the point where we are able to see patterns emerge from our research, it may be necessary to use *I* in the evolution of a piece of writing through various drafts. Let me explain.

In research projects where only secondary research is required, students seem to establish their distance from their work by refraining from writing themselves into the sentences. Take, for instance, Amy's treatment of her topic on the success of single-parent children. She writes:

> Many of the world's lost children come from single-parent environments. In these types of environments the child has more responsibilities. If the family is not well off, they are sometimes required to help out with bills; in which case they would have to get a job. Of course there are some who choose to relinquish their childhoods of their own free will. Some do this to have some independence from their family, and a little extra money in the pocket that they earned for themselves.

There may be a step in the writing process that your writing teachers never get to see because you and students like Amy revise. For example, Amy might have originally written, "I think many of the world's lost children come from single-parent homes. It seems to me that if the family needs money, the children must find a job to help with the bills." Amy may have revised to pull herself out by removing the *I* and creating a third-person stance; notice that she doesn't use *I* anywhere, which makes her relationship to the topic seem one of a distanced researcher, the sort of voice favored in academic writing. Like Amy, Stefan has removed himself from his topic on specialized work, focusing on the ideas he is dealing with as opposed to focusing on himself. Stefan says:

> Just as in warfare, increases in organizational specialization can be used in commerce. Adam Smith, who is often referred to as the father of contemporary economics, explained the potential gains in productivity through the division of labor.

But what happens to the writing of students like Amy and Stefan when the topics change or the assignment asks for primary research? No longer comfortable distancing themselves from their projects by using a third-person voice, they repeatedly write themselves into their work. And, instead of being liberated, many of them experience a breakdown in the research and writing process, which obscures the real subject of the writing. Yet it is not as easy as taking out "I think" or "It seems to me." In other words, the comfortable third-person style that they have grown accustomed to can and often does lose its footing when primary modes of research are introduced. With this lost footing, many students suddenly see the entire research process anew—and their style often reveals the cognitive or mental changes that they are moving through as they adjust.

Justin's paper on good management and employee relationships in the fast-food industry illustrates well what I mean. Here are three sentences from one of Justin's drafts (I've highlighted portions for discussion later). You should know that in this part of the paper he is trying to figure out how to integrate his findings from observations that he conducted in one particular fast-food restaurant.

> The first relationship <u>I researched</u> was between managers and employees pertaining to them *being disrespectful to each other.* <u>I found</u> that some *businesses closed down as a result* of problems that were occurring on the inside of the business.

And

> <u>I discovered,</u> in my observations at McDonald's, that there were *a lot of disrespectful employees.*

What you may quickly notice about these three sentences is how Justin is the subject of each sentence (the parts I underlined). Justin makes himself—the *I*—more important than his actual discoveries about businesses (the parts I italicized) by writing, "I researched," "I found," and "I discovered." In other words, when research methods (in this case, observation) ask Justin to be more physically involved in collecting the data than secondary research might, he puts himself first in his writing over the research subject. The real research subject—McDonald's, its managers and employees, and their relationships—is given secondary attention. Justin's process and discovery appear to be replacing critically thought-through assertions about the issue under discussion.

Justin's approach to writing his participation in the research process is, in my experience, typical of many students who take part in research activities relatively new to them. It is a necessary step and yet obscures the discovery. Note how the following sentences remind us of Justin's, even though they are written by a completely different student, Nikki, about a totally different subject: a university day care center. The underlined parts call attention to the researcher.

> <u>Walking</u> down a long, sloped ramp in the basement of the building <u>one</u> can hear the laughter of small children's voices. <u>Entering</u> the room, the children appear to be sitting in chairs at a long narrow table eating their snack, which today happens to be cookies.

And

> <u>Studying the children as they eat, I notice</u> that most of them cannot sit still for more than a couple minutes at a time.

Nikki seems to understand that overusing *I* might be troublesome. Yet she continues to struggle with how to remedy the problem of focusing on the researcher. Notice that while these short excerpts show only one use of *I,* the student is physically present with words like *walking, entering,* and *studying.* In an effort to not repeat *I,* Nikki has even substituted the word *one.* Yet this substitution still calls attention to the person doing the observing and listening—"one can hear the laughter of small children's voices"—as opposed to focusing on the children themselves, who should be the real subject of the analysis. Also, in trying to write herself out of the passages, Nikki has only complicated the grammar problems (dangling modifiers) without realizing it. For example, "Entering the room, the children . . ." is incorrect because the children aren't the ones entering the room; the one entering is the researcher.

Interviewing, another type of primary research, can befuddle students who are new to it in the same way that observation research does. In the following excerpt, a student writes himself into the project by making it clear that he was the interviewer, as the parts I've underlined show. In doing so, he loses the potential focus of the paragraph, which should be about good communication, by focusing instead on his own questioning of the interviewee.

> The job of running and maintaining the everyday affairs of the recreation center is a grueling one. The boss is constantly dealing with people in one way or another. Whether he is on the phone, answering e-mail or handling issues face to face, the *leader is always communicating* with someone. Sometimes *good communication can be hard*, especially when people are close-minded. When I asked the leader if he enjoyed his job, he replied by saying, "if you don't enjoy the company of people or you can't *communicate* well you wouldn't enjoy my position. Luckily for me I enjoy to do both." Sometimes it can be hard to *communicate* with others. When I asked him his personal opinions about good *communication*, the leader said, "yes, it can be hard to communicate with some people. I try to put myself in their position. I don't try to become better than the person. I want to make them feel special when I get done talking with them."

The underlined portions above show how the student has strung his questions and the interviewee's answers along linearly, instead of looking closely for patterns in the answers that he has collected. The parts that I put in italics show that, in fact, a pattern is emerging, one that is obscured by the intrusion of the *I*. That pattern should be what ties the paragraph together. Being able to recognize that pattern will help this student more aptly revise his work and write himself out.

So what can you do when you are asked to use a research method, like primary, that might be new to you and you have to decide whether you can use *I*? First, expect that writing using the first-person *I* might just be an absolutely necessary part of the drafting process. Even expert researchers and writers realize this. For example, in my first draft for this chapter (which, you may have noticed, is based on my own primary research), I wrote it this way, positioning myself front and center as the subject:

> I have underlined portions of the above passage to show how the student has not yet looked closely for patterns in the answers that he has collected from the interviewee.

Then I revised it, writing myself out, so it read:

<u>The underlined portions</u> of the above passage show how the student has not yet looked closely for patterns in the answers that he has collected from the interviewee.

In fact, I would argue that using *I* and spending time with early drafting stages are more important than ever when you are involved in unfamiliar research methods because those are the stages where a lot of the discovery about the writer's process and actual topic happens.

Second, and this point is founded upon my first, keep a writer's notebook (even if your instructor doesn't require one), so you have a place to comfortably say *I* as much as you like. This notebook might contain individual reflections on your research and can be written following each research session. This way you have a space to privately explore what patterns you might be seeing in your data, patterns that will eventually become the subjects of your writing.

Looking for Patterns

Finding patterns may seem at first a difficult task, if not a conundrum. The following passage was written by a student I mentioned earlier, Stefan, who completed an in-class observation in response to a class exercise that was designed to get students comfortable with looking for patterns. Stefan was asked to consider this research problem: "To find out how first-year university writing students handle the pressure of having to complete a timed, in-class writing task." Instructed to watch a student who was engaged in a different and timed writing assignment, Stefan collected the following notes. The italicized parts of the observation were identified in a postobservation exercise, and they reveal a pattern that Stefan will have to consider seriously if he wishes to further pursue the research question. Notice too that Stefan does, indeed, write himself into the research process (see the underlined parts).

> Starting with an observation from a distance <u>I can see</u> that the subject is a fairly well-built, tall male with glasses. He is wearing a white collar shirt and khakis. To begin his observation of [the statue of] the traveling Buddha, he gets up to inspect it at close range. After a close inspection he returns to his seat and starts to type on his computer. He then gets back up and starts to examine Buddha with his hands. He is running his hand over Buddha's chest and belly. After he is done feeling Buddha *he starts to discuss it with others standing around Buddha*. Then he sits back down to continue typing on the computer. As he types he would occasionally glance over at Buddha. *He then starts conversing with a female two seats down from him*. They are discussing the type of clothes Buddha is wearing. They come to the conclusion that Buddha is wearing a robe. Moving to a closer view <u>I notice</u> that he types while eyeing the keyboard. While typing *he questions the teacher about correct word choice*. Looking at the screen <u>I see</u> that he has typed "Buddha has a big belly," for his first sentence in his notes. He momentarily stopped typing when the teacher handed him a paper to glance over it. Returning to his screen *he declares that he has enough information and wants to know if they are to switch*

computers now. He has to type up his data paragraph yet. For his first sentence in the data he has typed, "The statue of Buddha is made of ceramic and is hollow inside." <u>Before returning to my own computer,</u> *he asks my partner and me if we have to type things up or just take notes,* therefore ending <u>my observation</u>.

This excerpt could end up in a more polished version of the paper, but it shouldn't since the writer hasn't yet become aware of what he noticed, and therefore, the passage hasn't yet been rewritten for clearer focus. By returning to his own written observations, his raw data, to look for patterns recorded in his notebook, he could potentially be headed toward finding the bigger issue that is important to his research question. A brief rewrite concerning the pattern—where the pattern or issue becomes the focus as opposed to the researcher—might read this way:

People might need to communicate with each other when engaged in such a research task. For instance, Subject 1 *"listened and conversed with other researchers," "discussed"* the object *"with others standing around Buddha,"* and *"started conversing with a female two seats down from him."* In addition, *"he questioned the teacher about correct word choice," "declared that he had enough information, and wanted to know if they are to switch computers now."* Finally, he *"asked a research partner"* if researchers *"have to type things up or just take notes."*

While the student is far from having enough research information, this focus on pattern over process makes space for tweaking thesis statements and exploring further particular questions:

- Is communication a way of relieving stress in an otherwise stressful situation?
- Does this sort of activity (data recording and research writing), which is sometimes perceived to be solitary, demand communication?
- Do the student researchers feel they are more productive when they are communicating with someone else about their work?
- Does positive discussion give people a feeling of collaboration and motivate their confidence?
- Does this particular kind of assignment demand more communication with others than other writing assignments?

Mandy demonstrates how interview data, like observation data, can be managed so that it focuses less on the researcher and more on a main pattern or point. She uses her findings from interviews to express her thoughts on working parents who also care for children. She writes:

Most parents understand that they need to work in order to adequately care for their kids. Even though their jobs may not be satisfying, parents are working because they want to properly care for their children. These parents are taking responsibility. A worker at Wal-Mart said that he is working "because I need to support my daughter." Tony worked hard so that he could financially support his daughters at college, away from home. By helping to pay for their education, he made his daughters' dreams come true.

Let's return now to Justin's brief comments about workers and management at McDonald's. Consider how Justin might revise his initial sentences to focus less on himself and his research process and more on the topic under discussion itself. It seems that instead of "researching," "finding," and "discovering," Justin may want to focus on the fact that *some businesses closed down* because of employee-manager problems, which grew out of *disrespect*. Similarly he may have noted that *disrespectful employees* abound in such places. Had Justin taken a little more time to search for and highlight patterns in his own work, he might have discovered that a line of investigation and discussion was already there waiting for him.

So, to answer the nagging question, "Can I use *I* in my papers?": Yes, if you use it to explore your own writing to find the real subject you want to write about and to discover the patterns that emerge from writing about your observations.

Sharing Ideas

- When you were in high school, were you allowed to use *I* in your writings? Were there rules for when you could and couldn't?

- Have you done any papers based on primary research? If so, discuss how you handled referring to yourself as the researcher.

- Do you agree that engaging in research methods that are new to you, like primary research, makes it even more important that writers consciously work through multiple drafts before considering their work done?

- Teachers speak of writing as discovery. Stefan used his writing to record what he discovered about the student he was observing, but how could he use his own written notes as the subject of investigation, a second stage of discovery?

- Brainstorm what secondary and primary researchers might *physically* do when they are involved in their research. Could the distinctions account for some of the reasons for the use of *I*?

- Style is linked to purpose and audience—why you are writing and who you are writing for. Imagine the various purposes and audiences for Justin's paper. When and why might it be useful for Justin to use *I* in his paper?

- A teacher named Ken Macrorie developed the term *I-Search* to describe research papers that include descriptions of the processes of finding information and making sense of it along with a report of the research itself. If you had to write an I-Search paper, what would you do first?

21

What Is a Grade?

Pat Belanoff

Pat Belanoff is Professor of English (and former director of the Writing
Program) at the State University of New York at Stony Brook, which is on
the north shore of Long Island, a little more than an hour from New York
City. She has coauthored several textbooks with Peter Elbow, the latest of
which is *Being a Writer: A Community of Writers Revisited*. With Betsy
Rorschach and Mia Oberlink she has coauthored a somewhat off-beat
grammar book called *The Right Handbook*. And fairly recently, she
coedited a collection of essays that bounce off the ideas of Peter Elbow,
titled *Writing with Elbow*. Pat also writes about the women of Old English
poetry and spends more time than she should doing crossword puzzles and
watching tennis matches.

Grades and school seem synonymous. Grades are the evidence educators, parents, politicians, and other citizens cite to demonstrate that students have (or
have not) learned what they should learn. Such reliance on grades presumes
that the student who gets an A has learned more than the student who gets a B,
who in turn has learned more than the student who gets a C, and so on down
the line to an F: The student who gets one of those has obviously not learned
much. Many in our society and in the schools accept without question these
connections between grades and the quality of student learning.

But those who accept these connections argue for their validity within
some fields far more strongly than within other fields. For example, most
people are more willing to credit a ninety on a math or physics test than on
a composition or on a paper responding to some piece of literature. Students,

reflecting this societal attitude, often complain to me about the nature of English studies—both literature and composition. It is the objectivity–subjectivity contrast that they usually bring up, lamenting that they wish grades on compositions could be objective like their math and physics grades. In those classes, they tell me, you know for sure what's right and what's wrong. In a writing class though, these same students say, everything is subjective: how well one does depends on what the teacher likes and dislikes—there's nothing substantial to guide one to better grades. Students come into my office to complain that a paper they got a poor mark on would have gotten an A or B from a previous teacher. And I suspect that among themselves they confess to the opposite: that some paper they just got an A or B on would never have gotten such a good grade from a previous teacher. They know from personal experience how greatly grading standards differ from teacher to teacher. Reacting to this, some students tell me that it isn't possible to get grades that mean anything in English classes and that they've come to hate English as a result.

Teachers of other subjects sometimes express similar judgments. I remember well, as a beginning faculty member, attending an interdepartmental meeting at which a member of the history faculty said that he envied English teachers because they didn't have to be bothered with "covering" a set range of materials every semester. When he was pressed to explain himself, he continued by saying that there was no "real" subject matter in English classes, only opinions and subjective ideas, no "facts." "How do you decide what grade to give?" he asked me. "It's all so subjective!"

How do I respond to these charges of subjectivity? First, I agree. I know, even better than they, that teachers do not give the same grades to the same pieces—particularly when these teachers work in unlike schools. But, rather than apologize for this lack of conformity, I actually celebrate it. I'll get back to why later in this essay.

After conceding the truth of these charges of subjectivity, I encourage those who make them to consider whether other subjects are as "objective" as they appear. Not all biology teachers cover the same material; not all of them focus on the same subjects when they make up their tests, and not all of them weigh answers in the same way. Biology teachers differ not only about what to teach but also about what's most important in the classroom. Some teachers think that how we discover information is more important than the information itself. They will teach and test quite differently from teachers who see their main goal as transferring information into the heads of their students. Furthermore, the deeper one goes into any subject, the less objective issues become. Astrophysicists look at the same data, but some posit a "big bang" theory for creation and others do not. Paleontologists study the same geology and the same bones and disagree about why dinosaurs disappeared from the earth. Newcomers in these fields gradually join these debates and earn the right to interpret data in their own ways.

Literature classes sometimes mimic the sequence I've just set forth for physical science: less and less agreement or objectivity as one moves deeper into the subject. Perhaps the teacher will give a test on the facts of a piece of literature: who wrote it, when, which character does what, where the figures of speech are, and so forth. Even literature teachers who approach their subject this way, however, move fairly quickly to interpretation, to an assessment of what the piece "means," which is equivalent to what the geologist does as he "reads" old bones and old geological formations. English teachers do seem to move to the level of interpretation more quickly than mathematicians do; but both fields deal with facts *and* interpretations. Both fields, that is, are objective *and* subjective.

I'm mainly a writing teacher, not a literature teacher, and must acknowledge that the objectivity–subjectivity issue is even more pronounced in a writing class than in a literature class. In the latter, there's at least some secure basis in that students are responding to published, established texts. But, in a writing class, there's a felt sense that the texts being produced are totally personal in a way nothing else in school is. We know, of course, that they're not totally personal: what we write is always partially determined by our backgrounds, our culture, our prior educational experiences, our past reading and writing activities. But all that is filtered through our sense of ourselves. Mikhail Bakhtin, a well-regarded Russian language scholar, once wrote that any word we use is only half ours, but that we can make words our own by saturating them with our own intentions and purposes. The more we're able to do that, the more individualized what we say and write becomes and the less likely it is to be like anything else a teacher has ever read. No A paper is exactly like another A paper in the same way as $2 + 2$ is always 4. Thus, the grades of English teachers can never be based on exact correspondences between papers.

I celebrate and encourage this diversity. A major goal of the humanities is to guide students—not just while they're acquiring facts, but also while they're learning to interpret them. As a writing teacher, my task is to help students gain control *through words* over their developing interpretations. All of us struggle with language when we need to express ideas new to us. My particular students struggle as their already established ideas and thoughts interact with the new ideas and thoughts a new world (college) presents to them. As they react, they will agree with some of their classmates in one way, with others in some different ways, and perhaps stand alone on still another issue. No one's ideas, opinions, and reactions are exactly like anyone else's. As a teacher I'm in the business of getting students to think, not of getting them to think like everyone else or even like me. Teachers who can get students to spit back information on tests will never know what these students are really thinking—or if they're thinking at all about what they're supposedly learning.

For the same reasons we do not react exactly like anyone else, none of us reads exactly like anyone else either. Thus possibilities multiply for diverse judgments—not only am I reading something I've never read before, I'm also reading in a way unique to me. It seems like common sense to see meaning as existing in the words on the page, but black marks on paper mean nothing until someone reads them. Meaning can only develop as a human mind interacts and inevitably interprets those black marks—and human minds come in all varieties. Quite simply, I never react to a student text exactly like any other teacher any more than I react exactly like anyone else when I read *Hamlet* or *The Color Purple*. And when the issue shifts to what these texts mean, differences multiply even more.

Many students do not like to hear this; it turns a world of seeming certainty into formless mush. It may be easier to have a teacher who tells you exactly how to write a paper. But once you realize that no teacher (because she is human) reads like any other teacher, you also realize that those directions for an A paper are valid only for that class. You don't learn much to carry to the next class if the teacher does not explain her standards for that A.

So far, I've written of the subjectivity resulting from the necessarily subjective acts of writing and reading. But subjectivity has other causes, one of which is the school setting. Because I've taught at a number of institutions of various kinds I've been forced to realize that grades are always relative to the institution where they're given. An A at one school isn't the same as an A at another school. What that means is that I'm judging each paper I read against other papers I've read at the particular school I'm teaching at. It also means that if that same paper were given to me at a different time at a different school, it would receive a different grade. And even within a department or program, grades are relative to the class in which they're assigned. A paper that earns a B in a developmental class will not be likely to get a B in freshman composition. And a B paper in freshman composition will not be likely to get a B in an advanced or upper-level writing class.

What's the alternative to the seeming unfairness or inconsistency? The alternative is to believe that somewhere out in the clouds is a model A paper, B paper, and so forth and that every paper I read (even though it is unique) can be graded relative to that model. Or, even more preposterous, that I was somehow born knowing what an A paper is. There are teachers who act as though they believe this is true, as though there is some absolute measure against which all student papers can be measured and that they know with absolute certainty what that measure is. Unfortunately for them no one seems to agree on any real, not-in-the-clouds paper which should serve as that model A paper. No sooner does a teacher offer one, than some other teacher finds fault with it and offers a different one. Usually teachers can only agree on the traits of good writing *in the abstract*. As soon as they start looking at individual papers, agreement disintegrates.

But even if we could get writing teachers together from all over the country and agree on a paper to which we would all give an A, we would not agree on how closely other papers approached our model, nor would we necessarily agree on what made that model A paper a model A paper. Some of us would cite its content first, some of us its organization, some of us its language, some of us the relevance of its arguments, some of us its originality, creativity, and imaginative power.

What I'm saying is that I inevitably judge the paper in front of me in terms of all other papers I've read. I make no apologies for that. That's the only way any of us ever judges anything: persons are beautiful in relation to others, movies are acclaimed or not in relation to other movies, scenery is lovely in relation to other scenes the observer has seen. I cannot know beauty, perfection, or loveliness apart from specific examples. It is hardly to be expected that decisions on the quality of writing could be made any differently. Thus the model of an A I have in my head is a product of all the papers I have read as well as of my own individual way of reading.

To be honest, I hate grading. I love teaching; I love talking to students about their writing, sharing my responses with them, discussing their subjects, listening and reacting to their ideas. But I hate grading papers. Most students work hard on their papers; many of them dig deep into themselves to express ideas and opinions important to them. It isn't easy to put "C" or "D" on such endeavors. It may be easy (I'm not really sure about this) for students and teachers in other classes to distance themselves a bit from the grades. A physics teacher gives problems to be worked out, formulas to be decoded and solved, and so forth. If a student does poorly, the teacher concludes that he didn't study or he's just not destined to be a physics student. The student can console himself by acknowledging that he should have studied more or that physics is just not his subject.

Somehow it's different when one writes a paper. It's hard to keep oneself out of it. The assumption—contrary to that about physics—is that everyone *can* "do" English. Everyone is assumed to have opinions and responses to events, to pieces of writing, to ideas presented by others; everyone is *not* expected to understand or master physics. Having an opinion on personal, social, and political issues or a reaction to a poem or an editorial is within the capabilities of all of us. We can't escape by saying that this isn't our subject. Thus we feel judged by grades on papers in ways we don't feel judged by a grade on a physics test. What we write (that is, if we genuinely commit ourselves to the writing) feels as though it comes from somewhere inside us; the answer to a physics problem feels like it comes from inside our heads only.

Perhaps the solution would be to abandon grading altogether in writing classes. I confess that this is a solution that appeals to me greatly. Instead of putting grades on a paper, I could simply respond to it: let the writer know my reactions to what it says and how it says it. If a student did all the assignments, met my attendance requirements, participated in class, and mostly got papers in on time, she would get a "Satisfactory" for the semester. There are colleges, universities, and even some high schools that have grading systems like this.

Perhaps some of you reading this article may even attend such a school; if you do, you undoubtedly have an opinion about the value of it.

Unfortunately (for me, at any rate), most colleges and universities require grades. Mine does. Therefore, I've been forced to do a lot of thinking about what grades are and how to make them as fair as possible. Almost every time I sit down to grade papers, I ask myself: "What *are* grades; what do they measure?"

Despite my questions and doubts (or perhaps because of them), I argue for the validity of two kinds of grading in writing classes: grading by groups of teachers and grading by individual teachers who have worked through standards with their students. I am not going to argue that such grades are *not* subjective, but I will argue that they can be meaningful within the environment in which they're given.

If grades are only meaningful within limited environments, it's logical to argue for the joint awarding of grades by those within the environment. Gymnastics competitions come to mind as a possible model. For each performance of each gymnast, six or seven people give independent scores, and these are averaged or added up in some way. (It's interesting to consider that in gymnastics scoring the highest and the lowest scores are eliminated before the averaging is done.) In such situations, I don't have to convince anyone of my opinions; I just vote. Perhaps students' papers ought to be judged like gymnastics contests: six or seven teachers would give each paper a grade, and the actual grade would be an average or total of those given, after discounting both the best and the worst grade. The problem with such a scheme, as far as I'm concerned, is that I would be spending all my time grading papers! Since I hate grading, my enthusiasm for teaching might be considerably dampened. Although it isn't feasible to have every student's paper graded by six or seven other teachers, it *is* feasible for teachers to share grading once or twice during a semester. If two or three teachers jointly grade a set of each other's papers during the semester, both they and their students will develop a sense of community judgment.

Even teachers within an isolated classroom can make grades useful for themselves and their students. A teacher can, of course, simply put grades on papers and leave it up to the students to figure out what she rewards and punishes. Some students are quite good at this. Quite a few are not. I believe that if students are going to get better, I have to explain the standards I use to arrive at grades. I consider this part of my responsibility.

I sometimes ask college freshmen to bring to class a graded paper they wrote in high school, especially if the paper has some comments on it in addition to the grade. Then the class and I together analyze the paper and draw some conclusions about what the teacher who graded it valued. I may also give my students some papers from other years and ask them to arrange them in order from the one they consider the most effective to the one they consider least effective. We then talk about our personal standards, where we agree and disagree and why. Often I do need to introduce some standards into the grading process that may not grow out of our discussions simply because freshmen are new to the academic community. At the same time, I aim to help them understand how the standards I introduce may be different from the standards of other writing teachers. I cannot do this honestly unless I make it my business to be more familiar with the standards of those with whom I work most closely: my colleagues in the department who are teaching the same courses I am and my colleagues who are assigning writing in other subject areas.

On the basis of all these discussions, my students and I strive to reach some conclusions on standards without privileging any particular set of standards: mine, theirs, their former teachers. I then give them some papers to judge on the basis of the standards we've developed together. And, finally, I give them several assignments that will be graded on the basis of these standards. In the process, I am teaching what may be the most important lesson of all: the ability to write for a particular audience. If I can help students understand how to get an A or B in my class, I will be helping them learn to figure out how to analyze and impress other audiences too, both in and out of school. When I give assignments that will be judged by different standards, the class and I again discuss these fully.

No matter whether I grade individually or as a member of a group of teachers, putting one grade on one paper can be misleading because others (including the student who writes the paper) may deduce more from the grade than is warranted. Since neither I nor the student author can know whether she can write with equal skill on a different task, a grade can be meaningful only as a judgment of a particular paper, not as a judgment of a writer's overall skills. For this reason, I prefer to give a grade to two or more papers at a time. In fact, I prefer to grade a portfolio of a student's work at mid- and end-semester and give one grade for all the work with commentary explaining the strengths and weaknesses of the whole portfolio. Students can then get some sense of how I assess their overall skill in terms of what I, their classmates, my program, and my particular school value.

I recognize that not all teachers have either the time or the desire to discuss standards with students. If you have such a teacher, you can find ways to get at these standards. You can analyze graded papers and draw conclusions about what the teacher likes and dislikes and then make an appointment with the teacher to test these conclusions. (You'll learn more if you do some analysis too, rather than just taking a paper in and asking for an explanation of the grade or for advice on getting a better grade.) Or you can ask a teacher if she is willing to read a draft of a paper several days before it's due. The worst she can do is say no. But most teachers are gratified to talk to a student who's willing to put in the time to improve his writing. My final suggestion in such situations is that you form study groups (research has shown that such groups result in better grades for participants) in which you share papers with one another before they're submitted for grading.

When I have this discussion with students in my classes, there's always more than one student who interprets me as saying that only conformity will lead to a good grade. My answer to that is not usually what they want to hear, for I tell them that language use always involves conformity. Speaking words others can understand means conforming to built-in rules of language. I can't give words my own meaning and adjust grammatical rules to my own liking. Creativity and originality can only develop *within* established meanings and rules. But that doesn't mean a language user cannot use the meanings and the rules in new, exciting ways—writers have been doing this for centuries. Taking into consideration a teacher's or class' standards is the same as being tuned in to your audience. Once tuned in, you can decide whether to play to it or whether to try to influence these standards themselves—but, at least, you have a choice. And if you do strive to persuade your teacher and classmates of the validity of somewhat different standards and are able to meet them and thus demonstrate that validity, you may succeed in altering classroom standards. I've had students who could do that.

Frankly, I would be frightened about the future of our culture if we ever arrived at a point where I was sure that the grades I gave were the same as those all other teachers would give. This would suggest some rather unpleasant things about the future of discussion in the world. Not all of us think Shakespeare was the greatest writer the world has ever produced; not all of us think Jacqueline Suzanne is the worst writer the world has ever produced. Most of us fall somewhere in between on both these points. And most of us like it that way; but that means we have to accept and learn to value varying evaluations of student texts also.

Most decisions we make in our personal and professional lives are more like the problematic ones we wrestle with in English and writing classes; they're not usually as clear-cut as the answers on math tests. I'd like to think that coming to terms with the subjectivity of grades is good training for living with the subjectivity inherent in the world around us. But perhaps that's stretching my point too far. What is important within the world of the individual classroom is that grades can be useful and meaningful to students who understand the basis for them and who recognize that one grade on one paper can never be a judgment on all their writing.

Shared Ideas

- Using Pat Belanoff's discussion, design your ideal writing class—how would grades work, matter, be assigned?

- Tell some stories of you, your writing, and grades.

- Have you encountered the subjectivity–objectivity problem before? What do you think about Pat's analogy to paper grading and gymnastics competitions?
- Are you "graded" in other (nonacademic) areas of your life? List the ways this happens. For instance, we may feel we receive grades in the workplace, on a date, when we go hunting and fishing, within our relationships, and so on.
- Are you willing to abolish grades and just get on with learning? What, for you, is at stake in earning grades in school?
- Have you ever learned in a nongraded and noncompetitive situation? Describe how that felt.
- How do you know when writing is "good"?
- Have you ever had to grade someone else? What did you do and what did it feel like?
- If writing is a way of thinking, if writing is a recursive ongoing activity, leading to more and more revision and discovery through revision, what does it mean to stop the process and grade a paper?

22

That Isn't What We Did in High School
Big Changes in the Teaching of Writing
Donald A. McAndrew

Donald A. McAndrew spends his work days teaching writing to undergraduates and the teaching of writing to college and secondary teachers. When not teaching, he works in his garden, listens to classical music and jazz, fishes from his boat or kayak, beats his three kids at tennis, and enjoys his wife's gourmet cooking. Currently he is writing about the teacher as leader in writing classrooms and about teaching writing as a spiritual act.

When I sat down to start playing with this essay, I decided to write it directly to the students I have now—Diane, Shelley, and Lori; Eric and Darin; Julie, Leigh, and Ed; Dwight and Will and Chuck—to see them sitting there, me flopped in a student desk, sipping hot black coffee, gabbing about writing and the teaching of writing. I guess it's fair to say that this piece is dedicated to those students—they are the ones who asked the questions that got me thinking about how our class was different from their high school English classes. In fact, as you'll see below, I quote directly from written answers and comments they gave to questions I asked about our class. So, this essay will be both to them and from them, a testament to their risking tough questions and to their insights in helping us all find answers.

On the first day of our writing class, I pass out a course overview sheet, which shows what we will do in terms of work and grades. It doesn't take long for my students to realize that this course is going to be really different from what they expect. They expect a rerun of Grade 12 English, just a little tougher; after all, this is college. Well, very quickly they realized they are wrong—this course isn't going to be much like high school English, or at least most high school English courses. Here they will choose their own topics to write about. They will draft and revise in class. They will work with other students who will read their drafts and try to help improve them, and they will meet one-to-one with me to talk about their developing drafts. They will read what they decide they need to read to help with their pieces of writing and with their growth as a writer. They will turn in only their best papers for grades, and they will have a say in that grade. Here there won't be tests, lectures, raising hands, desks in rows, and a teacher up front. But there will be portfolios, peer response, talk, movement, groups, conferences, and everybody, including the teacher, writing things that are important to them, sharing those pieces for feedback and revision. This is different from most high schools, oh, yeah.

In what follows, I show you some of the differences you might see in a writing class that is taught like ours, taught as current theory and research on teaching writing would tell teachers to teach. I do this by letting you hear the voices of my students reporting on life in our class. After that, I also explain why our class is taught as it is—theory and research that is the basis for the new writing class that many of you will experience. So, let me start by showing you some of the things my students saw as different from English classes in high school.

Differences from Previous English Classes

Atmosphere of the Class

Students frequently told me that the biggest difference they saw between their high school classes and our class was that the atmosphere was more "relaxed and comfortable" and "wasn't as tense." As a couple of students said, "it's not a sit-down-and-shut-up class" or a "sit, listen, and take notes class." Many also reported that there was "a ton more interaction between the students" than there had been in their high school classes.

Class Activities

Students characterized the activities in their high school English classes as centered on analyzing literature, test taking, and grammar. Most often they mentioned literature, saying that they "read plays, learned about the different ages in history, and read certain works from these ages." After reading, the teacher "stood in front of the class telling us the acceptable interpretations."

Next most often they mentioned studying "pieces of English like vocabulary, grammar, and punctuation" and "taking objective tests on trivial facts that I memorized and repeated on the test." Finally, they mentioned doing some writing, but explained that "the teacher was more concerned with grammar, fragments, commas, etc., rather than really what was in the paper."

In our class, whatever reading was done, whether literature or anything else, was decided on by each individual writer because of a need they felt based on a piece of writing they were working on. In our class, we never study the pieces of English, only the wholes, like pieces of student writing or pieces written by professionals or previous students. And in our class, I'm concerned mostly with what is in the paper, its ideas and content, not fragments and commas.

Writing Assignments

In high school, students told me that "the teacher controlled the topic" and that "you had to write about what the teacher wanted which was usually about a book we had to read" or "something you didn't know much about." Even the topics concerning the book were "very regimented." In our class, students told me they felt that they "could write about what you feel like writing about and this is good because it forces you to really know what you are talking about." One student explained it this way: "I have to write about topics of known interest to me because, if I'm not interested in the topic, my paper usually isn't my best work." Other students reported that writing about topics that they chose helped them to "expand on your own individual ideas" and "to be able to explore my own writing more."

Students also reported that their high school teachers controlled the form of their pieces of writing by requiring papers "always in the same style and always five paragraphs." In our class, the form of the writing and its length are decided by the writer. Also, students repeated that in our class they just flat out did more writing, lots more. In high school they "didn't do much writing at all" except for "maybe a few stories and poems and essays about literature." In our class, they "get a *lot* of practice writing and revising every day."

Response and Revision

My students reported that in high school they "wrote and revised by myself and turned it in to the teacher for her feedback." They also reported that "it was rare that students read and responded to each other's papers; only the teacher did that." They found this system of response to be inadequate, complaining that "there was no second chance to revise or rewrite a paper; so you couldn't learn from your mistakes." In our class, as you've probably already guessed, we did things differently. While writers were working on pieces, they could ask me or peers for a response. They found the one-to-one conferences with me valuable; they gave them "help when it was needed" during the process of

writing the piece, helping the writers see "ways to better their work" and
"what we could do to improve them." Students found response from peers
equally valuable, stating that it was "beneficial to have your peers read and
criticize your paper" because writers are "simply too involved to realize an
error or another route to take" and because "being able to read other students'
writings is a good way to see and compare the way they write with the way
you write."

[handwritten: good stuff]

Outcomes and Improvements

Students reported that they felt "more comfortable to express themselves" and
that comfort "helped you become more of an individual" and that "by writing
freely on topics of our own choice, we are learning about ourselves." Students
also thought that the frequent interaction between peers "taught me a lot about
other people" and gave them "respect for the opinions of others and showed
me how to handle them in a mature and respectable way." Others reported that
the peer interaction taught them "to be a little more outgoing," "helped us
make friends," and "gave me a sense of belonging."

[handwritten in margin: High school concerned only with grades and test scores]

   In addition to these personal effects, students also reported that our course
had effects on their growth as writers. They reported that writing "was not so
intimidating"; so they "became more interested in it" and "put more effort into
it." They realized that "it's what goes in the paper, thoughts and feelings, that
are most important" and that they can "set aside worries about grammar and
spelling and get my ideas on paper instead." They realized "the importance of
receiving feedback and revising more than once or twice."

Theory and Research Behind Our Writing Class

One of the most important things for you to realize about our class is that it is
well grounded in the latest understandings about how teachers *can best teach
students to be better writers*. I like to think of our class as our construction of
a state-of-the-art writing class. Your college writing class will not be exactly
like our class, but you will see many parallels because your class and our class
are grounded in the same body of theory and research, state-of-the-art theory
and research, if you will. In what follows, I give you an overview of that theory
and research so you'll see that we have powerful reasons for the things we do
in our class. Then I close by tying that theory and research back to specific features of our class, showing you the theory and research behind a couple of
activities that are at the heart of teaching and learning writing.

Social Constructionists

When I think of the theorists and researchers who support our writing class, I
think of three groups, each with a fancy name and all overlapping each other

a bit. The first group of theorists and researchers are called "social constructionists." These people are probably at the center of current understandings about how writing works and about how people learn to use it. As their name suggests, they are concerned about two issues—society and construction.

With "social" they hope to emphasize the fact that language is a phenomenon of societies, created by them and serving them. Language exists at a social level as speakers/listeners and writers/readers communicate. All language use occurs in a social world, among language users. Even when we sit alone writing at our desk, we are constantly thinking of the people we are writing to, the people whose previous writing we have read, and the people we have talked to. We are always in society.

By "constructionist" this group hopes to stress that language, and society itself for that matter, are constructed by humans. This constructionist belief also extends to what society does with its constructed language—it constructs communication, meaning, knowledge. We make our own personal understanding in language, either speech or writing, and share it with others as they listen or read. From this sharing of our individual understandings, we construct still more complex knowledge, both as individuals and as groups. Social constructionists believe we are simultaneously both individual and social, individuals-in-society, and that we build our knowledge and beliefs as a result of our lives and language as individuals-in-society. Knowledge is something we build, we create; knowledge is a social construction. That means that there is no knowledge "out there"; it is only "in here"—in the mind of social beings constructing it through language, not in textbooks, not in libraries. When you learn, you are not taking something from "out there" and stuffing it "in here." Rather you are building, creating, constructing it as an individual-in-society.

Participationists

The second group of theorists and researchers behind the new writing class is the one I call "participationists." This group stresses that to know something, to have knowledge, means to participate in its making, constructing through language, reading, writing, and talking to others who are also participating in making knowledge. Participation is the key—being active, doing it, joining in history, accounting, nursing, sociology as a language user. For example, a discipline like biology is not in the biology textbook, something objective and outside people; rather biology is what participating biologists say it is as they use language in a community of other biologists to construct their discipline of biology. The biology textbook is just one person's construction of her understanding of the field of biology in written language. Others will read it, talk about it, and write about it. She will read, talk, and write about what they say. And it is this participation in the language interaction of these individuals-in-society that creates biology as a field of study.

Think about schools and classrooms. Participationists say that teachers can't give you knowledge; you have to make it by participating in language activities. Just as biologists have to make biology by reading, writing, and talking, by participating in the discipline of biology, so too you must participate in the language of your classes. Your General Psychology class is just that—yours; you construct it by reading, discussing, writing, in a group of others who are also making their General Psychology. It is the -*ing* on *making* that is important—the process and activity of making. Knowledge is an action—in this case a participation in the language of a certain subject. During language participation in psych class, all members, students and teacher, create General Psychology—it is a social construction made through participation in language.

Socio-psycholinguists ↙ *dang*

The third group of theorists and researchers who support our writing class are the "socio-psycholinguists." Where the social constructionists look at our world generally—society, knowledge, language—and participationists look at knowledge and language, socio-psycholinguists look specifically at language, trying to form the big picture of how language works. Many have studied reading/writing, and it is these people who give us a lot of support for what we do in our class. Socio-psycholinguists have demonstrated that reading and writing are processes by which we make meaning—writers construct their own meaning and readers construct their own meaning, both actively building the meaning we commonly think of as "in the print" when, in reality, meaning is in writers and readers, in people not ink on the page. Writers and readers bring their prior knowledge of the world and language to bear on the new language event as they make their meaning based on this prior knowledge.

Socio-psycholinguists also remind us that reading and writing are a social action, always involving others. Here they echo the social constructionists and participationists I described above. They also emphasize the significance of context, the environment in which language use occurs, showing us that all language is inextricably tied to its context. The word STOP is a lot different on a road sign than it is in a magazine advertisement; the context in which the word occurs really gives much of its meaning. They demonstrate that real writing and reading only exist in real contexts, the natural and complex events of whole language at work among a group of languagers.

And finally, socio-psycholinguists emphasize how important risk taking and ownership are in improving reading and writing. They argue that learners must feel comfortable enough to risk making a mistake because this is the only way to learn; without risk there is little important learning. They also argue how important ownership is in improving writing and reading. Writers and readers must feel as if they own the meanings they make; they should not feel that they are forced to make a meaning someone else wants. The class focus should always be their piece of writing, written their way, and their response to reading, constructed as their prior knowledge tells them.

A Final Look at Our Class

Above I showed you two things about our class: first, a portrait of our class based on how my students reported it was different from the classes they had in high school and, second, some of the theory and research that supports our class. Now let me try to draw these two together by explaining how the theory and research specifically supports two activities at the heart of our class.

In our class peers frequently respond to each other's drafts. Why is this a good thing to do based on our state-of-the-art theory and research? Peer response creates a minisocial constructionist world. Writing is social because you share it with other students and you may even have them in mind while you write. You, in turn, read their writing. All of this is done with much talk about your construction of ideas as peers have constructed it while reading your piece. Everyone is participating in making meaning while they write and while they read the writing of others. You and your peer responder make your meanings based on your previous experience of life and language. The class becomes a group of writers and responders, all writing and responding to the meanings constructed. The teacher also joins in the process of writing and responding, focusing on meaning as the highest priority and creating a comfortable atmosphere where risk taking is easy. I hope you hear the echoes of the theory and research I described above: "minisocial constructionist world," "participating in the construction of meaning as the highest priority," and "comfortable atmosphere for risk taking."

Let me show you another example. In our class, students write mostly about self-selected topics. How is this grounded in state-of-the-art theory and research? Since prior knowledge of the world and language is the starting place for all language and learning, as socio-psycholinguists explain, then choosing your own topics, forms, and lengths seems like the perfect place to begin improving your writing. Your prior knowledge is at the center. This creates a context for class writing that is more like real, authentic writing—you write about what you know and value. From the outset of each piece you have almost total ownership of ideas, form, and the processes of your writing. Since the atmosphere is relaxed and comfortable, making risk taking easy, and since you are writing about topics and in forms that you know about and are interested in, participation in the life of the class happens naturally. You become an active participant in the construction of your improvement as a writer, something that participationists tell us is essential to knowledge, to knowing how to write well. Again, listen to the echoes of theory and research: "prior knowledge of language and the world," "participation in natural context," and "ownership of ideas, forms, and processes."

I hope that the two examples of peer groups and self-selected topics show you that our class is firmly grounded in state-of-the-art theory and research.

Remember this, especially when your writing class is doing things that seem different from many of the things you did in high school. When your writing class shows some of the features I've talked about, be glad because you're getting your money's worth for your tuition. Be glad also because you have a great chance to improve your writing ability, and that's what a first-year college writing course is all about.

Sharing Ideas

- What did you read and write about in high school? Do you agree with Don McAndrew's students that your classes focused more on the form than the content of your writing?

- Did you ever have two writing teachers who took very different approaches? Tell the stories of those two classes.

- Do you agree with Don that reading in a writing class should be done *for* the writer's own purposes and that a writer should pick his or her own topics? Why or why not? What does that mean for you as a writer? How do you go about finding your own readings and topics?

- Before your current writing class, did you ever share your work with peers? How did that work? List some ways you could have made the sharing more successful.

- When you're sitting by yourself writing, what are the influences you feel? Do you agree with the social constructionists that you aren't writing alone? To what degree are you remembering other writers and teachers or things you've read and friends you've talked to about your writing?

- Try writing two descriptive scenes. In one, you're composing alone (What does the place look like, what are you doing, what in particular are you eating, listening to, feeling, thinking, and so on?). In one, you're composing—or talking about composing—with others (Who is there, what is each person saying and doing? How do you feel, what do you see, notice, or need?). Rereading each descriptive scene, how are you a different (more or less successful) writer in each scene?

- If you've never before thought of yourself as a participationist, what does that mean for how you act in the classroom, particularly the writing classroom? If you're shy, what might you do? If you're confused, what might you do? If you're not shy at all, how as a class member can you help those who are shy or confused?

- Now that you've thought about this new type of classroom, think of your strengths as a writer and as a class member. Explain what you contribute.

23

When All Writing Is Creative and Student Writing Is Literature

Wendy Bishop

Wendy Bishop worked with writers and writing teachers at Florida State University. She arrived in Tallahassee after some years living and teaching in Alaska, Arizona, Nigeria, and California. She wrote about the connection between composition and creative writing; she wrote poems, stories, and essays. And she enjoyed seeing her children—Morgan and Tait—grow into writing and reading. They take particular pleasure when her books include their names, which they always do.

Here are journal excerpts from two writing students:

June

If we are to accept the definition of a writer as one who writes, we must accept the fact that writers are not a special type of person. Those who write might be of any age, shape, background or interest. They may produce a technical manual or a provocative essay or a piece of artistic prose. The one thing they hold in common is the use of language.

If I write a letter to my friend, I am a writer. If I submit a term paper of the same caliber of technique to a committee judging a dissertation, they might dispute whether or not I am a writer! Perhaps writing, like beauty, is in the eye of the beholder.

On the other hand, I can consider myself a writer if no one beholds that I write. Emily Dickinson certainly was a writer during her lifetime, not just after the discovery of her wealth of poetry. The first grader who tells in scrawled words and pictures of the arrival of a baby sister should be encouraged to call herself and be called the writer of that piece.

Perhaps by widening the definition of writer and dissolving the aura of specialness as a prerequisite, we might better encourage possible writing artists to give it a try. Ah-ha! Now there is another category—the writing artist. All writers won't enter that category, due to lack of talent, or dedication, or luck or some mysterious something that can't be pinned down. But with a recognition of a larger pool of writers as those who write, we are more likely to find among us those who write well.

Chris

The suggestions about how "art" writing may be similar or different from regular writing particularly intrigues me. After spending this school semester learning about composing as a process, I am more apt to see similarities between "art" and regular writing. Similarities exist in the process itself. The stages are the same whether you are wring a sonnet or an essay, pre-writing, writing, and revision. It happens over and over no matter what the outlet. The stages may vary slightly but by and large they remain similar. By learning about the composing process a writer can become more fluent in the language of writing.

In journal entries like these, collected for several years, my writing students often voice strong ideas about what constitutes good and bad writing. Many feel, or have learned to feel, that a writer either has *it* or hasn't got *it*. Sometimes, students enter my composition classroom remarking on differences between essay writing and "literary writing." Sometimes, they don't see differences, easily calling their essays "stories" and their stories "essays." Equally, many student writers are confused about the distinctions between types of writing classes they may enroll in—creative writing or composition. Is a composition class a place where they won't be allowed to be "creative"? Or a place where they just can't write poetry and fiction? And, when they move from composition to creative writing, will they be asked to put away all their compositional skills and never again write essays?

Fran

Is creative writing stuff that is done for fun, and composition stuff that the teacher makes you do? That's what it meant in elementary school, and later. Composition was writing about a specific topic, picked out by the teacher and had to be a certain length and certain form. Creative writing was anything you felt like putting down on paper.

As someone who teaches both kinds of classes and does both kinds of writing, I know that in the past composition was often taught as a skills class. Students were asked to write in particular essay forms (narration, description, exposition, argumentation) and to bring in a finished essay each week for grading. Such classes are now labeled current-traditional. Being product-oriented, those classes resulted in formulaic writing and rarely offered students glimpses into the messy, generative, exciting process of writing. Creative writing classes, too, for many years were taught in predictable ways; master poets or fiction writers asked students to share and critique a story or poem each week (again, almost always this writing represented a "finished" product). Workshops were stimulating in that twenty or more writers examined a single work. They were also frightening since a traditional creative writing workshop could feel like a performance, making new writers eager to conform to what they assumed were the expectations of their teachers or the models of "excellent" literature found in their particular class anthology.

But I don't believe either of those teaching approaches serves the writer in you very well, and my teaching strategies for both classrooms have become increasingly similar and more process-oriented. I aim to let writers see how writing is put together and to explore the necessary risks of sharing multiple drafts. I think a well taught composition or creative writing class should allow you to explore writing beliefs, writing types (genres) and their attributes, and your own writing process. You will be successful to the degree that you become invested in your work. And you need to be willing to experiment and to study your own progress.

I realize not everyone feels this way, and I believe I know why. In some classrooms, teachers encourage writing students to believe that literature consists only of famous (old) examples of poetry, fiction, and drama.

Robbie

Student "lit" is not old enough. Student writing can be literature, if it's published and recognized, and read by a lot of people. If it's just in the classroom, then it's a bill and not a law. Literature is Shakespeare, Chaucer, Coleridge, Shelly, Joyce.

But in other classrooms, teachers broaden the definition of literature to include more than texts in the traditional categories of poetry, fiction, and drama; they include nonfiction and the writings of many modern experimental writers. Students then learn to broaden their definitions, too.

David

Literature, to me, is just about anything that has been published. There are, of course, different levels of literature ranging from journals to novels, comics to compilations.

And in still other writing classrooms, teachers expand categories to include student writing as literature, encouraging writers to consider how their work functions in a universe of texts and text categories.

Karen

Student writing can be literature—it just may not necessarily be "good" literature.

Sean

There's not a reason why a student can't do it [write literature]. In fact, judging from what I've read of the students here over the last couple of semesters, they are pumping out literature.

If, during the course of your college career, you encounter two or even three writing teachers who make you feel strongly but differently about these issues, you may reasonably be confused. This essay won't resolve your confusion, but it will begin to talk about these points by letting you hear some student writers, and teachers who are writers, voicing their opinions.

Risk Taking, Creativity, Engagement

Creativity involves risk taking. It's likely that in your writing past, you were not praised for taking risks. Rather, you were told that you had to follow the conventions for the type of writing focused on in that class, writing an academic essay, a short story, or a research report. You were rarely asked to "publish" several drafts of your creative writing in workshop; instead, you were asked to produce a polished research paper and a finished story.

When writing classes don't highlight risk taking, it's hard to see the complicated ways authors go about their work. Sometimes it's difficult to realize that the "finished products" you read in anthologies often went through days, weeks, months, and years of change, alterations, false starts, and even sometimes temporary abandonment. For most of us, risk taking in writing spells disaster and failure rather than excitement and discovery. We haven't often been graded A on our outrageously playful parodies or our intelligent-but-still-problematic third drafts.

Since you generally write within classrooms and under the direction of teachers who value particular models of excellent writing, it's no wonder that you want always to present your best, most polished, most finished work to peers and your teachers. In doing this, it's natural to play it safe, but safe work is often conventional and derivative.

All this is understandable, too, since the penalty for risk taking in the traditional writing class is failure if your work is judged ineffective, unfinished, inexpert. And no one wants to fail in a writing class. Most of us remember too many past failures. We all have stories of teachers correcting our grammar and marking in red ink across every white and open space in our texts. As we grew up as school writers, there was so much to learn about spelling and sentences and paragraphs and citation systems that trying and failing in order to find a new, better, more original way of saying something would have sounded like a recipe for academic suicide. Yet without risk and experimentation, most writers remain disengaged with their work.

Fran

Then I wrote a paper that was required, and it turned out to be fun. What??!? Yes, and it was an English (ugh! don't say it!) term paper. I chose my own topic, so I wouldn't get bored with it. Something totally off the wall, so fascinating that its appeal overwhelmed my intense hatred of term papers. It was on parapsychology.

Another writer found that writing expository prose and creative prose was not a matter of inspirational difference; rather, it was a matter of cognitive difference, thinking in somewhat different ways for different purposes.

Juan

> I don't find a difference when writing expository prose and when doing "creative writing." To me, it's all essentially writing. To me, they're very similar, just the writing research comes from two different areas: internal source or external source.

For Juan, the creative writer conducts mainly "inner" research while the expository essayist conducts mainly "outer" research to support his text-in-progress.

Writing teacher Stephen Tchudi (1991) also feels that his experience writing in several genres—children's fiction to essays on teaching writing—have shown him fewer differences than similarities: "It's okay to put a little jelly on your bread-and-butter writing. My nonfiction prose style has been greatly aided by my ventures in imaginative writing" (105).

I'm suggesting then that writers need classes that allow them to take risks and experiment with prose, and they need to see similarities between the types of composing they do, adding a little jelly to their bread-and-butter writing (and I might guess that sometimes their jelly writing would benefit if it grew from the solid base of bread-and-butter prose).

Genre, Subgenres, Popular Genres, and Literary Genres

None of these suggestions means, however, that in writing classes you should stop valuing the work of professional writers or fail to study the forms their writings take. Traditionally, a great deal of student time in English classes has been spent acquiring genre knowledge, examining strategies for making poems seem like poems, stories like stories, and essays like essays. So part of the writing classroom, too, always involves the study of exemplary or expert writing in the forms you hope to learn. But you also always need the opportunity to write against and experiment with those forms. *You have to try it to do it*, whether bread-and-butter *or* jelly writing.

All of us can learn to value literary forms just as all of us value nonliterary forms or literary subgenres. My own not-so-hidden secret is that I love the writing of women detective novelists as well as the finest, most famous academic poetry I've ever read (and I've read a lot of both). Within her genre, for my money, Agatha Christie is still tops. Just as within his genre of lyric English verse, Gerard Manley Hopkins produced writing of incredible power.

Further, I've seen that my students have the same ability to perform well in many types of writing—many genres—if they choose and therefore value those forms. Over several years of writing and publishing student work in books about writing, I've come to like the works of Ken Wademan, Pam Miller, and Sean Carswell—who were writing essays, journal entries, in-class writing experiments, nonfiction, and parody—as well as any writing I've ever read. And these writers have strong feelings about their work because they are involved with it; they take risks, but also they take writing seriously.

Sean

I like to think all of my expository prose is creative. I like to think that the only difference is that it's focused on something that bores the hell out of most people. Also, my expository prose generally doesn't have characters, a plot, or foul language. Not that the language in my "creative" writing is foul, just a bit more vulgar.

Everything I write is literature and I'm offended that you'd doubt me. Sure student writing is literature. F. Scott Fitzgerald wrote the first half of *This Side of Paradise* while he was at Princeton. I've seen pieces go through the workshops here that are better than any John Updike I've read. Langston Hughes poem "Poem for English B" or something like that was written in college, and that's a great poem. I think Kerouac started his first novel at Columbia. I guess all that literature is taking on a theme worth reading about, writing well, i.e., good images, powerful language, different levels of meaning, none of the shit that's in Danielle Steel. There's no reason why a student can't do it.

You can see from Sean's remarks that widening what we define as creative and literary and viewing student writing as literature doesn't prevent us from categorizing and judging writing; humans understand their world through categories and judgments. I would simply argue that we shouldn't assume that there is only one way to categorize or that those categories should (or could) hold fast for all people, in all cultures, in all historical times.

Current theories of reading and writing suggest that there is no ideal, exemplary "best poem" or "great American novel" out there, waiting to be written. Rather, once texts are composed, we find them more or less like other texts that we have already sorted by general categories, *and* we do this sorting by community agreement: We do it within the worlds of literary critics, the worlds of English departments, the worlds of writing classrooms, the worlds of independent reading groups, and so on.

Karen

Literature to me can be just about anything. The word "literature" is kind of lofty and snobbish to me. The distinction I'd make is between "good" literature and "bad" literature. I don't have any rules for that—I think for example, that something like an article in the *Enquirer* is bad literature compared to maybe *Moby Dick*—then, again, if an *Enquirer* article was taken from its context and issued as a satire of comedy piece, it might be good (author's intent can be important in *some* instances . . .).

Karen is grappling with a category system here that says *Moby Dick* is better than an article in the *National Enquirer* just as I for many years felt a bit silly that I enjoyed Agatha Christie (and the subgenre of detective novels) as well as the work of Gerard Manley Hopkins (academic poetry).

Of course, most writers aim for a genre at some point in their drafting process. These days, we know writers can incorporate a lot of what they hope to share, but not all that they wish to share; they are unable to *fix* a text so that each reader will read it in exactly the same way because readers bring themselves, their backgrounds, associations, experience with texts, and so on, to each reading occasion.

Since a text can never be completely fixed, it is open to interpretation. Readers can offer several possible readings of your text without doing the work a disservice, although certainly some readings appear more "sophisticated" or may turn out to be closer to your original intention than others. At the same time, often you fail in your intentions and are unable to incorporate some of the genre characteristics you had hoped to incorporate, leading to a less than successful text.

For instance, your argument may be based on shaky facts, your "serious" story may be sewn together from absurd and unbelievable events, your *free* verse may go "Ta-dum, Ta-dum, Ta-dum" with constrained regularity, or your informal journal may be knotted up with self-consciousness. It takes study and time and practice to turn out a "traditional" piece of work in an accepted form and style (essay or novel or newspaper article) just as it takes study and time and practice to loosen the bounds of accepted conventions to write an exciting, experimental, or exploratory piece.

Equally, readers depend on the conventions they have learned to understand your work, yet they also need to be willing to suspend their judgments in order to understand *each* new work they encounter. A reader has to identify the genre you are attempting as well as decide to what degree you *intended to deviate* from the standards of that genre.

Reading and writing are *both* interpretive acts, then, requiring intricate intellectual negotiations from all parties concerned. And literature, traditionally, has been a set of texts, all having features that a group of readers and writers have agreed upon. This set of texts changes as the community changes, for, over time, agreement about common features of those texts changes. It's always been that way, even though English teachers often prefer their set— called a canon—of texts fixed, and therefore easier to "cover."

But sermons and letters have gone "out" of the set and stories and poems *of certain agreed upon quality* have been put "in." Women and racial, ethnic, and class minorities have often been out but nowadays many are arguing for including them as in. Students have often been out, but they know better, seeing themselves as in. After all, *someone* has to write literature before it can be classified as such.

Charles

Student writing is definitely literature; Literature is not only found in textbooks, it has to start somewhere.

Gordon

Student writing is always literature, however, the quality of that literature is never determined by the writer, but by the readers of that work.

Bill

To me, if a piece of written work is read by even a few people and enjoyed by at least one—then it was worth writing. The amount of popularity a piece gets is not NECESSARILY how good a piece of writing is, but what is most readily accepted at that time. What I'm writing now is not literature, but it could be if I spent a lot of time editing, and rewriting it would probably sound a whole lot different. I think that student literature can be considered literature if the student perfects the piece through revision. Many students disbelieve this because a lot of work is involved and many papers turned in are not up to literary standards are discouraged.

I believe student writing is literature, too.

I understand that conventional standards for judging writing always affect us.

At the same time, we, in our classroom communities, always affect those standards when we discuss together what we know about and appreciate in the writing we review.

That's how writing and reading work.

I hope you can see how certain questions about texts—When should writers obey or break writing conventions? What is successful work and unsuccessful work? What makes a poem a poem, a story a story, and an essay and essay?—have always interested those who write and study writing. Such questions are perhaps answered best by the nonanswer of overlapping genre categories; that is, categories don't start and stop but shade into each other. You can learn to write a traditional poem, and you can take risks with that form, exploring prose poems and short fiction along the way. You can learn to write the traditional first-year writing essay, and you can enliven that form by taking risks with your voice and your style as you adopt first person (I), add some unexpected narration, and/or use logic lightly. Sometimes you'll fail, but you'll always find that you learn from exploring conventions, sometimes—often—you learn as much by breaking those conventions.

Literature in the Writing Student

The questions and voices I've shared here suggest that you should approach composition classes and creative writing classes in pretty similar ways. Overall, both types of classrooms need to encourage *and reward* risk taking and experimentation as you learn to conform to and break genre conventions. Mimi Schwartz (1989) writes:

> To value self-investment, to avoid premature closure, to see revision and discovery, to go beyond the predictable, to risk experimentation, and above all, to trust your own creative powers are necessary for all good writing, whether it is a freshman theme, a poem, a term paper. . . . Few of us reward risk taking that fails with a better grade than polished but pedestrian texts. We are more product-oriented, judging assignments as independent of one another rather than as part of a collec-

tive and ongoing body of work. No wonder that students interpret our message as "Be careful, not creative!" (204)

If you are creative before you are careful, you will be more likely to gain an understanding of the writing process of professionals. This will happen when your workshops focus on drafting (being creative), revision, style experiments, editing (being careful), and use of portfolio evaluation (which allows you to share both experiments and final products). And being part of such a classroom doesn't mean that you won't still have to examine and explore some of these issues for yourself.

Anji

Of course student writing can be literature. If critics consider some of the trash out today to be literature, you better believe that students can write literature too. The ability to write something that is considered literature is not only a God-given talent. Most people can do it if they just make the time and collect their thoughts.

Like Anji, most of us are given to grand pronouncements about the quality of this or that piece of writing, but we need to temper our value judgments with an understanding of genre conventions, how they developed, and how they have gained value in particular communities.

Summer

Literature what is canonized by the unknown people who create anthologies and textbooks, is a formal definition. In an informal definition, literature is a completed piece which has been published or disseminated to an audience, and has been read by a number of persons (which would include everything, even graffiti and advertisements). To narrow the definition, it is not intended for business or propaganda purposes, is received in a "legal" form (NO graffiti, etc.) and is meant to be enjoyed by readers and meets cultural standards of literature (circular argument). Unpublished works can never be literature, no matter how worthy.

You start acquiring this knowledge as you learn about category systems and how texts work in the classroom community; you also learn that it is possible for you to become part of that writing community. These questions you have, the beliefs you hold, the worries you may feel, can all be explored. Remember, risk taking and experimentation results in knowledge, not in anarchy. At the same time, if your writing goal is, ultimately, to become a mystery novelist, you won't be tempted completely to ignore the requirements and limitations of that type of writing. A consummate mystery writer, Agatha Christie (1977) once wrote:

If you were a carpenter, it would be no good making a chair, the seat of which was five feet up from the floor. It wouldn't be what anyone wanted to sit on. It is no good saying that you think the chair looks handsome that way. If you want to write a book, study what sizes books are, and write within the limits of that size. If you want to write a certain type of short story for a certain type of magazine you have

to make it the length and it has to be the type of story that is printed in the magazine. If you like to write for yourself only, that is a different manner—you can
make it any length, and write it in any way you wish; but then you will probably
have to be content with the pleasure alone of having written it. (334–335)

When you view your writing as literature—through a broad definition and
understanding of that word—you allow yourself to share a supremely satisfying human activity. For most of us, writing is never easy, but it is made worth-
while when we "publish" in the writing classroom and when we are "read by
even a few people and enjoyed by at least one."

Works Cited

Christie, Agatha (1977). *An Autobiography*. Great Britain: Collins.

Schwartz, Mimi (1989). "Wearing the Shoe on the Other Foot." In Joseph Moxley
(Ed.), *Creative Writing in America*. Urbana, IL: National Council of Teachers of
English.

Tchudi, Stephen (1991). "Confession of a Failed Bookmaker." In Mimi Schwartz (Ed.),
Writer's Craft, Teacher's Art. Portsmouth, NH: Boynton/Cook.

Sharing Ideas

- Choose any quote in Wendy Bishop's essay and write your own informal
  response to the issues the writer raises. Put yourself in dialogue with the
  essay and these writers; add to our conversation.

- Wendy recommends classrooms that encourage and reward risk taking as
  you learn. Have you ever been in such a classroom (maybe your current
  class is one)? Describe how this changes what you do as a writer.

- Wendy discusses the notion that literature, according to English teachers,
  is often a canon, or set of writings, that they've agreed should be studied.
  The individual writings and types of writings may change over time: some
  are in; others are out. But what about student writings—do you think they
  should be considered literature? Explain.

- Is all writing creative?

- Do the types of skills needed for success in a composition class differ
  from those needed in a creative writing class?

- Have you ever been in a writing class that celebrated (or even admitted)
  the messy, generative, false-start-filled, painful, multiple-draft aspects of
  writing? Write about times that have or haven't acknowledged this side of
  writing.

24

I Am Not a Writer,
I Am a Good Writer

Joe Quatrone

Joe Quatrone was a student at Boise State University when he wrote this end-of-term analysis of his writing.

I am not a writer. I don't do writer-type things. I don't drink coffee. I've never read Keroak. I don't even know how to spell Keroak. I don't enjoy lurking in second-hand book stores, pretending I'm waiting desperately for delivery of one of my top-ten favorite writer's long-lost out-of-print fifth editions that will finally complete my vast comprehensive home collection. I don't have an opinion. I prefer ads to articles. I don't know what *hyperbole* really means. I like pictures. I have no interest in writing the great American novel. I don't "get" Hemingway. I think poetry is bunk. I've got bad grammar. And, I happen to believe a burp *is* an answer.

I am a good writer. I like to write what comes out of my head. I like to write about things that are goofed up in the world (not wrong, nor tragic, nor sad, nor socially unacceptable—just goofed up). I like writing with my pen on a legal pad. I like bad grammar. I like to write like I'm a camera. I like to write like I'm a Mac truck. I like to write like I'm not a writer. I like observing things. I like being a sniper. And, I like a warm, cuddly blanket with a book on a couch on a rainy day although I've never done it.

I think before I started this class, I always had this kind of defensive attitude about college writing that made me hate the prospect of it. I have always had a sort of laisez-faire attitude about grammar and style that I enjoy on a personal level, but that didn't usually go over well with my former professors. It's been refreshing to be able to write like I want to and not have to worry about comments like, "what do you reeeeeeeealy mean . . . ?????" I tend to just say stuff and not flower it up, and have comfort in knowing that anything written can be considered "interpretive." I've learned that it's okay to have a style and preference in my writing, and that I don't have to write like a secretary (not an administrative assistant—a secretary) to write successfully.

I think that one of my biggest weaknesses as a writer is my attention span. George Lucas has been quoted as saying that a motion picture is never really finished, it can only be improved upon. I think the same way about writing. However, I don't have the attention span to revise and revise. Granted, I know that revising is critical and I do it with everything (sometimes to a ridiculous degree), but often I lose interest in a piece soon before it's perfected. Excuse me: improved upon.

Another weakness I have is with what I call my hootie-tootie voice. It's the voice that sounds like I'm a motivational speaker and that I live in a transparency projector. It's that voice that you have to use when writing a formal document used in a big meeting with suit-types that say words like "kudos" and "Cool beans." Barf. It's the same voice you read in retirement home brochures and oral hygiene literature. I find myself using phrases like, "point-of-interest," "key to success," and "such as." Icch. I haven't any examples to illustrate my point, other than what's above.

Most of my peers and classmates say I have a pretty good grip on writing, with a fun and witty style. The really obvious critical comments tend to focus on confusing material or stuff that comes out of nowhere in a given piece of writing. While I'm happy to have my writing received optimistically, I fear that same witty, sarcastic voice that most people like, is getting a little "old hat" for me.

I frequently wonder whether I could be a beautiful writer. Write beautiful things that make people think deeper and more emotionally. I wonder if I could write about a walk down a dirt road and make it both interesting and beautiful. I know how the greats do it. I just wonder if I have what it takes to hit those things that everyone reads and goes, "Yea! I know exactly what he's talking about." It's that one thing that any reader can identify with and understand on an emotional level, exactly what I'm describing about that one rusted hinge. Or that leather boot that caressed the foot like a long-lost kitten. Hands touching cold, lifeless steel in the moonlight, burning like a hot iron in a calf's tender hide.

Hmm. That's not so bad. I guess I'm not that bad a writer. I guess I have a lot to learn, too, though.

Sharing Ideas

- Read Joe Quatrone's statement in light of Wendy Bishop's essay in the previous chapter. What assumptions does he seem to have about art and writing and himself as a writer? How do you think he'd respond to that essay?

- How do you think you've changed from the beginning of your writing class to the end? Do you hold contradictory opinions about your own work like Joe does? What do you think your classmates think about you as a writer? What do you think at this point in time?

- Good teachers like to read writers' self-analyses because they can always tell teachers something about their work that can't be seen from looking at the products alone. What have you learned about writing this term that couldn't possibly (or just doesn't) show up in your written products?

- Now, read your products—what do you like best, want to celebrate, think you'll enjoy rereading in the future and why?

25

Access: Writing in the Midst of Many Cultures

Hans Ostrom

Hans Ostrom is Professor of English and codirector of African American Studies at the University of Puget Sound. He has also taught at the University of California, Davis, and at Johannes Gutenberg University in Mainz, Germany. In 1994 he was a Fulbright Senior Lecturer at Uppsala University, Sweden. His books include *Three to Get Ready* (novel), *Langston Hughes: A Study of the Short Fiction*, and *Lives and Moments: An Introduction to Short Fiction*. With Wendy Bishop, he edited *Genres of Writing*. He likes to garden and listen to the radio.

I listen to the radio every day, and every day I hear at least one advertisement for this or that company "offering" (selling) "Internet access." Great word, *access*, as verb or noun. *Internet*, as a word, I can take or leave. *Access* seems to be a crucial word these days. Consider:

access to quality education

access to health care

"access denied"

breakdowns in security that allow terrorists access (to embassies, for instance)

computer crashes that prevent access to the hard drive

"freeway access"

"easy access!"

"let me access your account"

"don't go there" (i.e., access inadvisable)

Jerzy Kosinski wrote a novel, later turned into a film, called *Being There*, but it seems our lives have become all about Getting There. In the magical place of There, *there* is something we need or something we need to protect from others or protect others from. All the action, though, is in the access: a key; a door; an on-ramp; the right software; a map; a code; a password; an account; a card. Ours is not the Age of Information, Chivalry, Reason, Innocence, Space, or X. Ours is the Age of Access.

Naturally, once we "get" (access) There, we learn that There is a place from which we shall require access to other theres. The Internet especially seems to be an infinite string of accesses. The *Oxford American Dictionary* (1980), page six, warns me not to confuse *access* with *excess*. Okay, I promise. However, I am bound to observe that our culture's concern with access seems excessive, to the point of being obsessive.

Offered access to this book, I hereby announce my interest in how we access the many cultures around us—how we do so especially in college, particularly through writing and reading, specifically in first-year writing courses. Let me now move the mouse of this essay and click twice on the *Anecdote* icon and share some microstories with you. (Names of students are fictitious.)

Place: Departmental Reception for Graduating English Majors, on the morning before graduation. A father comes up to me. He is a native of Charleston, South Carolina. He is wealthy, polished, polite. His daughter, Grace, transferred to the University of Puget Sound when she was a sophomore. He thanks me for the wonderful experience she has had, but his face is grim as he continues: "Her beliefs were really challenged here." "Oh," I say. He moves on to talk with others. Although "Oh" was probably an appropriate response, given the context, other responses came to mind: "We'll try not to let that happen again." "You're entitled to a full refund." "Which beliefs?" Or, "It must have been an accident" (for Puget Sound is a small liberal-arts college; the student body is 85 percent white; the curriculum is most traditional). Or, "Her beliefs were challenged and—what?—what was the result?"

Place: First-Year Composition Class. We've been reading Primo Levi's book, *Survival in Auschwitz*. This day our conversation drifts to the subject of anti-Semitism in the contemporary United States. A student mentions that she heard someone on a talk show claim that "Jews control the media." Most students greet her report as she intended it: as an example of an unsupported claim in service of stereotyping and anti-Semitic lore. But one student, Stan, says, "Well, they pretty much do control the media." The discussion heats up. My contribution is to encourage the students to interrogate, not Stan, but the claim.

What is meant by "control" and "media"? The use of the word "they"—what does that suggest? Who owns NBC, CBS, ABC, CNN, BET, MTV, TCI, your favorite radio station, the company that produced your favorite CD, your hometown newspaper, the campus paper (an interesting question, this), the local avant-garde weekly? On the ownership question, we come up with answers like General Electric, Ted Turner, Rupert Murdoch, Time/Warner, I don't know, the McClatchy Family, doesn't Time/Warner own Ted Turner? Knight-Ridder papers, and so on. The claim evaporates before our eyes. But we move on to ask why some people (in general, not Stan) seem to need to believe that "Jews control the media." We discuss, and try to define, scapegoating. We discuss *theyspeak*, as in "they control the media." Eventually we get back to the unforgettable book by the Italian chemist, to our journal writing about stereotypes, to the hard work of developing topics based on *Survival in Auschwitz*.

Place: Another First-Year Writing Class. We've been reading Lorene Cary's book, *Black Ice*, much of which details her experience as an African American woman attending a virtually all white, upper-crust boarding school in New England. One of the men in class blurts out, "I'm from Idaho—black people just *look* at me and get mad!" Another student—Kathy, the only African American student in the room—says, with friendly exasperation, "Jay. I'm black. We've been in class together all term." Jay responds, "I know—I'm not talking about you!"

I'm interested in—grateful for—how guilelessly Stan and Jay recapitulate notions of "we" and "they," how they act out—no one could script it so well—issues raised in the reading and discussion, how they demonstrate a collision between beliefs they brought to college and studies they do here. I'm interested in students who keep their views to themselves, playing it safe, or holding back, or being confused, or just not caring. I'm interested in the way Kathy spoke, as a colleague, directly to Jay—in how strange (or familiar) it was for her to realize, as the class did, that for Jay the "black people" in his mind were, even after a month or more of class, disconnected from her. Ironic that, in the book, the famous lawyer Archibald Cox visits Cary's school, and while chatting with the students, turns to Cary and, about Richard Nixon, says, "He hates us, you know." Cary is thrown off balance as she realizes that Cox is talking about upper-class New Englanders and including her, a black middle-class woman not from Cox's turf.

I'm frustrated sometimes by how little difference the reading and writing seem to make, astonished at other times by how much they make, never sure how to tell one way or the other.

Place: (One More) First-Year Writing Class. We've viewed the film, *Come See the Paradise*, which concerns the internment of Japanese American citizens in "relocation camps" during World War II. We talk about how Hollywood seems to need to put a white person in the middle of stories regardless of the subject matter. In this case, it's a character played by Dennis Quaid. The character does help highlight issues of cultural differences and brings in interesting labor issues. But still. We talk about how, just fifty-some years ago, several Puget Sound undergraduates were removed from the college and sent with their families to a camp in nearby Puyallup (pronounced *Pew-al-up*), then on to an Idaho prison camp. Their families' businesses, farms, and homes were taken from them and in most cases never returned.

A student, Lori—extremely capable, thoughtful, and well read; a graduate of an ostensibly "good" West Coast high school—says, with a mixture of sadness and disbelief, to the other students, "Had you all heard about this [internment of Japanese Americans]? I'd never heard of this before we saw the movie." If it was news to other students, too, they aren't saying.

The drafts and essays that materialize impress me by how they distinguish between the movie and history, how they focus on a variety of issues—absence of due process and other illegalities, absurdities, what is "American"? tragedies, bitter ironies. After the reading, talking, and writing are all done, I find I focus on Lori's comment, "I'd never heard of this before. . . ." I am forced to remember that multiculturalism depends on information, on plain old news—some of it very old indeed.

Click Twice on *Interview* Icon

Q: What do you mean by *multiculturalism*?

A: May I plead the Fifth Amendment? I mean an active awareness of many cultures, and of cultures within or beside cultures. I mean a willingness to acknowledge cultural differences and similarities, a willingness to acknowledge what we don't know or what we think we know as opposed to what we know we know. I mean read, read, read, learn, learn, learn, write, write, write.

Q: What is *culture*?

A: A cluster of learned behavioral traits.

Q: Huh?

A: Example: *Swedish culture*. That would include geography (its influence on such things as farming and shelter), language, art, music, history, a people's sense of history, laws, attitudes toward sex/marriage/education/children/theft/murder/guns/hockey, toward Norwegians/monarchy/copper/crystal/potatoes, and so on. Swedes have a Swedish answer to the following questions: If someone invites you to come to dinner at 7:00 P.M., when do you arrive? (Exactly at 7:00, not even five minutes before or after.) Once you arrive, what is among the very first things you do? (Take off your shoes.) Maybe arrival times and shoe removal are trivial bits of the trait-culture; maybe they symbolize more significant traits.

Q: Is there such a thing as cultural purity?

A: No. Everything in one culture came from another culture—no exceptions (he said, issuing a challenge to find examples to the contrary).

Q: So all cultures are the same?

A: No. Absence of purity does not mean absence of difference or sameness of history.

Q: Why all this talk of differences? That causes trouble and just keeps dividing us.

A: Not necessarily. To observe differences—to discover, explore, even enjoy them—is not by nature a trouble-making affair. What we do with the information is our choice. We can choose to make trouble—or not. And trouble needs defining—another story.

Q: *Multiculturalism* seems so trendy, so politically correct. Such a buzzword.

A: I have been on the lookout for more than ten years, but I have yet to hear or read a definition of *politically correct* that makes any sense to me, so I can't help you there. If the *M*-word buzzes, ignore the buzzing. Consider the ideas. One idea is to study histories, customs, perspectives, beliefs. Trendy? Perhaps. But a trend is a pattern, and patterns aren't inherently good or bad. If multiculturalism suggests awareness of different histories and such, then it is not trendy in the sense of a fad. Anyone who ever tried to learn about and from other people was essentially multicultural. Anyone who ever caught the travel bug was multicultural. Anyone who was ever aware of "the many" who always, without exception, lie behind the illusion of "the one" (nation, people, kingdom, culture, state, city) was multicultural.

Q: So, the big *M*—it's a good thing?

A: Not necessarily. It's a little *m*. A perspective, a practice. It can be used for bad ends. One might become aware of a cultural difference and decide to exploit it unethically. One might equate the discomfort of being left-handed with the difficulties and pain associated with racism. This is to trivialize.

Q: What does multiculturalism have to do with first-year writing?

A: Let us now visit the Argument Web site.

A List. Racism. Anti-Semitism. Religious conflict. Terrorism. Police "profiling." Affirmative action. "English only." Immigration policies. People from different backgrounds trying to make their way in ever more populous cities. The relative ease with which we travel and communicate globally. The abundance of translated literature and subtitled cinema and television/radio in numerous languages. The terrifying ease with which ethnic conflict becomes genocide. "The race card." Segregated communities/neighborhoods. White supremacists. Haves and have-nots. Adoption of children as a global affair. This is the world in which we live.*

If one purpose of first-year writing is to reinforce your readiness to thrive in college, * and if one purpose of college is to educate you as a *citizen*, * and if a citizen should be multiculturally aware, * then multiculturalism is not, to say the least, out of place in first-year writing—*if* you buy those four premises, each marked by an asterisk (*).

More. First-year writing is the contemporary version of rhetoric. * Rhetoric is, in part, the art and craft of public discourse: persuading; discussing; debating; asserting as a citizen (member of communities). * Communities = an internet of cultures. * Therefore (*if* you buy the definitions/equations [*]), multicultur-alism plays a big role in our writing, bears directly on what, why, for whom, about whom, and to whom we write.

Also. To enter college is, literally, to enter a new culture, a new cluster of learned behavioral traits (some of which I shudder to think about). It is to encounter persons from different cultures. It is, as the father at the reception noted, to enter an arena in which your beliefs, attitudes, morals, hopes, dreads, prejudices, weaknesses, strengths, fears, ambitions, "family values," and so on, are tested. By tested I don't mean, necessarily, challenged or attacked. I mean *tried*. I mean seen in a new light. Placed in comparison and contrast.

Connection. "Essaying" is *trying* (sometimes very trying indeed). It is testing ideas—your own, someone else's: written; heard; read. It is expressing, link-ing, supporting, questioning ideas. First-year writing, then, is a fine test site where essaying and the multifaceted culture of college can meet and begin a beautiful friendship.

And Finally. Let us return to access, not to be confused with excess. Writing may be the ultimate access-software package for your cerebral hard drive. With it, you access images, memories, arguments, ideas—your own, others'. To write about a book is to access it, more powerfully than just to read it. To write *out* an idea is to see it anew. To write about yourself is to meet and greet yourself anew. Therefore, if we assume that surviving and thriving as a citizen in and of many cultures requires this capacity to access, then writing is one of a citizen's most important tools.

Click Twice on *Advice* Icon

Be the primary tester of your own beliefs and attitudes. Rely on writing to do this. Recall the father at the reception: He perceived his daughter to be a holder of beliefs and college to be a force threatening to take them away. It is com-mon to see multicultural questions pictured in such a way—as attack and defense, even as warfare. He implied that his daughter had weathered a storm or survived an onslaught.

But if we see being a citizen in and of many cultures in terms of adaptation, evolution, and discovery, then it is quite natural, productive, and smart for us to test our own beliefs and attitudes. We become more culturally nimble. We prepare ourselves for those rare genuine moments when our beliefs really are challenged. We become less defensive, in the negative sense of that term: jumpy. We see that changing beliefs is neither necessarily good nor necessarily bad, that it's a process over which we have some control. And truly, even when our beliefs and attitudes remain the same, they change. For example, a person can hold fast for a lifetime to a religious belief but also change within that belief. If you are a Muslim, Buddhist, Jew, Hindu, Christian, polytheist, agnostic, or atheist, are you the same Muslim, Buddhist (and so on) you were last year?

Find *Practice What You Preach* File

Okay, there I am at the reception. I know a little bit about the father from some things Grace has said. To this I add first impressions, then his comment about challenged beliefs and one about how sorry he is that the Citadel (a university) now has to accept women cadets. I begin to label him: conservative Southern man; wealthy; probably Republican; conservative Christian; views of race and gender probably different from my own.

As I write this essay, though, I have to admit how much I don't know about him. Truly I don't know what his views of race and gender are. I don't know to which of Grace's beliefs he was referring. Republican? Perhaps. But he could have voted for a Democrat or no one. What exactly do I mean by *conservative* and *conservative Christian*? Such imprecise terms. Also, there's what I know. I know from Grace that her father moved from Charleston some years ago to the Pacific Northwest for business reasons. Extended family members refuse to visit the Northwest. Sometimes Grace and her family feel shunned, therefore. So the father has experienced his own variety of cultural conflict.

Also, I know that visitors from France, let's say, if they were spectators at the reception, might note how similar the father and I are. We speak American English. Our sense of space and posture is probably American in some tell-tale way. We are garrulous. We're big.

I know I'm a father, too. At the reception, I think the father is overdramatizing the extent to which his daughter's beliefs were really challenged. Will I be so sanguine a decade later when my son comes home from college and talks about his classes?

Lastly, I know that by writing this essay, I've accessed the reception scene and scenes under the anecdote icon differently and more thoroughly than before. I've changed my sense of those scenes. I've recalled particulars and subtleties. I've had to think about the audience for whom I'm presenting the scenes. Matters have become complicated, in a good way.

Go Back to *Interview* Mode

Q: Yeah, yeah, but I just want to learn to write well enough to do okay in college and get a good job. Multiculturalism, multischmulturalism.

A: Practicality. I like it. Very American, culturally speaking. But even from your practical viewpoint, *Q*, writing about multicultural topics for different audiences and in different modes is excellent writerly training—or training okay enough to help you get an okay job, okay?

And there is what I call deep practicality. When you Get There—access your degree and your job—*there* will be a dizzyingly multicultural place, regardless of what and where the job is. Bet on it. As worker and citizen, you will travel strands of a multicultural internet that makes the Internet look like mere child's play—Legoland.

Click Twice on *Conclusion* Icon

The many cultures, and cultures within cultures; and beliefs, and beliefs about beliefs; and stereotypes and fears, and fears and facts and misinformation and conflicts and coalitions: these are the heart of our social, political matter. Writing as access is the heart of our educational matter. This is my conclusion, and I'm sticking to it, as now I move the mouse's arrow to the *Writing Tasks* icon.

1. Write a self-interview in which you 1 interrogates you 2 about certain beliefs—religious, political, or cultural. Make sure you 1 is as smart, logical, and articulate as you 2. Assume you 1 is not predisposed to agree with you 2.

2a. About what ethnic, religious, or political group that you do not consider your own do you find yourself making pretty hefty assumptions? List the assumptions in column A. List the support (evidence) for the assumptions in column B. In column C, admit to and list what you don't know for sure about the group. This will be a long list. Make column C the topic of an essay, the working title of which will be "What I Don't Know About [the group]." Devote part of the essay to probing how useful and accurate the Group label itself is.

2b. Write a researched essay, again based on column C (above); the working title will be, "What I Have Found Out About [the Group]."

3. Write a journal entry or an essay that recounts your having been excluded from a group (any group). Or write a journal entry (or essay) that recounts your having been accepted by a group that was initially unwelcoming.

4. Let's assume there is such a thing as "American (United States) culture." Working with other students, develop a big list of specific items you associate with this culture. Don't edit; just brainstorm. The items can be large or small, central or eccentric, major or minor. Then go back and discuss some of the items. What qualifies a given item as "American"? Even if an item

withstands scrutiny and seems still to qualify as American, discuss its source in other cultures. Write in your journal about this item. Also, write in your journal about one element of American culture that does not appeal to you.

5. There is such a thing as culture shock, something we often experience when we travel to other lands or even within our own land. We encounter differences in those infamous "learned behavioral traits," and the differences seem so abundant that we get frustrated, fatigued, stunned, homesick, even angry. Write about a personal experience of culture shock. Perhaps some thoughts about how, in time, the experience may have changed you or altered your beliefs in a good way.

6. Choose a favorite food of yours. Then search out facts about it, tracing it as far back in history and through as many cultures as you can. Let's say you choose fast-food french fries. You would research not just the culinary and cultural history of thin-sliced, deep-fried potatoes but also the history of potato-eating, of how "french" got in there, of deep-frying, of the origins of "fast food."

7. Read a book about slavery in the United States or about one significant aspect of it. Write an essay that summarizes and analyzes the book.

8a. Write a review of one (or more) of the following movies or television series: *The Black Robe*; *The Chosen*; *The Color Purple*; *Come See the Paradise*; *Do the Right Thing*; *Eyes on the Prize*; *Foreign Student*; *Gentleman's Agreement*; *Geronimo* (the most recent film); *Get on the Bus*; *The Great White Hope*; *The Holocaust*; *The Immigrants*; *Jungle Fever*; *Little Big Man*; *Malcolm X*; *The Milagro Bean Field Wars*; *Mississippi Burning*; *Mississippi Masala*; *El Norte*; *The Picture Bride*; *Pinky*; *Reservation Blues*; *Roots*; *School Ties*; *The Scottsboro Trial*; *Shoah*; *Six Degrees of Separation*; *Smoke Signals*; *Stand and Deliver*; *To Kill a Mockingbird*; *Tuskegee Airmen*; *The Wedding Banquet*; *Zebrahead*.

8b. What other kinds of writing about a film or several films might you do, and how might these be more useful than a review? Write one of such pieces.

9. Read Nikki Giovanni's book, *Racism 101*, and write an essay about the extent to which it applies to your college campus.

10. Based on personal observation, write an essay about exclusion. Many clubs, fraternities, sororities, cliques, and organizations are based as much on whom they exclude as on the alleged common interests they serve. (But perhaps your essay will take issue with this premise.) Chances are you have belonged to, been excluded from, resigned from, or observed closely such a group. Why do people practice exclusion (assuming they do so)? What are the stated and unstated criteria of exclusion? How do people justify, deny, and/or manipulate exclusion? When and on what grounds is exclusion appropriate? How would you describe the "culture" (learned behavioral traits) of exclusion?

Works Cited

Cary, Lorene (1991). *Black Ice*. New York: Knopf.

Come See the Paradise (1991). Motion picture. Twentieth-Century Fox, 1990. CBS/Fox Video. Director: Alan Parker. Writer: Alan Parker. Principal roles: Dennis Quaid; Tamlyn Tomita; Sab Shimono; Shizuko Hoshi.

Giovanni, Nikki (1994). *Racism 101*. New York: Morrow.

Kosinski, Jerzy (1972, 1985). *Being There*. Rpt. New York: Bantam Books.

Levi, Primo (1956). *The Reawakening: A Liberated Prisoner's Long March Home Through East Europe*. Trans. Stuart Woolf. Boston: Little Brown.

——— (1971). *Survival in Auschwitz: The Nazi Assault on Humanity*. Trans. Stuart Woolf. New York: Collier.

Sharing Ideas

- When you read Hans Ostrom's ten writing suggestions, which did you warm to most, and why? Which would you assign to a writing class if you were teaching, and why?

- Tell a story about you and culture. Move this story from an oral sharing to a written position statement to share with your writing group.

- How do you think Hans' style suits his argument? Were you intrigued or irritated, amused or worried by it? Is it closer to yours or farther away from your own writing preferences than other essayists in the book? Some of his discussion is about very important topics—would you approach these topics in a similar way? Why or why not?

- Think about your city—what are the big topics—the issues that garner letters to the editor? Take one up and wrestle with it. In fact, you might choose a letter to the editor and write back—exploring how you feel about a local and cultural issue. Then, ask someone in your writing group to respond to your response, and so on, around the group. Swap your "casebook of responses" with another group and read their dialogue on local issues.

- What readings would you include in a multicultural reader? (You may be taking a class that uses one right now—analyze what is included and why you think the collection is arranged and organized the way it is.)

- Tell a story about political (in)correctness—now extend that to the culture of school. What is the correct and incorrect way to be/act as a student? (You can specify the location, situations, of course.)

Part VI

Hint Sheets for
Students and Teachers

Right there, in the center over my workbench are four words in big black letters *NULLA DIES SINE LINEA*. The Latin command—"never a day without a line"—is attributed to both Horace and Pliny. Never mind who said it, it is the motto of most writers, ancient and modern, men and women. Jogging and writing require habit. And it is more productive to write every day for a short time than one day for a long time.

Brief writing periods can be amazingly effective. One prolific—and excellent—writer, Anthony Burgess, pointed out that by writing only one page per day, you can have a 365-page book drafted in a year. I find that I can get an amazing amount of writing done in bursts of half-an-hour a day, twenty minutes, fifteen; three pages a day, one page, half a page; 500 words, 300, 200, 100.

—Donald Murray, Pulitzer Prize–winning journalist

Hint Sheet A:
Inventing Inventions

The Journalist's Five Ws or Kenneth Burke's Pentad

Who? Ask who are the players involved; explore each actor involved with the subject.

What? Ask yourself how you would fully explain what the subject actually is.

Where? What is the location in which this subject occurs or the players are involved?

When? What time frame is involved in considering your subject? Ask if time is important.

Why? Ultimately, you will want to consider why your subject occurs or why it is important.

How? A sixth question is often added (although it only *ends* in a *w*). Explain for your reader how the subject occurs or how the action takes place.

Some Classical Questions for Discovery

Change Questions

What was your subject like in the past (years ago, months ago)?

What is your subject likely to become in the future, or what could it never be?

How much could your subject change before you'd have to say it was something else?

Sequence Questions

What caused your subject?

What happened just before your subject occurred?

What are the consequences of your subject?

Context Questions

Where is your subject likely to be found? Where would you never find your subject?

What is your subject's relation to its surroundings? Does your subject fit in? Is it appropriate?

Contrast Questions

In what way is your subject different from other things (persons, places) that I might know or feel are similar?

In what ways is your subject different from what I expected?

How does the way you feel about your subject differ from that of other people?

Classification Questions

In what way is your subject similar to things I know? What does your subject remind you of?

What other things would you group your subject with? What is the larger category your subject could be considered a part of?

Analogy Questions

Analogy is a special kind of comparison; its questions put more weight on the word *like*.

Your subject is like what? His loyalty was like a plant's turning toward the light, imperceptible but certain.

Your subject is as what as what? His outrage was a fierce as a mother robin protecting her nest.

Hint Sheet B: Understanding Writing Assignments

Dan Melzer

Seven Tips for Understanding Writing Assignments

1. Look for key verbs in the assignment.

2. Figure out what genre—what type—of essay you've been assigned.

3. Figure out who the audience for the writing assignment is.

4. Pay close attention to how the teacher will evaluate the assignment.

5. Think about the assignment in terms of the class as a whole.

6. Don't be afraid to ask the teacher questions.

7. If the teacher lets you choose the topic, pick something that's original and that you're genuinely interested in.

Some Questions to Ask a Teacher to Help You Understand an Assignment

- Can you explain what you mean by (summarize, define, compare, etc.)?

- What genre would you consider this assignment to be?

- Do you have any examples of this genre?

- Who is the audience for the assignment?

- What will you focus on when you evaluate the assignment?

- Will you evaluate the writing process, or just the final product?

- Can I use personal experience in my writing?

- What citation format should we use to cite sources?

- How much emphasis do you place on correct grammar and spelling?

- What kind of format are you looking for in the final paper?

- How is this assignment similar to/different from previous assignments?

Hint Sheet C: Your Journal

Names Include. Learning logs; to-do lists; dialogue journals; day books; travel journals; double-entry journals; reading logs; diaries; collage journals; field-notes, daily planners; e-mail journals; letter correspondences; audit books; dialogue journals with teachers; letters as journals (please feel free to add to this list).

Uses. To keep track and keep records; to keep in touch with yourself; catalog the world; make connections (between something being studied and seen and you); to create places to learn (to write, to read, to analyze, to speculate); to create places to play, to digress, to speculate; places to experiment, to take risks, to be excessive, to be safe, and to be personal (add to this list; try some new options).

Useful Habits. Use the first person; don't worry about looks or worry about looks only if it's fun to play with typography and mixed media; write regularly; write informally and explore leads and digressions; write in your own voice(s), that is, use slang, dialect, comfortable sayings and language; make use of chronology and explore time constraints; don't worry about correctness and grammar and punctuation and readers—you don't have readers unless you choose to share with someone (add to this list; make a version that is appropriate for you).

What Not to Do. Don't grade them, correct them, or force writers to publicly share things meant to be private without warning or permission; don't let them turn into busywork; don't make boring catch-up entries or give up because a pattern is broken—just plunge in again; don't be pedantic, over-precise; don't pay more attention to form than content or forget to be playful (add to this list).

Hint Sheet D: A Sampler of Creative Ways to Respond to a Literary Text

1. Choose a resonant phrase or crucial word and begin clustering in response.

2. Write a letter to a character or author—ask questions, give responses.

3. Write a reversal—change gender, actions, scene, or simply reverse language.

4. Write an extension—take the piece an hour, day, or week beyond its current ending.

5. Write a treatment—what contemporary movie stars would you have star in this text and why?

6. Explore the narrator or a character—use the following metaphoric prompts to add to your understanding of the narrator/character:
   - He/she is the kind of person who wears . . .
   - He/she is what color?
   - He/she is keeping what secret(s)?
   - He/she has this dream . . .
   - He/she would like to say but never says:
   - He/she is what kind of fruit? what kind of landscape? what kind of time of day?
   - What job should this person never have? what kind of a car does he/she drive?
   - This person is what kind of weather?
   - And so on.

7. Choose five words from the text you're studying—words that resonate or have odd significance, interesting locations. Freewrite on each for one minute. Then choose one of the freewrites to continue into an initial response writing.

8. Recast an issue or scene.
   - If the text talks about love and food, freewrite about love and food.
   - If a text talks about moral and ethical decisions/turning points, freewrite about those in your own life.
   - If the text has a lyrical description of x (summer, winter, the coast, and so on) freewrite about x in your own life.

- Draft your own text in a situation contemporary to you (create a word meal for a current lover, describe a current living landscape for a distant friend, and so on).

9. Explore the text's rhetoric and style.

10. Write a parody (new subject, same linguistic style).

11. Change genre (turn a poem into a prose passage by filling in gaps and re-creating sentence patterns; turn prose into a poem by lining out, cutting, repeating, altering the rhythm).

12. Write a reply to the text using the same style (or a reply for a character in the text).

13. Collage your text (any of the above exercises) with those of members of a group.

Hint Sheet E: A Discussion of Drafting Levels

In workshop and process-oriented classrooms, you'll want to develop your own classroom language for revision—zero draft, rough draft, first draft (I call these full-breadth drafts nowadays; complete enough to merit discussion but really an initial trying on of ideas that will be revised after readers' responses), professional drafts, portfolio-quality draft, and so on—because so much writing classroom time these days is spent in drafting and response sessions.

Early Revision. In early drafts, a writer is primarily involved with developing ideas although also making initial decisions about what form might best communicate those ideas. A writer tries out options, lots of them, options and ideas that are never seen by a reader. This happens because a writer at the beginning needs to look at the big picture and it takes some time to plot out that picture.

During early drafts, a writer is not very concerned with the fine details—mechanics, spelling, punctuation, and word choice. The writer pushes on to discover. The writer is not worried about perfection. To do this type of drafting, the writer must be flexible, try not to worry about the product, and learn to trust the process of setting out on a writing journey.

Late Revision. Late revision is a relative concept. For some writers, late revision happens in the second draft and for others it happens during draft twenty-five. During late revision, a writer finalizes ideas, fits those ideas to the form the writer has chosen, and becomes concerned with smaller style options, particularly at the paragraph and sentence level. After the big picture is blocked out, it's time to look at the nuances, the precise effects this text will have on an intended reader, asking, will he understand or enjoy this?

During later revisions, the writer starts looking seriously at audience issues but does not become overly concerned with the finest of details of mechanics, spelling, and punctuation; there is still time to move a paragraph or a sentence, to think up a more effective phrase. The writer is not yet concerned with perfection, but the writer is getting close to that point.

Editing. It's most efficient—and generally most satisfying—to edit a piece of writing immediately before relinquishing it. When we give a text to a teacher or publisher, we must be concerned with perfection. This is, at least momentarily, a writer's best opportunity to focus on surface-level clarity. Editing is the smallest picture of all; the writer is concerned with detail and mechanics—getting a dark print from the printer toner, setting standard margins, having a title, including a writer's name, proofreading for spelling errors, checking for unintentional punctuation and/or grammar errors.

A writer edits so as not to alienate a reader by making the reader do the writer's work. During editing, we strive toward some standard of perfection. Editing is not a time to remove paragraphs four through seven and rewrite them or to dramatically change the genre or focus of a piece or to add a new set of research issues.

Hint Sheet F: Revising Out— Expanding and Amplifying a Draft (Before Revising In)

My argument: We tend to stop down our texts too soon. To tire out, to play it safe, to not invest, to not develop enough text to truly revise. Thorough revision means to revise at the global level (paragraph to whole text) as well as the local level (word and sentence). These exercises allow you to generate more text before you close down and finalize your options. I ask writers I work with to choose one of these options after their first full-breadth draft has been shared in a small group response session.

A Fat Draft. Arbitrarily double your text. Turn a one-page poem into a two-page poem. Turn a five-page essay into a ten-page essay. Turn a one-act play into a two-act play. It doesn't have to be "good" or "better" or "finished" it just has to be honestly twice as long.

A Memory Draft. Read your text carefully. Say two times. Once silently. Once aloud. Then you put it away. Immediately (or if you prefer, after you've dreamed upon it), sit down and write another text of at least the same or longer length—you can try to "remember" your text, go off on a tangent, or do both. This is a memory draft; it may closely shadow the original or strike off in a new direction. Again, this does not have to be "good" or "better" or "finished" it just has to be as long or longer and written without a single turning back to the original, except for what you have retained in memory.

Move from Participant to Spectator. Narrate an earlier memory, event, scene, and then move between that time and the present to turn an *event* into an *experience*. Variation 1. Set yourself at a certain age and remember beliefs, way of life, attitudes, scene and then move to the present and reflect on how those beliefs, actions, attitudes, scenes have shifted and why. Variation 2. Revisit an actual site. Tell a past story from that site while actually there. Look around and draw on the present physicality of your location which may require that you shuttle back and forth through time—how it was then, how it is now.

Fragments and Extensions. Reread what you've written. Along the way, collect five words or phrases from your text and freewrite on each word. Let the

263

word or phrase take you anywhere. See if any of this new material helps you open up the draft; can you insert the new material at the point you find the original word or phrase? Somewhere else?

Burrow. Find a place where readers asked for more (or said they were confused). Imagine that every sentence contains its own next sentence. You can hear it if you listen. Begin with a single sentence, to which you add, by the sheer force of language itself, just another sentence, which adds a little bit to the first. Now in place of a single sentence, you have two, to which you add a third. Each time you increase your text, you are adding on to the whole that precedes it, and each time the whole is transformed. Burrow into the sentences you write as if on an archeological dig. Turn your words and their sounds and their sentences over and over. Listen for the spark, for connections, for the force of your own desire. When the initial impulse of your sentence has exhausted itself, stop. Go to the next sentence marked by readers, proceed as described above, add a new sentence, and continue . . . for a while.

Try Like an Essay Tries. Contradict, associate, use one or more voices, offer multiple truths, digress, argue, stay open, define, redefine, digress, imply, perform. You may want to try all these options on a single word (a core word) from your original text.

Write Between the Lines. Begin with a text you have written. Begin by convincing yourself you have only just begun to know anything about what you have written. Now begin again by writing in between the lines of your text. Between every two lines, insert a new line that adds to, or deepens, or further explores what the lines on either side of it have started. Variation 1. Break each sentence into two sentences, adding to the middle to fill them out. Variation 2a. Identify the basic organizing unit of the text—if you are writing prose, make it paragraphs; for poetry, stanzas. Open the text at the joints of each unit and write something new at each break. Add paragraphs, or stanzas. Repeat as necessary. Variation 2b. Add a different genre between each unit. Variation 3a. Have someone make random slash marks on your text—at each slash mark, break open the text. Variation 3b. Proceed as in Variation 2b above, only at the slash marks.

Hint Sheet G: Revision Exercises

What do you do when you have to revise a paper?

Add

- Add material. Add sentences to further explain or give examples. Fill in what was left out.
- Trade papers with another writer and suggest two places where information could be added that will make the writing better. Mark places with a big star (*).

Subtract

- Take out material that doesn't really fit or material that isn't really necessary to the point of the essay or story. Take out excess words.
- Find two places where excess material could be cut. Draw a line through it.

Move

- Rearrange what you already have in the writing. Move sentences around. Move phrases within sentences around. Move paragraphs to make a different order.
- Find two paragraphs that could be switched or reordered.

Shape

- Sculpt the sentences so that they are as clear as possible, as elegant as possible, as interesting as possible.
- Make the essay or story have a rhythm or sound that captivates the reader, a voice that captures your interest.

Revision means to look again, to view what was there in a new way. *Re-viewing* is an active process; you have to see what is present and what isn't there, what your writing needs. *Re-seeing* includes seeing again for the first time. And *revision* means:

Replacing

- After you've had a chance to add, cut, and move, try replacing.

- Look for five pronouns that could be replaced with the nouns they refer to. Circle and then replace five of them. For example, *I* and *It* are pronouns:

  When I think of loyalty, the first thing that comes to mind is a dog, man's best friend. It can also mean to stick up for what is right.

  Can become

  When I think of loyalty, the first thing that comes to mind is a dog, man's best friend. Loyalty can also mean to stick up for what is right.

Continue Replacing . . .

- Add adjectives and then even replace them with a noun phrase that expands the idea. For example:

  These traits are what make Brooke my friend.

  What kind of traits? What kind of friend?

  These *admirable* traits are what make Brooke my *best* friend.

  These *admirable* traits are what make Brooke my *best* friend, a person to whom no one else compares, someone that I could not imagine living without, the sister I never had.

  Another example:

  Love is a *magical* feeling; it comes from the heart.

  Love is a *magical* feeling, the mushy gushy sensation that comes from the heart.

  Coming from the heart, love is a feeling, a magical emotion that startles and amazes you.

  Now try it....

- Circle five adjectives and replace with a noun phrase that expands the idea.

Hint Sheet H:
A Few Words About Verbs

To be or not to be . . . That's the first verb we're looking at. The *to be* verb is the basic connector that affirms something exists, for example, Ricky is the quarterback. The trouble is that the *to be* gets overused—in place of action words. Verbs are action words. But even in that sentence, I just used a *to be* verb: *are*. I could've written: verbs create action; verbs convey action; verbs energize sentences; verbs counteract boredom.

Let's look for *to be* verbs; circle them in your writing. Some *to be* verbs: *Is, am, was, were, will be, are, have been, has been*, and negatives, *won't be, haven't been, hasn't been, ain't, isn't, aren't, weren't, wasn't, to be*. Replace those tired *to be* verbs with some action. Think of what it is that you're trying to create for your reader; what word is more concrete that would allow someone to visualize what you're writing?

For example, "Monday came around and *it was* the activity period" could be revised to read, "Monday came around and I waited in the activity period room." And verb phrases. Remember, sentences can be expanded using verb phrases. Find a sentence that is somewhat short, go to the end, add a comma, and start a verb phrase with a word ending in *-ing*. In the earlier example, it might look like this: "Monday came around and I waited in the activity period room, looking out the corner of my eye for his entrance, trying not to stare at the door; finally, Matt spotted me from across the room, entering with a bounce in his stride, looking fabulous in jeans and a sweater, preppy-boy outfit."

Expand three sentences with verb phrases. For example,

- "When separated from her, my thoughts constantly focus on Rita" can become "When separated from her, my thoughts constantly focus on Rita, making me feel tingly inside, giving me a goofy look on the outside, one that others might characterize as the look of a lovesick fool." (I added two verb phrases and a noun phrase for good measure [thirty-five words up from ten].)

- "He is shy and self-conscious but is also obsessive and controlling." can become "He seems shy and self-conscious but also acts obsessive and controlling, waiting for me to return home, calling me thirty minutes after I leave him, asking me questions that make me somewhat nervous, and interrogating me like he's Judge Judy or something." (Forty-two words up from eleven.)

- "Friends often switch roles and become the encouragement to our encouragers. " can become "Friends often switch roles and become the encouragement to our encouragers, allowing each person to give an equal contribution to the friendship, helping when she has problems, lifting her up when she's down in the dumps, guiding her when she faces a fork in the road, giving support when the road gets tough." (Fifty-three words up from eleven.)

Now here's some practice. Try adding verb phrases where the blanks are. Be creative, but if you have trouble, you can use one of the suggested verbs that are listed at the end to start the phrase.

As the curtain opened, Jessica stood like a statue, _____ .

_____ , she listened for the initial notes of her song to resonate through the auditorium.

_____ , her chin lifted and she began to dance.

_____ , she executed each move precisely. Her shadow followed her like an angel, a dark blur created by the constant spotlight on her. Her costume, a pressed blue-velvet long-sleeve leotard with a skirt, matched the tone of her dance, simple and understated. As the performance came to a close, she returned to her angelic pose. _____ , she gave a huge smile to the audience.

As the curtain closed, an older woman sitting next to me leaned over and said, "That was beautiful."

Suggested verbs: *waiting, beginning, leaping, raising, looking*

Hint Sheet I: Description

To use description means to sketch a picture, give an account, provide an explanation. To learn how to do it, look at how writers describe things: "For the first time since I'd known her, her honey-colored hair wasn't pulled back into a tight bun. Instead, it was hanging loosely, longer than I imagined, reaching below her shoulder blades. There was a trace of glitter in her hair, and it caught the stage lights, sparkling like a crystal halo."

What's being described? A woman.

What about her? How she looked:

* terrific and free

* hair not in a tight bun but flowing down to her shoulder blades with glitter that sparkled like a halo

So, description answers a question. The woman; the question: How'd she look? Like an angel (and it never has to actually say that).

Description is done with visuals, adjectives that let you see. Actually it is done with sense information; sight is simply the most common. There's also taste, smell, feel, sound. Look at this example from Tim O'Brien: "They stared down at the rucksack. It was made of dark green nylon with an aluminum frame." The dark green gives a visual; the aluminum gives the weight, the feel. But then he adds: "They stared down at the rucksack. It was made of dark green nylon with an aluminum frame, but now it had the curious look of flesh." Something else is going on. When considered with an earlier description— "The pack was heavy with mud and water, dead-looking"—you realize there's a metaphor working too.

Metaphors compare one thing to another to try to convey descriptive information: "He jumped over a low place in the hedge at the bottom, and took to the meadows, passing through the night like a rustle of wind in the grass." This description tells how he moved—silently, like a breeze.

Sometimes writers let adjectives pile up: "One gorgeous, buff, commitment-phobic actor blowing out of town. One overweight, insecure, commitment-obsessed secretary left behind." Too much of this gets annoying.

Sometimes the description doesn't tell you much at all: "It was a fine night, and the black sky was dotted with stars." What made it fine? Black with stars, oh, like every night. Well, maybe not every night because there are clouds this time. A better description of the sky might be: "The sky was a haze of different colors: black directly above him like a mountain peak, then blues of infinite range, becoming lighter until it met the horizon, where gray took its place."

Description serves a purpose: to tell the reader the answer to a question; to let the reader see what is unseen in print; to convey metaphoric information that goes beyond visual, sense-oriented information.

Hint Sheet J: Responding to Peer Writing Before a Full-Class Workshop

Please respond to each essay with a letter (or paragraph, or note) from you to the author (suggestions for things you may want to discuss follow). Also, annotate the writer's text. Return the text and letter after each discussion.

1. Each writer will read a paragraph aloud.

2. All class members will share in the discussion.

    a. Try to offer the writer a sense of how you read the piece.
       Among many other things, you might tell her:

- how you understood or enjoyed the text
- what sentence or image seemed crucial to the text and your understanding of it (essentially, identify the center of gravity)
- where your attention lagged (and perhaps picked up again)
- how you felt as the audience for this piece (were you the right audience? do you need to know more about the writer's intended audience? and so on)
- where you felt gaps, wished for more, felt something was being held back, and so on

    b. Try to offer the writer a sense of possible revision directions.
       Among other things, you might tell him:

- how to lengthen or shorten the piece, if the beginning and ending are effective, and so on
- how he could experiment in a way you'd find interesting
- if you sense any risk taking going on and how to keep capturing that sense of working dangerously (but also productively)
- where breaking the conventions works (usage, sentence structure, invented words, punctuation) and/or where you're worried by broken conventions (are they intentional/effective?)

    c. Try to offer the writer insight into her prose style.
       Among other things, you might tell her:

- what you notice about word choice

- which sentences are effective (and why) and which ones are choppy, tangled, confusing, or so on
- about the strategies you notice (metaphorical language, repetition, balance, circular movement, self-consciousness); suggest whether they should be used more or less often
- about style or technique by saying how the writer's prose differs or seems similar to your own

There is always something to say about a piece of writing. All writings can be studied and, through careful response, be strengthened. Your comments will help other writers challenge themselves.

Hint Sheet K: Suggestions for Submitting Writing Portfolios

Your final portfolios should be in a plain, inexpensive, two-pocket folder. They're due at the beginning of our last class. *I will not be returning any material in the portfolio so please be sure to photocopy anything you want to keep or give me photocopies and keep the originals.*

1. In the left pocket of the portfolio, I'll expect to see your final course work. Each essay should have a process cover sheet attached to it (the story of how you wrote the essay—about a one-page narrative). Each essay should have your name, date, the course number, and the title on it, followed by the typed body of the text. I'll also want either the radical revision/or a "script" for the radical revision and the extended process cover sheet for the radical revision.

2. In the right side of the pocket, I'll expect to see, clipped together, early drafts and class materials for each essay. I'd like no more than two earlier drafts—first full-breadth draft and one professional quality workshop(ed) draft (shared with a small or large group) and copies of the most useful responses peers made. Essentially, this side represents the raw material of your drafting and process cover sheets. This is where you can store a copy of your executive summary for the essay you shared with us all.

3. In the right side of the pocket, I also require a final letter from you to me, maximum two, single-spaced pages. I would like your letter to address all of the following issues (in whatever order you like):

   • Read the final drafts of your essays and cover sheets. Take me through each of these essays pointing out what you learned, what worked and didn't work, where you think your writing and reading of writing (ability to improve your own texts) improved. If you didn't see much growth, tell me why that is and how the class could be changed to help future students improve as writers and readers of writing.

   • What were your favorite class activities? In what ways did they help you as a writer/reader?

   • Revisit some of your earliest class journal entries/exploratory writings about reading and your first essay, and discuss what—if any—has changed in your understanding of yourself as a reader of texts.

- What in the class activities and assignments would you urge me to keep and what should I change?
- How did this course meet or disappoint your expectations about what you'd accomplish?
- Think about your own participation in all the class elements—discussion, reading, writing, responding to peers' texts, reading group, researching, and so on. Talk about your strengths and your weaknesses in participation.
- Who in the class influenced you, helped you, taught you the most? What specifically did he/she do? In turn, whom do you think you influenced, helped, interacted with most usefully?
- Reread the course information sheet. Given the class design and your own knowledge of your participation and progress in class, give yourself a grade using any scale you like: check, check minus, or check plus; 1–10 (ten is high); A, B, C, D, F—(you know how those work); and so on. Explain in some detail the basis for your decision.
- Tell me one or two things about the class that I should know but didn't ask about.

Think of this letter as a "user's guide" to your portfolio. Your answers will help me to read your work with more skill and appreciation and will help me improve the class for future students.